IRA CHERNUS
MYSTICISM IN RABBINIC JUDAISM

STUDIA JUDAICA

FORSCHUNGEN ZUR WISSENSCHAFT
DES JUDENTUMS

HERAUSGEGEBEN VON
E. L. EHRLICH
BASEL

BAND XI

WALTER DE GRUYTER · BERLIN · NEW YORK
1982

MYSTICISM
IN RABBINIC JUDAISM

STUDIES IN THE HISTORY OF MIDRASH

VON
IRA CHERNUS

WALTER DE GRUYTER · BERLIN · NEW YORK
1982

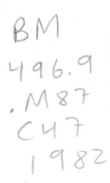
Library of Congress Cataloging in Publication Data

Chernus, Ira,   1946–
    Mysticism in rabbinic Judaism.
    (Studia Judaica ; Bd. 11)
    Bibliography: p.
    Includes index.
    1. Merkava in rabbinical literature. 2. Mysticism—Judaism. 3.
    Midrash. I. Title. II. Series: Studia Judaica (Walter de Gruy-
    ter & Co.) ; Bd. 11.
    BM496.9.M87C47   1982   296.7′1   82—14034
    ISBN 3-11-008589-5

CIP-Kurztitelaufnahme der Deutschen Bibliothek

Chernus, Ira:
Mysticism in rabbinic Judaism : studies in the history of midrash /
by Ira Chernus. — Berlin ; New York : de Gruyter, 1982.
    (Studia Judaica ; Bd. 11)
    ISBN 3-11-008589-5
NE: Studia Iudaica

IN MEMORY OF MY FATHER
SOL CHERNUS

PREFACE

The chapters which follow were originally written as separate essays. Each was occasioned by my interest in tracing the history of one particular midrash or midrashic motif. In reviewing these essays, however, I became aware that they were all dealing with more or less the same set of concerns, so that each might be read more profitably in light of the others. Therefore I have assembled them here, with a few additions and revisions, in what seems to be their most logical sequence. While this sequence does imply a single general line of argument, the argument was not really developed until after the essays had been written. The content of the essays generated the overall argument, rather than vice versa.

The basic issue with which all these essays are concerned is the relationship between Merkabah mysticism and rabbinic Judaism as reflected in rabbinic midrash. I have concentrated on two general themes within the midrashic literature: the revelation at Mount Sinai and the eschatological rewards of the world to come. My general conclusions are that the development of the former theme shows many striking affinities with the literature of Merkabah mysticism, while the development of the latter theme shows very few. In discussing these conclusions I shall suggest some of their possible implications; here I want to mention only one.

Gershom Scholem has made an invaluable contribution to our understanding of the rabbinic era with his illumination of a broad range of esoteric concerns, which he labelled "Merkabah mysticism." But there is a growing scholarly sense that he has not served us equally well in calling this phenomenon "Jewish Gnosticism." The evidence presented here from rabbinic midrash will indicate, I think, that Merkabah mysticism was integrated into rabbinic Judaism precisely to prevent the development of a true "Jewish Gnosticism." The term, therefore, may well be misleading as a characterization of any developments within the rabbinic community. I hope that these essays, in developing this rather modest point, will shed helpful light on related questions as to the nature of rabbinic Judaism.

Unfortunately I can not claim to have any definitive contributions to two of the most crucial and most baffling problems facing us in this area. We would certainly like to know whether the leading rabbis of the classical rabbinic era (the first three centuries CE) were actually involved in Merkabah mysticism. While Scholem has consistently affirmed this, others have denied it as valid for the tannaim, and recently mysticism among the amoraim has been seriously questioned. My own sense of this debate is that, while Scholem perhaps has a preponderance of the evidence on his side, neither side will ever be able to prove its point irrefutably, for sufficient evidence just does not exist. In interpreting the amoraic materials, I have made the assumption that they do in fact reflect the existence of some kind of Merkabah mysticism among the rabbis, since the evidence points so strongly in that direction. But I am aware that this remains merely a likely hypothesis. In dealing with tannaitic data the evidence is not as convincing, and I have therefore felt obliged to interpret it without making such an assumption. Others may, of course, read the data presented here differently than I do myself. In particular, those disposed to find Merkabah mysticism in rabbinic circles may find significant material here to support their arguments.

One major difficulty in solving this problem of Merkabah mysticism among the rabbis is that we do not yet have a precise definition of just what Merkabah mysticism was. The term "Merkabah mysticism" is, of course, a modern coinage. The rabbis themselves spoke of *"ma'aseh merkabah,"* but we still can not say exactly what that phrase meant to them. In any event, it may well have meant something more narrow than the wide range of phenomena intended by Scholem in his usage of "Merkabah mysticism." Yet Scholem's term does seem helpful, since it clearly points to a number of significantly related, albeit vaguely defined, phenomena. Many scholars have found it helpful to label these as "esoteric" concerns, although that term too is variously and sometimes vaguely defined. The studies presented here are not intended to define what Merkabah mysticism was (although they do suggest some things that it was not), but neither do they presume any precise definition. Since we are still studying the phenomena in order to arrive at a definition, it would be methodologically unsound to presume any definition *a priori*. I have chosen, therefore, to use the terms "Merkabah mysticism" and "esotericism" roughly interchangeably, assuming only that they denote a broad range of experiences, all in some way related to ecstaticism and the realm of the divine in the "upper world."

For practical purposes, I have assumed that Merkabah mysticism includes those words and images found in the texts which seem to be central to it, and I have looked for those same words and images in the midrash. Admittedly, this means searching out parallels between rabbinic texts of late antiquity and mystical texts of the early medieval period. If Merkabah mysticism as reflected in the extant mystical texts was known in substantially the same form to the classical rabbis, then we can draw some important conclusions about rabbinic religion from these parallels (or their absence). If, on the other hand, Merkabah mysticism did not develop until after the classical rabbinic period, we can draw significant conclusions about its development, although this may not illuminate the early rabbinic era itself so clearly.

One other problem which remains unsolved here is the basic methodological one of using rabbinic midrash as an historical source, and in particular the question of the validity of the attributions to specific rabbis. Since methodology in this area is still rather unsophisticated, we are left with two options: either suspend substantive research entirely and work only on problems of method, or else use an *ad hoc* method which offers a reasonable assessment of each text on its own terms. Like most scholars, I have chosen the latter course, although this may lead in some cases to an over-reliance on the attributions in the text. But it seems to be the lesser of two evils. Those who are more methodologically rigorous may choose to regard the conclusions presented here as hypotheses awaiting testing.

A number of people have offered me valuable assistance which made the completion of this book possible. Research and publication costs were underwritten in part by the University of Colorado through its Council on Research and Creative Work, its Committee on University Scholarly Publications, and its College of Arts and Sciences, by the American Philosophical Society, and by the very generous assistance of Miriam Chernus. My colleagues in the Department of Religious Studies at the University of Colorado, Boulder, have offered their consistent support and encouragement; the continuing assistance of Maxine Kluck has been invaluable. Sami Schachter, David Goldfischer, and Denise Straus helped to prepare the final manuscript; Alison Greene helped to prepare the index. I wish to express my sincere appreciation to all these people and, above all, to Ann, for proof-reading the manuscript and for much, much more.

Ira Chernus

Boulder, March, 1980

TABLE OF CONTENTS

ABBREVIATIONS

ARN = Abot d'Rabbi Nathan
Dt. R = Deuteronomy Rabbah
Ecc. R. = Ecclesiastes Rabbah
Esther R. = Esther Rabbah
Ex. R = Exodus Rabbah
Gen. R = Genesis Rabbah
HR = Heikalot Rabbati (ed. A. Jellinek)
Lam. R = Lamentations Rabbah
Lev. R = Leviticus Rabbah
Mek. = Mekilta d'Rabbi Ishmael
Mek. RS = Mekilta d'Rabbi Simeon bar Yohai
MM = Ma'aseh Merkabah (ed. G. Scholem)
MT = Midrash T'hillim
M = Mishnah
Num. R = Numbers Rabbah
PA = Wilhelm Bacher, *Die Agada der Palästinensischen Amoräer*
PR = Pesikta Rabbati
PRE = Pirkei d'Rabbi Eliezer
PRK = Pesikta d'Rab Kahana (ed. Mandelbaum)
Ruth R = Ruth Rabbah
RY = Re'uyot Yehezkiel
Sifre Dt. = Sifre on Deuteronomy
Sifre Num. = Sifre on Numbers
Song R = Song of Songs Rabbah
Tan. = Midrash Tanhuma
Tan. B = Midrash Tanhuma Haqadom (ed. S. Buber)
TB = Babylonian Talmud
TP = Palestinian Talmud
Tos. = Tosefta
Y = Yalkut Shimeoni

I. REVELATION AND MERKABAH MYSTICISM
IN TANNAITIC MIDRASH

One of the most common and most important themes in rabbinic midrash is *matan Torah* − the revelation of the Torah to the Israelites at Mount Sinai. If we look at the midrashim concerning *matan Torah* which were developed during the second century, we find that the event was described in terms strikingly similar to those used in the literature of Merkabah mysticism.[1] In these midrashim the experience of the Israelites at Sinai appears to be in many ways analogous to the experience of the "descenders to the Merkabah."

The earliest trace of this theme in the extant texts seems to be a discussion of Psalm 68:18 between R. Eliezer of Modiʿim and R. Elazar b. Azariah:

> R. Elazar b. Azariah and R. Eliezer of Modiʿim were engaged in interpreting the verse, "The chariots of God, twice ten thousand, thousands upon thousands, the Lord among them, Sinai in holiness." R. Elazar b. Azariah asked R. Eliezer of Modiʿim: But could Mount Sinai hold them? He said to him: . . . [God] said to Sinai: Lengthen yourself, enlarge yourself, receive my angels.[2]

This particular verse from Psalms came to be an important crux for the influence of esoterica on amoraic midrashim on Sinai.[3] Here, however, its significance is merely the suggestion of the close proximity of the angels to the Israelites; such proximity to the angels is, of course, a dominant feature of all the literature of Merkabah mysticism. In fact, it has been suggested that the tradition of ascending to the Merkabah may have begun with Temple priests who "joined in with [the recitation of the hymns in] the liturgy of the angelic world."[4] Here, however, rather than humans ascending to join the angels, we find the idea that the angels descended to join the humans.

In the same generation of tannaim was R. Elazar b. Arak, who, according to one tradition,[5] expounded on the "*maʿaseh Merkabah*" before his master, R. Jo-

---

[1] Cf. Saul Lieberman, "Mishnat Shir Hashirim".

[2] PR 21.8, 103b; cf. Tan. B. II, 77, Tan. Zav 12, PRK 12.22.

[3] See, e.g., MT 68.10 and PR 21.7 and 21.8, 102b−103a.

[4] Johann Maier, *Vom Kultus Zur Gnosis*, p. 134.

[5] Mek. RS 158; Tos. Hagigah 2.1 and parallels.

hanan b. Zakkai. A tantalizing fragment in the late compilation Pirkei d'Rabbi Eliezer[6] says:

> R. Elazar b. Arak says: When the Holy One blessed be He descended to give the Torah to Israel, 600,000 angels descended with him, corresponding to the 600,000 men of Israel, and in their hands they had weapons and crowns, and they crowned Israel with the crown of the ineffable Name.[7]

The traditions concerning the weapons and the crowns recurred, as we shall see, in later generations. Since this passage occurs only in this late text which consciously stressed esoteric traditions,[8] we can not accept the authenticity of the attribution with any certainty. Yet it is tempting to trace these later traditions back to R. Elazar b. Arak, a known participant in the earliest stages of rabbinic esotericism.

The first rabbi who made a clear and significant contribution to the theme being studied here was R. Akiba, whose role in esoteric pursuits is most well-known from the story of the "four who entered Paradise"; only R. Akiba "entered in peace and left in peace."[9] Scholem has insisted on this story as evidence for an actual ecstatic ascent,[10] and he has concluded: "So R. Akiba, a central figure in the world of rabbinic Judaism, is also the legitimate representative of a mysticism within its boundaries."[11] R. Akiba taught explicitly that the "glory" — a *terminus technicus* "for God when He is the object of profound mystical enquiry"[12] — descended on Mount Sinai:

> "While the king was still at his table" (Song 1:12) . . . R. Akiba says: While the King of king of kings, the Holy One blessed be He, was still at his table in the firmament, already, "And the glory of the Lord dwelt upon Mount Sinai" (Ex 24:16).[13]

Professor Lieberman remarks on this passage: "Even though R. Akiba's words are unclear, nevertheless it is clear . . . that he interprets [the verse] with reference to the giving of the Torah at Sinai."[14] A tradition preserved in the Mekilta expresses R. Akiba's view in a somewhat different way:

---

[6] Joseph Heinemann, *Aggadot V'toldotaihen* p. 205, has recently assigned it to the eighth century. Cf. Gerald Friedlander, *Pirke de Rabbi Eliezer*, p. liv, and Louis Ginzberg, *On Jewish Law and Lore*, p. 72.

[7] PRE ch. 47, 112a.

[8] Cf. Scholem, *Kabbalah*, p. 30.

[9] Tos. Hagigah 2.3–4; TB Hagigah 14b.

[10] Gershom Scholem, *Major Trends in Jewish Mysticism*, pp. 52,53; idem., *Jewish Gnosticism, Merkabah Mysticism, and Talmudic Tradition*, pp. 14–19. But cf. the counter-arguments of E. E. Urbach, "Hamasoret al Torat Hasod Bit'kufat Hatannaim," *Studies in Mysticism and Religion presented to Gershom Scholem*, ed. E. E. Urbach.

[11] Scholem, *Kabbalah*, p. 14.

[12] *Ibid.*, p. 13.

[13] Song R 1.12.1.

[14] Saul Lieberman, "Mishnat Shir Hashirim," p. 120.

> R. Akiba says: One Scriptural passage says: "That from heaven I spoke with you" (Ex 20:19), and another passage says: "And the Lord descended upon Mount Sinai at the top of the mountain" (Dt. 4:36). It teaches that the Holy One blessed be He bent down the lower heavens upon the top of the mountain and spoke with them from heaven.[15]

Although this passage does not use the term "glory" specifically, it is another indication that R. Akiba had gone beyond R. Eliezer of Modi'im's view and claimed that God Himself, not just the angels, was in a special proximity to the Israelites at Sinai. We may also note here an anonymous passage in the Mekilta which seems to combine the views of R. Akiba cited here; it may reflect a later synthesis or a more accurate version of R. Akiba's original midrash:

> Is it possible that the glory actually descended and reclined upon Mount Sinai? That is why Scripture says, "That from heaven I spoke with you." It teaches that the Holy One blessed be He bent down the lower heavens and the upper heavens upon the mountain, like a man who spreads out a cushion on top of a bed, and like a man who speaks from on top of the cushion.[16]

In all three of these midrashim we see an attempt to claim a special proximity to God Himself and His glory and at the same time an attempt to preserve the divine transcendence; this dialectic of *tremendum* and *fascinans* is a principal feature of the "numinous" quality of much of Merkabah mysticism.

The clearest parallel between R. Akiba's midrash and the esoteric tradition, however, appears in another passage in the Mekilta:

> "And all the people saw the thunderings" (Ex 20:18) − R. Akiba says: They were seeing and hearing the visible − seeing speech of fire coming out of the mouth of the Power and being hewn onto the tablets, as it is said, "The voice of the Lord hews out flames of fire" (Ps. 29:7).[17]

In this case the same specific image occurs in both the midrash on Sinai and the Merkabah mystics' literature. In Heikalot Rabbati we find:

> And His words shall drop as perfume, flowing forth in flames of fire . . . You are He who revealed Your secret to Moses, and You did not hide any of Your power from him. When the word went out of Your mouth, all the high mountains would shake and stand in great terror, and all of them were burned in flames of fire.[18]

The contention that the Israelites actually saw the divine glory may also be reflected in another of R. Akiba's midrashim:

---

[15] Mek. Yitro Bahodesh 9, p. 238; cf. MT 18.13.

[16] Mek. Yitro Bahodesh 4, p. 216; cf. Mek. RS 145.

[17] Mek. Yitro Bahodesh 9, p. 235; cf. Midrash Shmuel ch. 29 and Mek. RS p. 154. Noteworthy here is the use of the term "Power" − "*g'burah*" − which is, like "glory," a *terminus technicus* for God in the Merkabah tradition, according to Scholem, *Gnosticism*, pp. 67−69.

[18] HR 24.3, cited in Scholem, *Gnosticism*, p. 62;

"My dove in the cleft of the rock, in the hidden place of the cliff" (Song 2:14) . . . R. Akiba says: These words were not said anywhere else but in front of Mount Sinai — "Let me see your face" (*ibid.*).[19]

Professor Lieberman has shown that this passage is an early example of the esoteric interpretation of Song of Songs, which indicates a tannaitic origin for the Shiur Komah tradition.[20] Whether in fact this midrash is part of the Shiur Komah tradition must remain doubtful, given the difficulty of fixing the original text.[21]

Another tradition known in R. Akiba's time, although he himself apparently did not support it, claimed that the Israelites at Sinai had seen the ox in the divine chariot which descended to them (cf. Ezek. 1:10) and had made the "golden calf" as a replica of that ox. Although direct assertions of this tradition only appear in much later texts,[22] its existence is indirectly attested in a conversation between R. Akiba and R. Pappias:

R. Pappias interpreted the verse "They exchanged their glory for the image of an ox" (Ps. 106:20): I might understand this to mean the supernal ox; that is why Scripture says, "that eats grass" (*ibid.*).[23]

Similar disagreements must have existed among the rabbis about the validity of other such traditions. Evidence of one such disagreement even among the students of R. Akiba has been preserved for us:

R. Jose says: Behold it says, "The heavens are the heavens of the Lord and the earth He has given to human beings" (Ps. 115:16). Moses and Elijah never ascended to heaven, nor did the glory ever descend below.[24]

While R. Jose opposed his master on this point, another of R. Akiba's great disciples, R. Simeon b. Yohai, seems rather to have followed the lead of the master. He claimed that the Israelites at Sinai had actively sought a direct vision of the "glory": "R. Simeon b. Yohai taught: This is what they asked: They said: Our whish is

---

[19] Song R 2.14.4; Mek RS p. 143; cf. Mek. Yitro Bahodesh 3, p. 214.
[20] Lieberman, "Mishnat Shir Hashirim," p. 119.
[21] The text in the Mekilta clearly refers to the "face" of the Israelites when read in context, while the text in Song R. refers to the "face" of God; the latter text reads:
"R. Akiba interpreted the verse as referring to the Israelites when they stood before Mount Sinai. "My dove in the cleft of the rock" means that they were hidden in the secret place of Sinai. "Let me see your face," as it is said, "And all the people saw the thunderings.""
Only if the Song R. text is the original version would we have clear evidence of an early source for the Shiur Komah tradition here.
[22] Ex. R. 3.2, 42.5, 43.8; Tan. Ki Tissa 21.
[23] Mek. Vay'hi B'shalah 6, p. 112; Song R. 1.9.3; Mek. RS 68; cf. Lieberman, "Mishnat Shir Hashirim," p. 122, n. 24, and Louis Ginsberg, *Legends of the Jews,* vol. VI, p. 52, n. 271.
[24] Mek. Yitro Bahodesh 4, p. 217; cf. TB Sukkah 5a and TP Sukkah 51d; Mek. Yitro Bahodesh 9, p. 239; Mek. RS 145.

to see the glory of our King."[25] Lieberman has cited this passage as evidence that "those who think that the Song was [first] recited at Sinai also say that they [i. e., the Israelites] saw Him, as it were, in actuality."[26] The validity of this claim is supported by an anonymous version of this tradition in the Mekilta, which may or may not reflect the original version of R. Simeon's tradition:

> They said: Our wish is to see our king; one who hears is not comparable to one who sees. God said to him: Give them what they have requested — "For on the third day the Lord will descend in the sight of all the people upon Mount Sinai" (Ex. 19:11).[27]

Another tradition widely attributed to R. Simeon b. Yohai says that "He gave [the Israelites] a weapon with the ineffable Name inscribed upon it."[28] Scholem has described the importance of the theurgic use of the ineffable Name (the Tetragrammaton or expanded forms of it) in Merkabah mysticism; he notes that "the magical element was strong in the early stages of Heikalot literature only, becoming weaker in later redactions."[29] In an early text which is "most characteristic of this material,"[30] the Ma'aseh Merkabah, we find consistent stress on using the magical names of God, for it is only through the proper recitation of these names that R. Ishmael claims to be able to make the ascent to the divine chariot. Moreover, R. Ishmael in this text employs seals tied to various parts of his body on which are inscribed these theurgic names. While there is no text which calls these seals "weapons," there is a strong sense in which they function as weapons for the "descenders to the Merkabah," since the seals are primarily to enable the "descender" to pass in safety the angels guarding the thresholds of the heikalot:

> R. Ishmael said: . . . Who has been able to gaze upon Padakras the angel of the presence since the time the secret first existed? Padakras the Lord God of Israel said to me: Descend and see. If a man like you descended without the permission of Padakras the Lord God of Israel they destroyed him. R. Ishmael said: There were seven seals with which I sealed myself when Padakras the angel of the presence descended.[31]

---

[25] Song R 1.2.3; cf. Ex. R 29.4 and 41.3.

[26] Lieberman, "Mishnat Shir Hashirim," p. 121.

[27] Mek. Yitro Bahodesh 2, p. 211; cf. Mek. RS 140.

[28] Ex. R 45.3 and 51.8; PR 33.10, 154a; Lam. R Proem 24; MT 103.8; Tan. B II, 99 and IV, 76. This passage is usually found in pericopes dealing with various objects that the descending angels gave to the Israelites, all of which are amoraic traditions and all of which refer to the objects in the plural. Therefore this passage has been taken by English translators to refer to a plurality of weapons; cf. S. M. Lehrman, *Midrash Rabbah, Exodus*, pp. 520, 570; A. Cohen, *Midrash Rabbah, Lamentations*, p. 39; W. G. Braude, trans., *Pesikta Rabbati*, p. 648. However all versions of R. Simeon b. Yohai's tradition end with the prepositional phrase in the singular — "inscribed upon it."

[29] Scholem, *Kabbalah*, p. 20; cf. *idem.*, *Gnosticism*, pp. 54—55 and 75—83.

[30] Scholem, *Gnosticism*, p. 76.

[31] MM pars. 14, 15.

It seems reasonable to conclude, then, that R. Simeon b. Yohai was ascribing the possession of some kind of magically effective and protective object to the Israelites at Sinai.[32]

Roughly contemporaneous with R. Simeon b. Yohai was another disciple of R. Akiba, R. Judah b. Ilai. He also asserted that the Israelites had seen God: "At Sinai they saw Him face to face, as it says, 'And he said: The Lord came to Sinai' (Dt. 33:2)."[33] The choice of this particular prooftext is interesting, for the conclusion of the verse reads: "at His right hand a fiery law." We have already seen R. Akiba's view that the speech of God at Sinai was fire, and R. Judah b. Ilai seems to have developed the implications of that view:

> R. Judah b. Ilai says: Since Israel was scorched by the heat of the fire of the upper world, the Holy One blessed be He said to the clouds of glory: Drip down the dew of life on my children, as it says, "Earth trembled, even the heavens dripped before God," and it says, "A bounteous rain You did pour down, O God." (Ps. 68:9,10).[34]

We could assert R. Judah's dependence on R. Akiba more definitely if we could accept the attribution in the following passage:

> R. Judah says: . . . Israel heard the voice of the Holy One blessed be He and saw the voice coming out of the mouth of the Power with lightning and thunder, as it is said, "And all the people saw the thunderings and lightnings."[35]

However, since this passage appears only in the Pirkei d'Rabbi Eliezer, we must again be skeptical about the attribution. In any event, it seems likely that R. Judah did point specifically to phenomena of fire and burning in his midrash on the revelation.

The motif of being burned by heavenly fire also appears in the literature of Merkabah mysticism. One text has a "descender to the Merkabah" say, in reference to the guardian of the "first gate": "When I saw him, my hands were burned and I was standing without hands and without feet."[36] Another text says that "the fire which comes out from the man who beholds, this enkindles him and this burns him."[37] It seems plausible that the description of the transformation of Enoch may also represent such an ecstatic experience:

---

[32] In two texts — Ex. R 51.8 and Tan. B IV, 76 — R. Simeon b. Yohai's tradition is immediately followed by the assertion that this weapon provided immortality, but the absence of this assertion in the other versions of the tradition makes it likely that it represents a later addition.

[33] Song R 3.9.

[34] Mek. Yitro Bahodesh 9, p. 236; cf. Tos. Arakin 1.10.

[35] PRE ch. 41, 98a.

[36] Heikalot Zutarti as cited in Scholem, *Gnosticism*, p. 63; cf. *ibid.*, p. 60 and *idem.*, *Major Trends*, p. 52.

[37] HR 2.4, p. 84.

My flesh was changed into flames, my sinews into flaming fire, my bones into coals of burning juniper . . . the hair of my head into hot flames, all my limbs into wings of burning fire and the whole of my body into glowing fire.[38]

More generally, there is an enormous amount of fire imagery throughout the literature of Merkabah mysticism.[39] We may cite briefly some representative examples:

From the utterances which proceed out of the mouth of the holy ones, and from the melody which welleth out of the mouth of the servants, mountains of fire and hills of flame are piled up and hidden and poured out each day.[40] Your power is fire and Your innermost chambers are fire. You are fire devouring fire, Your throne is fire, Your storehouses are fire, and Your ministers are fire, and Your Name is hewn out in flaming fire.[41]

Related to this theme is the frequent mention of lightning as a feature of the realm of the Merkabah; the guardians of the gate to the seventh *heikal* are described as having "lightning which leaps forth from their eyeballs, and balls of fire from their nostrils, and torches of hot coals from their mouths."[42] Another text claims that the "descender to the Merkabah" would be able "to walk in rivers of fire, and to know the lightning."[43] A third text says: "The seraphim of the glory surround the throne on all four sides with walls of lightning, and the ophannim surround the throne of glory with fiery torches."[44] These dual themes of fire and lightning are also found in a series of anonymous midrashim in the Mekilta; while the texts as we have them may or may not be tannaitic, it is likely that they reflect ideas known in the tannaitic era:[45]

"And Mount Sinai was completely smoking" (Ex. 19:18) — It might only refer to the place of the glory; that is why it says "completely." Why? Because "the Lord descended upon it in fire" (*ibid.*). It tells us that the Torah is fire, and it was given out of fire, and it is compared to fire . . . "And its smoke rose up" (*ibid.*). It might only refer to ordinary smoke; that is why it says "a furnace" (*ibid.*). But it might only refer to an ordinary furnace; that is why it says, "And the mountain burning with fire unto the midst of heaven" (Dt. 4:11).[46] "And there was thunder" (Ex. 19:16) — thunder upon thunder,

---

[38] III Enoch 15.1, p. 20.

[39] Ithamar Gruenwald, in "Knowledge and Vision," *Israel Oriental Studies* 3 (1973), p. 89, has pointed to the close link between fire imagery and ecstatic experience in rabbinic material relating to Merkabah mysticism.

[40] HR 2.4, p. 84.

[41] MM, par. 4 end.

[42] HR 15.8, p. 94.

[43] Heikalot Zutarti as cited in Scholem, *Gnosticism*, p. 78.

[44] III Enoch 33.3, p. 49.

[45] For a recent summary of the problem of dating Mekilta texts, and arguments for accepting them as tannaitic, see E. P. Sanders, *Paul and Palestinian Judaism: A Comparison of Patterns of Religion*, pp. 63–69.

[46] Mek. Yitro Bahodesh 4, p. 215; cf. Mek. RS 143, 144.

many different kinds of thunder. "And lightning" (*ibid.*) – lightning upon lightning, many different kinds of lightning . . . "And they took their stand" (Ex 19:17) – they huddled together. It teaches that the Israelites were awe-struck by the storms and earthquakes and thunder and lightning which came.[47]

In addition to these midrashim concerning fire, there are two other relevant traditions ascribed to R. Judah b. Ilai. Expounding the verse "While the king was still at his table," which we have already seen in R. Akiba's midrash, R. Judah said:

> While the King of king of kings, the Holy One blessed be He, was still at His table in the firmament, Israel gave off a pleasing odor before Mount Sinai and said, "All that the Lord has spoken we will do and we will obey" (Ex 24:7).[48]

We noted a passage earlier from Heikalot Rabbati in which God's revelatory word is said to be both fire and perfume; thus the motif of "a pleasing odor" may indicate a parallel with esoteric traditions.[49] There is also another passage in Pirkei d'Rabbi Eliezer attributed to R. Judah:

> R. Judah says: As long as a man is wearing the clothes of his splendor he is beautiful in his appearance and in his glory and in his radiance. Thus were the Israelites when they wore that name – they were as good as ministering angels before the Holy One blessed be He.[50]

This passage reflects many esoteric motifs:[51] the special clothing, the "glory," the radiant light, the name (apparently the ineffable Name of God), and the equality of the Israelites with the angels. It is most tempting here, as previously, to hypothesize that the Pirkei d'Rabbi Eliezer preserves traditions which are in fact authentic, but the absence of parallels in other texts leaves us unable to do so.

There is better ground for asserting that a tradition concerning special clothing at Sinai was known in the last generation of the tannaim, for we find such a tradition attributed to R. Simai in several texts; he said that God "clothed them in royal purple."[52] R. Simai may have based this remark on a similar tradition of R. Simeon b. Yohai which appears only once in the extant texts,[53] although R. Simeon b. Yohai used the term "*argavanim*," while R. Simai used the synonymous "*porporia*'." While the terms "*porporia*'" and "*argavanim*" do not appear in the esoteric texts,

---

[47] Mek. Yitro Bahodesh 3, p. 214; cf. Mek RS 142.
[48] Song R 1.12.1.
[49] Cf. TB Shabbat 88b, in which two traditions attributed to the amora R. Joshua b. Levi are juxtaposed, one reflecting this theme and the other R. Judah's midrash on the "fire of the upper world."
[50] PRE ch. 47, 112b.
[51] Cf. especially the parallels in III Enoch 12.1 and 2, p. 17.
[52] Ex. R 45.2 and 51.8; Tan. B II, 99 and IV, 76; cf. MT 103.8 where the attributions are probably erroneous.
[53] PR 33.10. It is possible that "Simeon" is a scribal error and that the original text here too read "Simai."

there is reference to special clothing, such as the "garment of exaltation and . . . robe of glory with all kinds of beauty and splendor and radiance and glory set in it" which is said to be given to Enoch-Metatron.[54] Perhaps more interestingly, there is also reference to the "robe" worn by God, whose quality of "royalty" is an over-riding theological concern of the Merkabah tradition.[55] Thus we find God addressed as "resplendent King, robed in splendor"[56] and described as wearing a garment (*ḥaluq*) whose "beauty is as sweet as the beauty of the appearance of the splendor of the glory of the eyes of the image of the living creatures."[57]

Scholem has asserted that the rabbinic tradition about the royal purple garment has direct affinities with the esoteric tradition, since "The garment of purple which Israel received came 'from the splendor of His glory.'"[58] Unfortunately we can not accept this opinion, since the phrase "from the splendor of His glory," though it appears in the same pericope as R. Simai's tradition in Exodus Rabbah, is clearly a later addition to a separate tradition of R. Eliezer b. Jose the Galileean, which is cited in the same pericope but is unrelated to the purple garment.[59] Nevertheless, Scholem is correct when he goes on to say that the original version of R. Simai's tradition may have read: "He clothed them in royal purple and the ineffable Name was inscribed upon it."[60] If this is the original version, it bears a striking resemblance to a passage stressed by Scholem which describes "the garment of Zoharariel JHWH God of Israel, who comes crowned to the throne of His glory, and it is every part engraved from within and from without JHWH JHWH."[61]

This juxtaposition of the garment and the crown may have been known to R. Simai, for he seems to have been the first to assert that the Israelites at Sinai had special crowns too:

> R. Simai expounded: When Israel put "we will do" before "we will listen" 600,000 min-istering angels descended, and they affixed on each and every Israelite two crowns – one for "we will do" and one for "we will listen."[62]

---

[54] III Enoch 12.1, 2.

[55] Scholem, *Major Trends*, pp. 44, 55.

[56] HR 24 as cited in Scholem, *Gnosticism*, p. 26.

[57] HR 3.4, p. 86.

[58] Scholem, *Gnosticism*, p. 131.

[59] R. Eliezer's tradition appears without the phrase "from the splendor of His glory" in Tan. B IV, 76, Ex. R 41.7, and Num. R 16.24.

[60] Scholem, *Gnosticism*, p. 132, citing Benzion Luria, *Beth Mikra*, VII, fasc. 4 (1963), p. 108. This is the reading in Num. R 16.24 and in Tan. Shalah 13 (attributed, probably erroneously, to R. Huna), which concludes "the ineffable Name was inscribed upon them." Cf. Tan. B IV, 76, n. 9.

[61] HR 3.4, p. 86; cf. Scholem, *Gnosticism*, pp. 59, 60. It is interesting that in Jellinek's edition just the key phrase "*JHWH JHWH*" is omitted, although it is retained in the edition of S. Wertheimer, *Battei Midrashot*, I, 72.

[62] TB Shabbat 88 a.

This motif of crowns is also widespread in the esoteric texts; Odeberg says: "'Crowns' often termed 'crowns of glory' are frequently, one might say regularly, ascribed to angel-princes."[63] More specifically, one text tells us that these crowns are "affixed" (QŠR) to the heads of the angels, using precisely the same term found in R. Simai's midrash.[64] Moreover, as we would expect, the crown of God is an important theme in these sources; God is described, for example, as "crowned with magnificence and majesty, a crown of sublimity and a diadem of fearfulness"[65] and "surrounded with chains of crowns."[66] In fact, it would seem that "crown" was one of the esoteric names for God in the Merkabah tradition.[67] The most precise parallel to R. Simai's tradition, however, appears in the late addition to Heikalot Rabbati called the "Prince of the Torah."[68] There we find the Prince of the Torah telling the "descenders to the Merkabah": "I know what you are seeking and my heart understands what you desire: you are seeking a great amount of Torah and heaps of Talmud . . . to affix crowns to your heads and diadems of royalty."[69] God Himself says to the "descender": "Sit before My throne as you would sit in an academy and take a crown and receive it and study this tractate of the Prince of the Torah."[70] These passages from the "Prince of the Torah" are especially noteworthy for their connection of the donning of crowns with the learning of Torah. Although the statement of this connection in such explicit terms is apparently a late phenomenon, the general notion that esoteric learning is linked to Torah study is probably much older.[71]

In reviewing R. Simai's contribution we may say this: R. Simai depicted the Israelites at Sinai as receiving royal crowns and garments. We have no direct evidence that the "descenders to the Merkabah" claimed to wear such royal apparel, although it is plausible that they might have done so. We do know that both God and the angels are depicted in this way. So we can conclude that R. Simai's description implies (whether intentionally or not) that the Israelites became in some way more like God and the divine beings as they were known in the esoteric texts.

Having surveyed the tannaitic midrashim on Sinai which have parallels in the esoteric literature, we may now offer some concluding remarks on the significance of this material. First, it should be said that there may very well be other relevant midrashim which have some link with esoteric concerns. I have discussed here

---

[63] III Enoch, p. 32 (English Text), note to 12.3; cf. the many references given there.

[64] HR 11.1, p. 91.

[65] HR 24 as cited in Scholem, *Gnosticism*, p. 26.

[66] *Ibid.*, as cited in Scholem, *Gnosticism*, p. 62.

[67] ARN version A, ch. 12 end; cf. Scholem, *Gnosticism*, pp. 54, 78.

[68] On the dating of this text, see Scholem, *Kabbalah*, p. 374.

[69] HR 28.1, 2, p. 105.

[70] *Ibid.*, 29.6, p. 106.

[71] Cf., e.g., HR 20.1, p. 98; Tos. Hagigah 2.1; Urbach, "Hamasoret," p. 3; and Chap. III, Sec. III below.

only those which seem to show fairly obvious parallels. As our knowledge of the esoteric traditions continues to grow, there may well be other midrashic traditions which deserve to be included here, but at present these seem to be the only ones which are fairly certain. In addition, I have been concerned here only with traditions speaking of the Israelites at Sinai as a whole. There is a very rich and complex tradition concerning the ascension of Moses to heaven which surely has close parallels in the esoteric literature but which deserves to be studied separately.[72]

Within these limits, it seems clear that nearly all of the important themes of Merkabah mysticism are also to be found in the tannaitic midrashim on the revelation at Sinai. The Israelites are said to be on the same plane as the angels, in an environment of fire, lightning, and thunder, in the presence of the divine chariot and "glory" and the fiery word of God, which they see. They are given a weapon with the theurgically powerful ineffable Name, as well as the royal apparel of crowns and special garments. Their response to this is one of numinous awe and the singing of a hymn to God — the Song of Songs. And, very importantly, all of this takes place for one purpose: so that they may learn the divine teachings which have hitherto been unknown to human beings. We have seen that some form of most of these motifs was known by the time of R. Akiba's death, though they continued to be developed by his disciples in various ways. Given the pervasive influence of R. Akiba and his disciples, it seems safe to conclude that by the end of the second century these traditions were well-known among the Palestinian rabbis and, taken as an aggregate, made it easily possible to interpret the experience at Sinai as something very much like the "descent to the Merkabah" (with the important exception that the Merkabah and its attendant environment had descended to the people at Sinai). And such a possibility for interpretation might easily have existed as early as the lifetime of R. Akiba himself.

At this point it is tempting to hypothesize that in fact these midrashim were consciously modeled on the experience of ecstatic ascent which was the source of Merkabah mysticism. This would follow the general model offered by Scholem: when an early midrash is found to have a parallel in the esoteric literature, he has generally assumed this to demonstrate that the midrash is rooted in and reflects the esoteric tradition. However, in our particular case such arguments need not be compelling. Urbach has argued that the various elements such as the descent of fire and of angels were not combined with the learning of Torah to produce an esoteric tradition until the third century.[73] Maier has claimed that the numinous features of the Sinai midrashim originated independently and were not applied to ecstatic

---

[72] For a compilation of relevant sources see Ginzberg, *Legends*, vol. VI, pp. 47—49, nn. 247—257. For a study of some of this material see Joseph P. Schultz, "Angelic Opposition to the Ascension of Moses and the Revelation of the Law," *Jewish Quarterly Review*, vol. LXI (April, 1971), pp. 282—307.

[73] Urbach, "Hamasoret."

ascents until the third century.[74] Gruenwald has expressed a more cautious mediating view:

> In the words of the tannaim on the revelation of the Shekinah at Mount Sinai it is already possible to find elements drawn from mystical sources alongside elements which are not linked in any close or direct way to the thought-world of the mystics. But even in the latter case one may conjecture that they also have some points of contact with mystical matters.[75]

It is perfectly possible that individual elements of the midrashic traditions we have examined do have their origin outside the esoteric tradition. It has been suggested, for example, that the concept of God's word as fire is based on Greek philosophical conceptions.[76] The stress on fire and lightning and thunder could be merely an elaboration of the plain meaning of the Biblical text. The "royal purple" garment has no direct analogue in the extant esoteric texts and so may reflect some other tradition (with political implications?). On the other hand, it is equally possible that all of these traditions are consciously drawn from a developed esoteric tradition centering on the Merkabah and well-known to the second century rabbis. In that case, we might have, in midrashim such as R. Simeon b. Yohai's on the sword or R. Simai's on the purple garment, evidence about the Merkabah mystics which is not obtainable from strictly esoteric texts. So, given the present state of our knowledge, either of the arguments on historical priority seems tenable, as does a mediating position which would claim that the influence worked both ways simultaneously.

But I want to suggest that questions of historical precedence and filiation, while important, are not crucial here. Regardless of the historian's judgments the striking number of parallels between exoteric and esoteric traditions can tell us something important about rabbinic Judaism and the place of esotericism within it. Let us assume first that the ecstatic experience and the esoteric tradition it spawned were not in existence in the tannaitic era in rabbinic circles. Then we must ask why, when that tradition did originate, it took as one of its important models the experience of the Israelites at Sinai (as described in midrash). The answer to this question, it seems to me, is most probably to be found in the very difficult predi-

---

[74] Maier, *Vom Kultus*, pp. 131–146.

[75] Ithamar Gruenwald, review of *Rivalität zwischen Engeln und Menschen* by P. Schäfer, in *Kiryat Sefer*, vol. 51 (September, 1976), p. 661. Cf. Gruenwald's general remarks on esoteric elements in rabbinic midrash in "Yannai and Hekhaloth Literature," *Tarbiz*, vol. 36 (April, 1967), pp. 257–277. P. S. Alexander, in "The Historical Setting of the Hebrew Book of Enoch," *Journal of Jewish Studies*, vol. 28 (Autumn, 1977), pp. 156–180, has also noted the close relationship between rabbinic midrash and ecstatic experience in Merkabah mysticism, stressing the "orthodoxy" of the mystics.

[76] Abraham Joshua Heschel, *Torah min Hashamayim B'aspeklaryah Shel Hadorot*, vol. II, p. 22; Ithamar Gruenwald, "Some Critical Notes on the First Part of Sefer Yezirah," *Revue des Études Juives*, vol. 132 (1973), pp. 500–504.

cament of the earliest "descenders to the Merkabah." If they did live in the third century, they must have been developing, quite consciously, a Jewish analogue to the many contemporary non-Jewish techniques for attaining ecstatic illumination. The similarities between Merkabah mysticism and these non-Jewish traditions of *"gnosis"* are so striking that they have led Scholem to label Merkabah mysticism a "Jewish Gnosticism." Yet we know that the interpretive frameworks surrounding ecstatic experience in the Hellenistic world, particularly in the more strictly Gnostic circles, were often inimical to basic contents of rabbinic Judaism. Thus the early Merkabah mystics must have run a high risk of being labelled *"minim"* – heretics – and being excluded from the rabbinic community, a fate which they obviously wished to avoid. What better way could be found to assert one's legitimacy within the rabbinic community than to claim that one was actually repeating the experience of the Israelites at Sinai? Certainly other Biblical paradigms might be found as well (e. g., Ezekiel, Isaiah, Daniel). But the use of Sinai as a legitimating paradigm would create a chain of tradition going back to the very inception of the convenantal relationship, in much the same way as the chain of tradition invoked at the beginning of Pirkei Abot legitimated exoteric rabbinic Torah study. Moreover, these earliest Merkabah visionaries must have been rather overwhelmed by the intensity of their experiences, some of which purported to culminate in visions of the divine "glory" itself. Given the great importance of Biblical paradigms in rabbinic Judaism, it is unlikely that Jews attempting to stay within the rabbinic framework would arrogate to themselves the privilege of a relationship with God which was closer and more immediate than that of their Biblical ancestors. Thus they would have even stronger motivation to depict their experiences as repetitions of the Sinai experience, thereby giving themselves and others an interpretive framework in which to make sense of their experience.

Now let us assume, conversely, that the main features of Merkabah mysticism were already crystallized and known to the rabbis in the early second century. In this case we must ask why the rabbis chose to depict the Sinai event in terms drawn from that tradition. I would suggest, as one plausible interpretation, that here too it is basically a question of legitimation. Some of the rabbis, like R. Akiba, may well have had ecstatic experience of the Merkabah themselves; others no doubt had direct acquaintance with those who were having such experiences. They had, therefore, to accept the existence of such ecstatic experiences as a given which, in itself, was not schismatic. The danger surely existed, however, that the interpretive frameworks created by and for these experiences might become schismatic and even heretical, leading out of Judaism and into Gnosticism. The problem, then (and it may have been an overriding problem for the second-century tannaim), was to integrate these new experiences into the total gestalt of Jewish religiosity as the tannaim were attempting to shape it. One obvious way to solve this problem was to assert that these experiences were not in fact new, but rather could be traced back to the beginnings of Judaism at Sinai, thereby legitimizing them as indigenously and authentically Jewish. This could be done, of course, by describing the Sinai event in terms drawn from the experience of the Merkabah mystics. And here again the problem of the direct encounter with the divine had to be dealt with. The rabbis could hardly have admitted that these mystics were having a closer relationship with God than those who stood at Sinai. Thus they gave the Israelites at Sinai privileges which no contemporary of theirs could claim: they made God Himself descend to the people, as we have noted, and they asserted that the vision at Sinai was uniquely and unrepeatably great:

> "For on the third day the Lord will come down upon Mount Sinai in the sight of all the people" (Ex. 19:11). This teaches that in that hour they saw what Ezekiel and Isaiah never saw, as it is said, "And through the prophets I will speak in parables" (Hos. 12:11).[77]

I suggest, then, that regardless of the historical questions the same significance for the parallels between midrash and esoterica may be reasonably postulated: they demonstrate the attempt to legitimate a new kind of religious experience in terms acceptable to the wider religious community. Yet the choice of the Sinai event as a crucial legitimating paradigm has consequences which go beyond the formal appearance of legitimation and affect central questions of the meaning of the religious experience itself. By placing Sinai in such a central role, either the second-century tannaim or the third-century Merkabah mystics would have been affirming the centrality of the Torah and law revealed there by the Creator, whose goodness in giving this law is also implicitly affirmed. This would be, of course, a direct denial of the central tenets of Gnosticism, in which the creating and revealing God of the Bible is an evil being; his "tyrannical world-rule is called *heimarmene*, universal Fate . . . In its psychical aspect, which includes for instance the institution and enforcement of the Mosaic Law, it aims at the enslavement of man."[78]

Moreover, in rabbinic Judaism the moment of revelation plays a crucial role as a turning point in the movement of history from creation to redemption — a movement which is affirmed as ultimately positive in Judaism but wholly negative in Gnosticism, where "history is useless . . . Time is perceived and conceived as strangeness, servitude, and evil."[79] In this context, too, the choice of Sinai as a legitimating paradigm would have been a direct affirmation of fundamental Jewish belief in the face of Gnostic denial. If, then, the Merkabah mystics of the third century modeled their experience on the Sinai midrashim, they were clearly denying any relationship with the basic concepts of Gnosticism, though they may have borrowed some external techniques and features from the Gnostics. If, on the other hand, the tannaim were shaping their midrash to conform with existing Merkabah mysticism, they were saying implicitly that Merkabah mysticism was

---

[77] Mek. Yitro Bahodesh 3, p. 212; cf. Mek. RS 154.
[78] Hans Jonas, *The Gnostic Religion*, p. 43.
[79] H. C. Puech, "Gnosis and Time," in *Man and Time, Papers from the Eranos Yearbooks*, pp. 63, 64.

consistent (and must stay consistent) with a law-affirming and history-affirming Judaism in which Sinai must continue to be of central importance.

But we may take this analysis one step further and suggest that not only the framework of theological interpretation but also the meaning of ecstatic experience itself is at issue here. In Gnosticism, despite the wide variety of forms it took, there seems to be general agreement that the reception of esoteric revealed knowledge is in itself the central saving experience. The Gnostic myth, says Jonas, "claims saving power for itself *qua known*; it *is* in short, the *gnosis* . . . this knowledge of truth is as such held to be liberating."[80] The revealed knowledge, he goes on to say, may include techniques for ascent to the higher worlds, but this ascent will only take place after death — the ascent is a product, not a source, of saving knowledge.[81] Van Baaren suggests that the ascent of the soul is not in fact a saving experience in itself: "In gnosticism the ascension of the soul is placed after death and it forms a symbolic expression of the liberation of the spiritual part of man from the shackles of this material world."[82] In other words, the ascent is a sign that the individual has already been saved, rather than a salvific event in itself.

If the Sinai event served as paradigm for ecstatic ascent in Judaism, the significance of that ascent would be altogether different. While the mystic in his ascent gain revealed knowledge, that knowledge could not be redemptive in itself. For the fundamental knowledge necessary for redemption is that revealed in the paradigmatic event — the revelation of Torah. No other ecstatic experience could be allowed to supercede the primacy of Sinai. And the knowledge of Torah could never in itself be redemptive, because redemption depended on the decision of the will to obey Torah; even those who prized "study" over "doing" did so because "study leads to doing."[83] Moreover, the ascent in Judaism took place during life as a temporary event, rather than after death. Thus the ability to make such an ascent could never in itself be evidence that one had been in any sense "saved," as it may have been in Gnosticism. In general, we may say that in Gnosticism one received knowledge, then was saved, and then made the ecstatic ascent, while in Judaism the order was reversed: the Israelites at Sinai had the ecstatic experience, as a result of it gained knowledge of Torah, and then (if they obeyed Torah) were redeemed.[84]

---

[80] Hans Jonas, "Delimitation of the Gnostic Phenomenon — Typological and Historical," in *Le'Origini dello Gnosticismo*, p. 99.

[81] *Ibid.*, pp. 99, 107.

[82] Th. P. Van Baaren, "Towards a Definition of Gnosticism," in *Le Origini dello Gnosticismo*, p. 176.

[83] TB Kiddushin 40b.

[84] P. S. Alexander, in "The Historical Setting," offers a brief balanced summary of the similarities and differences between Gnosticism and Merkabah mysticism, concluding that it is "premature . . . to categorize the Jewish texts as 'Gnostic.'" (p. 180) In this context he points out that "Rabbinic 'Gnosis' is not soteric" (a point already made by Gruenwald, "Knowledge and Vision," pp. 99, 106), and that in Gnosticism "there is little or no

In conclusion, we may say that the midrashim on Sinai which we have reviewed seem to be important evidence for the ability and desire of the rabbis to
incorporate esotericism into their religious community without changing that
community's basic principles. Certainly there are formal affinities between Jewish
esotericism and Gnosticism, and these may well reflect substantive elements which
were held in common by the two. Both, for example, indicate the desire to leave
the mundane plane, to experience the divine as that which far transcends the
cosmos. In Judaism, however, this experience, whatever form it took, would be
only temporary, whereas the Gnostic would have seen it as a permanent salvific
state. More crucially, perhaps, as Jonas points out, "the Gnostic God is not merely
extra-mundane and supra-mundane, but in his ultimate meaning contra-mundane."[85]
While Judaism could apparently find room for the experience of God as both extra-
and supra-mundane, it could not tolerate a God who was contra-mundane. Yet it is
this last characteristic which seems to be the key to understanding Gnosticism in all
its varied forms. Thus we must conclude that the substantive differences between
Gnosticism and Jewish esotericism definitely outweigh both the formal and substantive similarities. Given the extent to which the rabbis illuminated and reinforced
these central differences through midrash, it is questionable whether the term
"Jewish Gnosticism" is helpful in our attempt to understand rabbinic esotericism.

---

evidence of the ascent being anticipated in mystic ecstacy in this life. In Heikalot literature,
on the other hand, the ascent is made during lifetime, and followed by descent." (p. 179)
The same distinction has been mentioned by Maier (*Vom Kultus*, p. 17):

 "It is not a soul essentially different from and detachable from the body which ascends
 to God's throne, but the mystic in his own total person. Only in very late texts
 can the heavenly journey of the souls of the dead be described by means of the old
 esoteric depictions of ascent. Thus in the phenomenology of religion the ascent of the
 mystics to the Merkabah belongs rather to the sphere of temporary ascensions than to
 the gnostic heavenly journey of the soul."

The emphasis on covenant and law in Jewish esotericism has been thrown into sharp relief
by G. A. Wewers, whose *Geheimnis und Geheimhaltung im rabbinischen Judentum*
(Berlin and New York: Walter de Gruyter, 1975) places the twin themes of Torah and
"chosenness" at the very center of all esoteric interests in rabbinic literature. If Wewers'
theory can be sustained, it would make the centrality of Sinai in rabbinic esotericism rather
self-evident and add an important dimension to the present study.

[85] Jonas, *Gnostic Religion*, p. 251.

II. REVELATION AND MERKABAH MYSTICISM
IN THIRD-CENTURY MIDRASH

In the period of the amorain, *matan Torah* continued to be a central focus of midrashic activity, and the pattern we have been tracing was very much alive. Among the Palestinian rabbis of the third century, it appears that R. Johanan was the first to take a serious interest in the traditions which seem to link the revelation at Sinai with Merkabah mysticism. His relevant midrash has come down to us in a number of different versions:

> "The chariots of God, twice then thousand, thousands upon thousands, the Lord among them, Sinai in holiness" (Ps. 68:18). R. Johanan said: On the day that the Holy One blessed be He appeared on Mt. Sinai to give the Torah to Israel, 600,000 ministering angels descended with Him, and in the hand of each one was a crown with which to crown each Israelite.[1]
> "Who satisfies you with good as long as you live" (Ps. 103:5).[2] R. Johanan began the exposition of Scripture by referring to Sinai: At the time when Israel received the Torah, 600,000 ministering angels descended and put crowns upon their heads.[3]
> R. Aba b. Kahana in the name of R. Johanan said: 1,200,000, and one would put a crown on his head while one would gird him with a weapon.[4]
> R. Aba b. Kahana in the name of R. Johanan said: 1,200,000 ministering angels descended with the Holy One blessed be He − 600,000 affixed crowns and 600,000 girded them with girdles.[5]

Since so many variants of R. Johanan's midrash are known,[6] it is probably impossible to determine an original reading. It is interesting to note that basically the same midrash is offered as an exposition of four different Biblical verses.[7] This may indicate that R. Johanan repeated this midrash on different occasions, thus explain-

---

[1] PR 21.7, 102b.

[2] The translation follows the RSV, which notes in the margin that the Hebrew is uncertain. R. Johanan interpreted the last word, *'adayik* ("as long as you live") as "your ornaments."

[3] MT 103.8; Tan. B T'zaveh 7; Y Ps. 858.

[4] Wilhelm Bacher, PA, I, p. 218, points out that R. Aba is a frequent tradent of R. Johanan's traditions.

[5] PR 33.10, 154a. "Girdles," Heb. *zoniyot*, is probably a corruption of "weapons," Heb. *zayin*; cf. n. 48 below.

[6] Cf. also PRK 16.3; Tan. B add. to Shalah 1; Ex. R 51.8.

[7] PR 21.7 − Ps. 68:18; PR 33.10−Ezek. 16:10; PRK 16.3−Lam. 2:13; MT 103.8 and parallels−Ps. 103:5.

ing the variants, or it may indicate that his midrash was well known and widely circulated, so that later redactors could attach it to various verses. In either case, the divergent readings make it quite likely that the substance of the midrash accurately reflects the view of R. Johanan himself. Thus we can say with some certainty that he first brought together several tannaitic motifs which we have examined:[8] the descent of the angels and of God himself to Mount Sinai, the crowning of the Israelites, and the presentation of weapons. (Because R. Johanan claimed that the angels gave each Israelite a weapon, he had to change R. Simeon b. Yohai's singular weapon into a plurality of weapons).

It seems reasonable to assume that R. Johanan combined these motifs because he saw some common thread tying them together. If he did in fact connect this same midrash with more than one Biblical verse, we can say that the common thread is not found in the Biblical text; at the very least we can be sure that later redactors did not see the common thread in any Biblical text, and it is hard to see how any of the verses used here could in fact offer a source of cohesion for the various motifs. It seems more likely that R. Johanan found the motifs to be related because they all had some potential for linking Sinai with the realm of esoterica.[9]

Further evidence that R. Johanan connected the revelation with Merkabah speculation has been offered by Professor Lieberman. In Song of Songs Rabbah we find: "'Let him kiss me with kisses from his mouth' (Song 1:2). Where was it first said? . . . R. Johanan said: It was said at Sinai."[10] In Lieberman's words:

> Those who think that the Song was [first] recited at Sinai also say that [the Israelites] actually saw Him, as it were. Thus in Song of Songs Rabbah 1:2: "Let him kiss me with kisses from His mouth" — R. Johanan began the exposition of Scripture by referring to the Israelites at the time when they went up to Mt. Sinai, etc . . . R. Simeon b. Yohai taught: This is what they asked: They said: Our wish is to see the glory of our King.[11]

The text of Song of Songs Rabbah itself does not give evidence here that R. Johanan was referring directly to R. Simeon b. Yohai's view. But we have just seen that he

---

[8] This assumes that the tradition attributed to R. Elazar b. Arak in PRE 112a is a pseudepigraph.

[9] The connection of the 600,000 angels with the crowns had already been made by R. Simai and thus forms an intermediary link between the tannaitic traditions and R. Johanan. E. E. Urbach, *Hazal, Pirke 'Emunot V'de'ot*, p. 127, n. 46, points out that "in fact we find that R. Johanan hands on traditions of R. Simai," but he goes on to deny that R. Johanan knew this particular tradition of R. Simai, because R. Johanan's midrash in TB Shabbat 88a is linked to one of R. Hama b. Hanina, not to the preceding one of R. Simai. However since both R. Hama b. Hanina and R. Simai used the same proof-text, Ex. 33:6, R. Johanan's use of Ex. 33:7 could just as well have been a response to either (or both), and the particular arrangement in the text is the work of a later redactor. Thus I fail to see the validity of Urbach's point.

[10] Song R 1.2.

[11] Saul Lieberman, "Mishnat Shir Hashirim," p. 121.

did draw on R. Simeon b. Yohai for part of his midrash on Sinai, and it was extremely common for R. Johanan to hand on the traditions of R. Simeon b. Yohai.[12] So it is at least plausible to agree with Lieberman that R. Johanan was asserting a direct vision of the divine glory at Sinai.

A younger contemporary of R. Johanan, R. Tanhum b. Hanilai, offered a brief but colorful amplification of the midrash on Ps. 68:18: "'The chariots of God, twice ten thousand, thousands upon thousands' — R. Tanhum b. Hanilai said: To the point where even a mathematician can not calculate them."[13] Since R. Tanhum b. Hanilai is known as a tradent of R. Johanan's midrash,[14] it is possible that we have here his own elaboration of the latter's teaching about the many angels. But another possibility is that R. Tanhum was elaborating a midrash of his teacher, R. Joshua b. Levi, many of whose traditions he transmitted.[15] For in the same pericope in Pesikta Rabbati we find, immediately following R. Tanhum's midrash: "R. Azariah and R. Judah b. R. Simon in the name of R. Joshua b. Levi: 'Twice ten thousand' — for there is no number to them."[16] In any event, it seems safe to conclude that by the middle of the third century the vast throng of angels, a common feature of the Merkabah texts, was also a common feature of midrashic elaborations of the revelation at Sinai.

R. Johanan's assertion that the Israelites saw God directly at Sinai seems to have been endorsed by his contemporary and close associate, R. Simeon b. Lakish: "Now on the day of the giving of the Torah, the Holy One blessed be He split open the heavens and showed Israel what is on high. R. Pinhas and R. Levi in the name of R. Simeon b. Lakish: The Holy One blessed be He split open the seven firmaments for them."[17] It seems likely that the attribution of this midrash is authentic, even though we have no attributed parallels to confirm it. There is frequent evidence in rabbinic texts of the close relationship between R. Levi and the school of R. Johanan, including R. Simeon b. Lakish, and also of the frequency with which R. Pinhas transmitted traditions known to R. Levi[18] So the chain of transmission cited here is certainly plausible. Moreover, this midrash appears in a rather artfully composed pericope whose redactor obviously chose existing traditions as the material for his composition. All of the traditions he used are anonymous in the extant text except for this one; it seems likely that the redactor included the attri-

---

[12] Bacher, PA, I, p. 206, n. 7.

[13] PR 21.8, 103a; Cf. PRK 12.22; MT 68.10; Y Yitro 286 and Ps. 736. The readings are rather confused — cf. the notes of Friedmann in PR and Buber in MT *ad loc.* — but this is clearly the original intent of the midrash, though it may have read "to the point where [only] a mathematician can calculate them."

[14] Bacher, PA, I, p. 219.

[15] *Ibid.*, pp. 130–131.

[16] R. Joshua b. Levi interpreted *shinan* as *she'ayn*, "for there is no."

[17] Dt. R ed. Lieberman pp. 65–66.

[18] Bacher, PA, II, pp. 296–305.

bution because he received the tradition this way. Otherwise we would have to argue that he arbitrarily made up this chain of transmission while leaving all the other traditions in his pericope anonymous — hardly a likely course of events.

Yet we must recognize that a similar tradition about the splitting of the seven firmaments appears in a number of later midrashic texts,[19] in every case anonymously (though two are attributed to "our sages"). If R. Simeon b. Lakish had in fact created this tradition himself, we would expect to find it cited in his name in other texts. Perhaps the best solution to this problem is to surmise that the tradition was already circulating anonymously in R. Simeon's day and that he incorporated it into his own midrashim, from whence R. Levi and then R. Pinhas heard it. Among the anonymous versions, one which is especially intriguing is discussed briefly by Scholem:

> R. Joshua ibn Shoeib quotes a passage from Midrash Hazita in his Derashot (ed. 1574, fol. 58 a) not found in our text of Song of Songs Rabbah on Song of Songs 2:4: "What is the meaning of 'His banner over me was love'? At Sinai He split open the seven firmaments for me, as it is written, 'To you it was shown, that you might know' [Dt. 4:35], and He showed me there the chambers of [ḥadrei] the Merkabah." The term "chambers of the Merkabah" for the object of the Merkabah vision was current in the second and third century traditions of several aggadists; cf. Major Trends p. 359. All these passages do not employ mere poetic figures of speech, but a consistent technical language developed by the Merkabah mystics.[20]

This does not prove, of course, that R. Simeon b. Lakish was referring explicitly to a vision of the "chambers of the Merkabah" in his midrash, nor that such a vision at Sinai was asserted in the third century. It does make both of these alternatives possible, however, and it shows at the very least that later generations would have had little trouble putting R. Simeon's tradition into an esoteric context.

We know that the splitting of the seven firmaments did play a role in Merkabah mysticism for we find in the earliest of the Merkabah texts, Re'uyot Yehezkiel: "While Ezekiel was gazing the Holy One opened up the seven firmaments for him and he saw the glory."[21] We can also point to several passages in the extant rabbinic literature which employ this motif in esoteric contexts.[22] As for R. Simeon b. Lakish himself, his cryptic interpretation of Gen. 35:13 — "The patriarchs, they are the Merkabah" — whatever its meaning, at least attests to his interest in the Merkabah.[23] When we combine this with his obvious awareness of the tradition that

---

[19] Noted by Lieberman in Dt. R ad loc.
[20] Gershom Scholem, Jewish Gnosticism, Merkabah Mysticism, and Talmudic Tradition, p. 68 n. 12. On "ḥadrei merkabah" cf. Johann Maier, Vom Kultus zur Gnosis, pp. 142–143.
[21] RY p. 111.
[22] These are listed by Lieberman in Dt. R p. 65 n. 13 and by Gruenwald in his comment on RY p. 111.
[23] Gen. R 82.6, p. 983, and parallels cited there; cf. Gershom Scholem, Major Trends in Jewish Mysticism, p. 79.

the Israelites had seen the divine glory at Sinai, and in light of the ease with which the splitting of the firmaments could be given an esoteric interpretation, it is hard to resist the conclusion that R. Simeon b. Lakish himself was referring to some aspect of the esoteric tradition. Again, however, such a conclusion must rest on its plausibility rather than incontrovertible proof.

Another variant on the theme of the vision of God at Sinai also seems to have arisen some time during the third century, or perhaps even earlier. Its history is relatively clear and quite interesting. In both versions of the Mekilta we find:

> "This is my God and I will praise Him" (Ex. 15:2). R. Eliezer says: Why can you say that a maid-servant at the Sea saw what Isaiah and Ezekiel never saw? For it is said, "And through the prophets I gave parables" (Hos. 12:11), and it is written, "And the heavens were opened and I saw visions of God" (Ezek. 1:1).[24]

The point of this midrash is that the prophets — even Isaiah and Ezekiel who claim to have had direct visions of God — did not receive as full or direct a revelation as did the lowliest Israelite at the Reed Sea. This direct revelation explains why the Israelites were able to identify God and say "This [and no other] is my God."[25] While it is difficult to ascertain the original intent of this midrash, the reference to Ezekiel 1:1 certainly raises the possibility of a link with *ma'aseh Merkabah*.

The later history of this midrash tells us little about its original intent, however, because it was removed from its context as a midrash on the crossing of the Reed Sea and turned into a midrash on the revelation at Sinai, one with a clear esoteric intent:

> "And the people saw" (Ex. 20:18). What did they see? They saw the great glory. R. Eliezer says: Why can you say that an Israelite maid-servant saw what the greatest of the prophets never saw? You learn it from what is said: "And the people saw" — What did they see? They saw the great glory.[26]
> "Before the eyes of all the people" (Ex. 19:11). It teaches that they saw at that moment what Isaiah and Ezekiel never saw, as it is said, "And through the prophets I gave parables."[27]

As noted above, anonymous traditions in the Mekilta are difficult to date; if they are not tannaitic, it is at least quite likely that they come from the third century. There is one attributed version of this tradition as a midrash on Sinai which, if the attribution is accurate, comes from some time in the third century:

> R. Hoshaiah said: The lowliest person in the days of Moses saw what Ezekiel, the greatest of the prophets, never saw — people with whom the Shekinah spoke face to face, as it is said, "The Lord spoke with you face to face" (Dt. 5:4).[28]

---

[24] Mek. Shirah Bahodesh 3, p. 126; Mek. RS 78. Cf. Max Kadushin, *The Rabbinic Mind*, p. 231, n. 44.
[25] This interpretation is confirmed by Song R 2.14.3.
[26] Mek. RS 154; cf. RY p. 113.
[27] Mek. Yitro Bahodesh 3, p. 212.
[28] Dt. R. 7.8.

We may be dealing here with the R. Hoshaiah of the first generation of amoraim, who was a teacher of R. Johanan. However it seems more likely that this is the R. Hoshaiah of the third generation, who was a student of R. Johanan; we shall see that a number of the latter's students asserted in some way the direct vision of God at Sinai.[29] In either event, we have an interesting connection with R. Johanan and an obvious attempt to take an originally unrelated midrash and relate it to his view that the Israelites had seen God. The historical relation between his attributed midrash and the anonymous versions in the Mekilta is unclear. But regardless of which is the original, we can conclude that in the third century (or earlier) a midrash with obvious esoteric implications was severed from its connection with the Reed Sea and intentionally brought into connection with Sinai.

In the third generation of amoraim, the students of R. Johanan handed on and developed midrashim on Sinai which seem to have esoteric implications. R. Elazar b. Pedat, who according to the Talmud was invited by R. Johanan to study *ma'aseh Merkabah*,[30] seems to have made explicit his teacher's implicit assertion that the Israelites did see God at Sinai:

> "The chariots of God, twice ten thousand, thousands upon thousands [*shinan*], the Lord among them, Sinai in holiness" (Ps. 68:18). R. Elazar b. Pedat said: What is the meaning of *shinan*? The most beautiful [*na'in*] and glorious among them [i. e., the angels who descended on Sinai]. But nevertheless, "the Lord among them" — the most distinguished among them. The Community of Israel said: "My beloved is all radiant and ruddy" (Song 5:10).[31]

We have already seen that Ps. 68:18 was a key verse for apparently esoteric midrashim on Sinai, but more important here is the reference to Song 5:10. In concluding his survey of tannaitic approaches to the Song of Songs, Lieberman states:

> Hence I find acceptable the supposition of Scholem that the mishnah of Shiur Komah is the early midrash to Song of Songs 5:10—16, which was included in the ancient "Midrash on Song of Songs." The Shiur Komah is laud and praise to the Holy One blessed be He in a form and manner beyond our grasp. And in Mekilta B'shalah Shira 3, p. 127: ("This is my God and I will praise Him") R. Akiba says: I will speak about the beauty and glory of He who spoke and the world came into being, in the presence of all the nations of the world, etc . . . And Israel says to the nations of the world: Do you know

---

[29] Herman L. Strack, *Introduction to the Talmud and Midrash*, pp. 120, 126.

[30] TB Hagigah 13a. David Halperin, in "Merkabah and Ma'aseh Merkabah, According to Rabbinic Sources" Ch. 6 n. 112, refers to "the story's claim that R. Elazar never learned *ma'aseh merkabah*." But Halperin himself notes that the meaning of the story, with R. Elazar's enigmatic reply, "I am not old enough," is not at all clear. It need not rule out some acquaintance with esoteric matters. Since R. Elazar was a student of Rav (TB Hullin 111b), it is at least plausible that he had begun the study of *ma'aseh merkabah* and for that very reason was invited to continue his study by R. Johanan after having arrived in Palestine.

[31] PRK 12:22; Tan. B Yitro 14; shortened version in PR 21.8, 103b.

Him? We will tell you a small part of His glory: "My beloved is all radiant and ruddy, distinguished among ten thousand" (Song 5:10).[32]

We can not trace a direct line from R. Akiba's midrash to R. Elazar b. Pedat's, but it seems likely that any third century rabbi who cited Song 5:10 in the context of the Sinai revelation would have been making a point with some esoteric dimension. Within the Shiur Komah tradition, the "beauty" and "glory" of God (note that both R. Akiba and R. Elazar used exactly the same words) would refer to an actual physical appearance of God as seen by the mystics. Both Scholem and Lieberman believe that such a physical vision is attributed to the Israelites at Sinai in tannaitic midrash, and certainly the same would hold true for amoraic midrash. We can not assert the validity of this conclusion quite so flatly on the basis of the evidence adduced here, but we can again say that it has a fair degree of probability.

A more explicit assertion that the Israelites saw God at Sinai came from another student of R. Johanan, R. Levi, who was apparently responding to another midrash on Ps. 68:18 by R. Elazar:

> "The chariots of God, twice ten thousand, thousands upon thousands." R. Elazar b. Pedat said: And they all descended keen [shinunim] on destroying the enemies of Israel. For if they had not accepted the Torah they would have destroyed them. R. Levi said: But they had seen the face of the Holy One blessed be He [and therefore could not be destroyed] since anyone who sees the face of the Holy One blessed be He does not die, as it is said, "In the light of a king's face there is life" (Prov. 16:15).[33]

It is surprising to find R. Elazar apparently offering such a completely different interpretation of the same Biblical verse; we must allow the possibility that one or the other of the midrashim on Ps. 68:18 attributed to him is pseudepigraphal, though this need by no means be the case. The one just cited has a good claim to be authentic, since it could very plausibly have evoked the response of R. Levi which has been handed on together with it. We have already noted that in the Merkabah texts the angels are depicted as willing to destroy humans who do not have the necessary spiritual prerequisites. Yet R. Elazar's interpretation here also fits into the context of a series of midrashim which tell of the imminent possibility of the Israelites' death at Sinai;[34] none of these shows any clear connection with esoteric traditions (although such a possibility should not be ruled out). It may be that R. Elazar was consciously trying to give an exoteric, moralizing turn to an esoteric tradition about the angels' presence at Sinai. Professor Scholem has pointed to the

---

[32] Lieberman, "Mishnat Shir Hashirim," p. 123.

[33] PRK 12.22; Tan. B Yitro 14 with minor variations. MT 68.10 reads "keen on destroying the world," and PR 21.7, 103b has the same reading but attributes the tradition to "the rabbis." R. Levi's retort indicates that the PRK reading is the original, since it makes no sense in the MT reading. Perhaps MT conflates R. Elazar's midrash with an earlier separate midrash of "the rabbis"; cf. MT 75.1; TB Shabbat 88a; PR 21.5, 100a for parallels to the midrash of "the rabbis." "The enemies of Israel" is a euphemism for "Israel."

[34] TB Abodah Zarah 2b; Song R 8.5.1; MT 68.9; and especially Dt. R 4.2.

existence of such a trend in the third century.[35] This suggestion would assume, of course, that there was an esoteric tradition about the dangerous intent of the angels at Sinai, and since there is no direct evidence of such a tradition, the suggestion is offered with caution.

R. Levi's response to R. Elazar is equally puzzling and intriguing, for it too seems to have no predecessor or successor in rabbinic tradition.[36] Both R. Johanan himself[37] and R. Isaac[38] commented on Prov. 16:15 in apparently esoteric contexts, but neither drew the conclusion of immortality for the Israelites from it. Nor do we find precisely the same idea expressed in the Merkabah texts themselves. We do find in the Shiur Komah: "Everyone who knows this measure [*shiur*] of our Creator, and the praise of the Holy One blessed be He which is hidden from the creatures, may be assured that he is a participant in the world to come."[39] And in the text Ma'aseh Merkabah we find:

> Every human being who has in his heart the praise of RVZYY YVY the God of Israel and to whom this great secret is revealed should study it every day at dawn and cleanse himself from wickedness and falsehood and every kind of evil . . . and he may be assured that he is a participant in the world to come.[40]

However neither of these passages say that the mystic will not die; in fact they imply that he will die, since only those who have died can participate in the world to come. Another passage in Ma'aseh Merkabah also appears to be relevant; it advises the "descender" to the Merkabah to "raise his eyes to heaven so that he will not die . . . and let him stand and mention a name and glorify . . . so that the demons will not come and seem to him to be angels and murder him."[41] Here the mystic is told how to avoid death in the "descent," but he is not told that having successfully completed it he will never die. If the avoidance of death were one of the rewards given to the Merkabah mystic it would surely be an important element in Merkabah literature. Yet such does not seem to be the case at all.

There is a tradition, dating from the latter half of the second century, that the Israelites at Sinai had gained immortality:

> When the Holy one blessed be He gave the Torah to Israel they were not subject to the rule of the angel of death, as it is said, "Graven [*ḥarut*] on the tablets" (Ex. 32:16). What is the meaning of "*ḥarut*?" R. Judah says: Freedom [*ḥerut*] from the exile. But R. Ne-

---

[35] Scholem, *Major Trends*, pp. 78–79.

[36] See the discussion by A. M. Goldberg, *Untersuchungen über die Vorstellung von der Schekhinah in der Frühen rabbinischen Literatur*, p. 264.

[37] Num. R 2.25; PRK 26.9; Y Lev. 524; Lev. R 20.10; Tan. Aharei 6.

[38] Num. R 21.16; PRK 6.1; PR 16.2, 80a and 48.3, 194a.

[39] Merkabah Shelemah 38b.

[40] MM par. 4.

[41] *Ibid.* par. 11. It is interesting that here it is not the angels themselves who are the potential sources of death, though in par. 9 of the same text we find: "that the ministering angels may not destroy me."

hemiah says: Freedom from the angel of death. R. Pinhas b. Hama said in the name of R. Johanan in the name of R. Eliezer b. R. Jose the Galileean: The Holy One blessed be He said: If the angel of death should come to me and say, "Why was I created?" I will tell him: "I created you to be the officer in charge of the other nations, but not of my children."[42]

There is no indication that this tradition was originally related to esoteric traditions; it may have been intended as one of the many midrashim drawing parallels between the Israelites at Sinai and the "righteous" in the world to come.[43] However at some point it was connected with the themes we have been examining, for a redactor added to the passage just cited the words: "for as soon as they accepted the Torah the Holy One blessed be He clothed them from the splendor of His glory [*meziv hadaro*]."[44] The same redactor or another then added a passage connecting this immortality with a number of themes which we have examined:

> And what was the clothing? R. Johanan says: He adorned them with crowns. And R. Simeon b. Yohai says: He gave them a weapon with the great Name engraved on it . . . And R. Simai says: He clothed them in royal purple. And R. Huna says: He clothed them with girdles. But when they sinned the Holy One blessed be He took away all this beneficence from them.[45]

This motif of immortality has been attached to one or all of these particular themes in a number of other texts,[46] but the pericope cited here seems to reflect most clearly the historical fact that this attachment is the work of later tradents and redactors. Yet it is possible that others in R. Levi's time also asserted the immortality of the Israelites in some esoteric context; perhaps the pericope discussed here may even reflect the substance, though not the exact wording of their assertions. The extant texts, however, do not give any support for this view.

The reference to R. Huna in this pericope should also be noticed. This is R. Huna b. Abin of Sepphoris, a fourth generation Palestinian amora who is known as a tradent of R. Johanan's traditions.[47] His statement that the Israelites at Sinai were girded with girdles ("*zoniyot*," a loan work from Greek "*zone*") is often repeated in our sources,[48] frequently as a midrash on Job 12:18. It always appears together with the midrashim about the crowns or the royal purple garments or the weap-

---

[42] Ex. R 51.8; cf. Ex. R 41.7; Song R 8.6.1.
[43] PRK 5.16 and 12.19; TB Abodah Zarah 5a; MT 92.2; Tan. Zav 12; PR 41.2, 174a.
[44] Ex. R 51.8.
[45] *Ibid*.
[46] Num. R 16.24; Tan. Shalah 13; Tan. B Va'ere 9 and add. to Shalah 1.
[47] Bacher, PA, III, p. 567.
[48] PR 33.10, 154a and 21.7, 103a; PRK 16.3; Tan. Shalah 13; Tan. B Va'ere 9 and add. to Shalah 1; Lam. R 2.17; Ex. R 45.2 and 51.8; Num. R 16.24; MT 103.8.

ons.[49] It is not at all clear what the meaning of this statement is and what, if any, its esoteric implications might have been.

There is one other interesting and enigmatic midrash attributed to R. Levi which seems relevant here; it is an exposition of Song 2:4, which we have already seen as the sources of at least one mystical midrash:

> "He brought me to the house of wine, and his banner over me was love." R. Joshua of Siknin said in the name of R. Levi: The Community of Israel said: The Holy One blessed be He brought me to the wine cellar — this is Sinai. There was Michael and his regiment; Gabriel and his regiment. They said: Would that we might journey in such a heavenly arrangement. Then the Holy One blessed be He said: Since My children desire to be in regiments, let them encamp by regiments, as it is said, "The people of Israel shall encamp each by his own standard, with the ensigns of their fathers' houses" (Num. 2:2).[50]

Here again R. Levi has taken an older midrash — which has its roots at least as far back as R. Judah b. Ilai[51] — and given it an explicitly esoteric turn, claiming that the Israelites at Sinai not only saw the angels who play such a central role in Merkabah texts but modelled themselves after these angels.[52] Beyond this, it is hard to say exactly what R. Levi might have meant by this midrash.

One final member of the school of R. Johanan to whom an apparently esoteric midrash on Sinai is attributed is R. Aba b. Kahana:

> While Israel had not yet sinned, what is written? "Now the appearance of the glory of the Lord was like a devouring fire on the top of the mountain in the sight of the people of Israel" (Ex. 24:17). R. Aba b. Kahana said: There were seven partitions [m'ḥizot] of fire grinding against each other and the Israelites saw them and were not awe-stricken nor afraid.[53]

A literary analysis of the entire pericope shows that R. Aba b. Kahana's midrash has been inserted here by a redactor as a parenthetical gloss on Ex. 24:17. Thus we can not say with certainty that it was originally a comment on Ex. 24:11, nor can we say anything certain about its original context. However it surely does refer to the Israelites at Sinai, and it therefore represents a more specific expression of the general motif of fire at Sinai which we have seen in tannaitic midrash.

---

[49] An interesting exception is Tan. B Sh'mini 10. In the case of the weapon tradition, this juxtaposition has often resulted in an erroneous reading, "girdle" (Heb. ZNY) being substituted for "weapon" (Heb. ZYN).

[50] Song R 6.10.1. The attribution is supplied on the basis of the parallel in Song R 2.4.1. Cf. the anonymous parallels in Num. R 2.3 and Tan. B'midbar 14.

[51] Song R 2.4.1.

[52] The term "troops [g'dudei] of ministering angels" in Merkabah texts is discussed by Gruenwald in his comment on RY p. 114; cf. PR 21.8, 103a.

[53] PRK 5.3; Num. R 11.3; PR 15.3, 69a; Song R 3.6; Midrash Shmuel 17; Y. Ex. 362. The verb "grinding" (Heb. kos'sot) is the most likely of the several different readings; cf. Friedmann's note in PR ad loc.

R. Abdima of Haifa, though perhaps not a student of R. Johanan, seems to have been in contact with a number of the latter's students.[54] His midrash on Ps. 68:18 is widely cited in rabbinic literature, often as the very first of the many comments on this verse: "R. Abdima of Haifa said: I learned in studying my mishnah that 22,000 squadrons of ministering angels descended to Sinai with the Holy One blessed be He."[55] Although the substance of this midrash does not add anything new to our study, it is interesting for two reasons. First, it is the only explicit statement from a Palestinian amora that the descent of the angels on Sinai is a tannaitic tradition. Thus it forms an important piece of evidence in Lieberman's argument that the esoteric interpretation of the Song of Songs originated among the tannaim. After citing R. Abdima's midrash, Lieberman says:

> In essence, the manifestation of the Holy One blessed be He as it were in His appearance and upon His chariot at the Sea and at Mt. Sinai is a tradition of the tannaim, and they are *mishnayot* . . . Although the geonim called the aggadic midrashim "*mishnayot*", in our discussion we mean actual *mishnayot* − *baraitot* of the tannaim, which were also called *mishnayot*.[56]

The second important aspect of R. Abdima's midrash is the alternative reading of it which appears in several sources: "R. Abdima of Haifa said: I learned in studying my mishnah that 22,000 chariots [*merkabot*] of ministering angels descended to Sinai with the Holy One blessed be He."[57] If this in fact were the original reading, we would have explicit evidence for a link between the revelation at Sinai and the *ma'aseh Merkabah*. Although we can not rule out this possibility, it seems likely that this version is an erroneous conflation of R. Abdima's midrash with another originally separate midrash.[58]

There seem to have been two authentic traditions which postulated the presence of "chariots" at Sinai:

> 22,000 chariots descended with the Holy One blessed be He, and each and every chariot was like the chariot which Ezekiel ben Buzi saw. In the name of the group which came up [to Palestine] from Babylonia they said: 42,000 chariots, as it is said, "the Lord among them [*bam*]" − according to the numerical value of "*bam*" [42]; thus taught [*shanah*] Elijah of blessed memory.[59]

---

[54] Bacher, PA, II, p. 536−537.
[55] PRK ed. Buber 107b seems to be the correct reading, also found in Y Ex. 286; Mandelbaum in his edition of PRK, 12.22, p. 219, relegates this to the variant readings and reads: "22,000 of ministering angels," as does PR 21.7, 102b and Y Ps. 796; cf. Num. R 2.3; Ex. R 29.2; Dt. R ed. Lieberman p. 68.
[56] Lieberman, "Mishnat Shir Hashirim," p. 122 and n. 24.
[57] Tan. Vayishlah 2 and Zav 12; Tan. B Yitro 14 and Zav 16; MT 68.10; BHM V, p. 73.
[58] This was pointed out by Buber in Zav 16, n. 71; it is also the opinion of Gruenwald in his comment to RY p. 132.
[59] BHM V, p. 73; MT 68.10; cf. Buber's n. 32 there and PRK 12.22. This passage is discussed by Urbach, *Hazal*, p. 126, n. 41 and by Lieberman, "Mishnat Shir Hashirim," p. 122, n. 20.

The tradition of the Babylonians, like R. Abdima's tradition, is particularly interesting because of the term *"shanah,"* which again seems to indicate a tannaitic origin.[60] Moreover, Urbach claims that "the group which came up from Babylonia were
amoraim who possessed mystical traditions and who emigrated to Palestine just as
Elazar b. Pedat emigrated from Babylonia."[61] This would not be surprising, since
Babylonia was apparently a stronghold of mystical speculation,[62] and it may very
well be that the Babylonians were less reticent in explicitly articulating the link
between Sinai and *ma'aseh Merkabah.* However it is quite possible that the Palestin-
ians already had their own tradition about the chariots at Sinai when the Babylonians arrived, since most of the Palestinian texts insist that there were 22,000 chariots,
the number being derived from the first part of Ps. 68:18. If this tradition had
first been learned from the Babylonians, we would expect the Palestinian texts only
to tell us about the 42,000 chariots, based on the latter half of the verse. We do not
know, of course, when the Babylonians arrived; since their tradition appears in
only two texts, it may be relatively late. On the other hand, Lieberman claims that
this tradition was deliberately deleted from other texts because it was no longer
understood at the time of their redaction.[63] Urbach asserts that the Babylonians
were "of the same generation as R. Elazar b. Pedat"[64] (i.e., latter part of the
third century). Thus it is likely, though not at all certain, that the Palestinian
tradition of the 22,000 chariots pre-dates a third century arrival of the Babylonians.

We can fix a *terminus ad quem* for this Palestinian tradition with some certainty,
because three appearances of it in the extant texts are attributed to R. Yannai b.
Simeon b. Yannai, the grandson of the first generation amora R. Yannai, the teacher
of R. Johanan.[65] Each of these three appearances has a similar context: the pericope
begins with R. Abdima's midrash, then cites a midrash attributed to R. Levi or R.
Berakiah deriving the number 22,000 from the population of the tribe of Levi,
which is followed by a rejoinder of R. Yannai b. Simeon b. Yannai. The rejoinder
is somewhat different in each version, though its substantive point is the same,
and it seems impossible to say which is the original. The simplest version reads:

> R. Berakiah Ha-cohen said that the Holy One blessed be He foresaw that none of
> the tribes would be steadfast in their oath[66] except the tribe of Levi. Therefore they

---

[60] Cf. Lieberman, *ibid.*

[61] Urbach, *Hazal*, p. 126.

[62] For an argument for the primacy of Babylonia in *Ma'aseh Merkabah*, see Halperin,
"Merkabah and Ma'aseh Merkabah."

[63] Lieberman, "Mishnat Shir Hashirim," p. 122 n. 20.

[64] Urbach, *Hazal*, p. 126.

[65] Bacher, PA, lists only one Simeon b. Yannai, and according to TP Mo'ed Katan 2.2
81a R. Yannai, the outstanding first-generation amora, had a son named Simeon. Strack,
Introduction, p. 119 notes that R. Yannai was sometimes called "the Elder" to distinguish
him from his grandson of the same name who was known as "R. Yannai the Younger."

[66] I.e., their oath of loyalty to God, following the reading suggested by Buber in Tan.
Yitro 14 n. 75 and Tan. Zav 16 n. 73.

descended [in a number] equivalent to the camp of Levi. R. Yannai said: If so, what is the significance of "the chariots of God, twice ten thousand, thousands upon thousands"? Rather, it must be the case that 22,000 chariots descended with the Holy One blessed be He, and each and every chariot was like the chariot that Ezekiel ben Buzi saw.[67]

It seem apparent that, in each of the three versions, R. Yannai's interpretation is a direct response to the midrash preceding it. Since R. Yannai was in the third generation of amoraim, and since R. Levi was in the same generation (and a student of R. Yannai's grandfather's student), it is fairly likely that we have here a record of an exchange between these two rabbis. Although the midrash preceding R. Yannai's is usually cited in the name of R. Berakiah, it is common for the latter to get credit for traditions which originated with his teacher R. Levi.[68]

The upshot of this is that the tradition about the 22,000 chariots seems to have been known in indigenous Palestinian circles, and very possibly in the school of R. Johanan, by the late third century. Though one might consider the possibility that the attribution to R. Yannai here is pseudepigraphal, it seems extremely unlikely, since this midrash fits so well as a direct rejoinder to R. Levi, and among all the rabbis who could have been chosen for a pseudepigraph there are few as obscure as R. Yannai b. Simeon b. Yannai. This obscurity, though, raises another question: Is it likely that R. Yannai, who was at best on the fringe of R. Johanan's school, would have independently created a tradition as potentially significant and powerful as this? Would he have taken it upon himself to make the first explicit connection between the revelation at Sinai and the chariot which Ezekiel saw? And if he had, is it likely that his name would have been forgotten in later times, when this tradition circulated anonymously? These possibilities must be considered, of course, but it seems more probable that he was drawing on a tradition which was already known to him and applying it to the exegetical needs of a particular moment. If the anonymous version of the "22,000 chariots" tradition were in fact R. Yannai's tradition with the attribution missing, we would expect to find it linked to the preceding midrash of R. Levi in the same way as the attributed "22,000 chariots" tradition. Yet in virtually all of its appearances, the anonymous tradition stands by itself as a distinct midrash unrelated to what precedes and follows it; e. g.:

R. Abdima of Haifa said . . . R. Berakiah Ha-cohen said that it is related to the camp of the Levites. The Holy One blessed be He foresaw that none of them would be steadfast in their oath except the tribe of Levi, and therefore 22,000 descended, like the camp of Levites. Another interpretation [dabar 'aḥer]: "the chariots of God, twice ten thousand, thousands upon thousands." It teaches that 22,000 chariots descended with the Holy One blessed be He, and each and every chariot was like the chariot that Ezekiel

---

[67] Tan. B Zav 16; the parallels are Tan. Zav 12 and PR 21.7, 102b, where the Parma ms. erroneously reads "R. Yannai b. Simeon b. Yohai." A similar error occurs in Y I Sam., as noted by Bacher, PA, III, p. 623, n. 6.

[68] Bacher, PA, III, p. 349, n. 1.

saw. "The chariots of God." R. Elazar b. Pedat said: And they all descended keen on destroying the enemies of Israel . . .[69]

All of the pericopes in which these and other comments on Ps. 68:18 appear seem to draw on a fund of old (usually third century) traditions about Sinai, all of which are attributed except for this one. These considerations make it likely that the anonymous tradition was a well established element in this fund of traditions, and quite possibly could have been known to R. Yannai b. Simeon b. Yannai. We can conclude, then, that there is a significant amount of evidence pointing to an explicit connection between what Ezekiel saw and what the Israelites at Sinai saw within the interpretive framework of third century Palestinian midrash.

If we compare the third century midrashim with the second century midrashim which seem to link Sinai and esoteric interests related to ma'aseh Merkabah, an interesting pattern appears. The second century midrashim are relatively indirect, relying on implication and allusion, and they are relatively fragmented; i.e., the same specific motif does not appear more than once or twice. The third century midrashim, on the other hand, are much more direct and explicit and center around two or three basic themes which were apparently often repeated. A number of the second century motifs were repeated in the third century (e.g. the weapons, the fire, the glory of God on the mountain), and we can assume that most (if not all) of the second century midrashim were known in the school of R. Johanan, where they formed the necessary foundation for creative development of the general theme. But the interests of the third century rabbis were drawn much more to the theme of the chariots (which we have just examined), and angels (mentioned by four rabbis), and the direct vision of God (mentioned explicitly or virtually so by five rabbis). In fact virtually every third century midrash we have examined is either a re-statement of a second century midrash or a reference to one of these three topics. (Each of these three does, of course, have roots in second century midrashim.)

Taken as an aggregate, then, the third century texts even more strongly than their second century predecessors provide a picture of the Israelites at Sinai as replicating the experience of the "descenders" to the Merkabah. The interest in peripheral details has given way to a concentration on the fundamental elements of the "descent:" the angels, the chariot, and the direct vision of God. Yet again we must note that each of these midrashim can be explained in other interpretive frameworks. The references to the chariots may reflect a purely exegetical interest in Ezekiel 1, unrelated to esotericism or ecstatic experience. Urbach has argued that the amoraim wanted to avoid excessive anthropomorphism and therefore assigned various actions to the angels rather than to God Himself, thus explaining the great interest in the angels. And the assertions of the vision of God might be seen as merely midrashic elaborations of the Biblical statements that the Israelites had in fact seen God at Sinai. But there are problems with each of these potential modes of explanation. If the dominant tendency among Palestinian rabbis was to

---

[69] Tan. B Yitro 14.

treat the first chapter of Ezekiel exoterically, this tendency would have been, as Halperin has argued, stronger in the second century than in the third. Yet we find that the allusions to the chariot are fragmentary and veiled in the second century but quite open and explicit in the third. Since no one has argued that Ezekiel 1 was esoteric in the second century but exoteric in the third, the most obvious explanation is that it was esoteric all along, but that the esoteric tradition was firmly enough established in the late third century to allow explicit references to it in occasional midrashim. In light of the frequent references to the vision of God, it is hard to support Urbach's view that the amoraim avoided anthropomorphism. In fact, it should be noted that the tannaim tend to speak more frequently of seeing the "glory" of God, whereas the amoraim generally found even this buffer against anthropomorphism unnecessary. And if the midrashim about the vision of God were motivated only by the Biblical assertions to this effect, we would expect the relevant Biblical verses to be the crux of the midrashim; yet this is not the case. In fact the only midrashim which cite these Biblical verses are those based on R. Eliezer's midrash about the "maid-servant," which originally did not refer to Sinai at all. This is not to deny that explanations of these midrashim outside the framework of the esoteric tradition may be valid. It is merely to say that such explanations may very well be problematic.

The assumption that all of these midrashim do in fact reflect interest in esoteric traditions has one principal virtue − it offers a single hypothesis to account for a wide range of data and to relate those data to each other in a coherent way. It does seem plausible that as an esoteric tradition becomes more firmly entrenched its adherents are more willing to refer explicitly to it, so that fragmentary and veiled allusions give way to repeated and consistent references. Yet we must remember that even the third century midrashim which seem to relate Sinai to esoteric interests are relatively sparse and somewhat indirect; this was still an esoteric tradition. This hypothesis would explain why the reference to the chariots did not appear until the latter part of the third century, and even then in such a form that the uninitiated could take it as mere fanciful elaboration. It might also explain the increased interest in the angels. Phillip S. Alexander has recently pointed out that the *ma'seh Merkabah* tradition showed an aversion not to anthropomorphism but to immanence, so that "the void left by God's withdrawal to the heights of heaven is filled in the Hekhaloth texts with hosts of angels who mediate between God and the world."[70] This is surely the most plausible explanation for the great number of angels in the Merkabah literature, and an increased influence of esoteric concerns in the third century would also explain the increased importance of the angels at that time. On this view, the stress on the angels would be accompanied by an increasingly anthropomorphic (and transcendent) concept of God as visible and describable, a tendency to which the texts we have discussed seem to point. More-

---

[70] P. S. Alexander, "The Historical Setting of the Hebrew Book of Enoch," *Journal of Jewish Studies*, vol. 28 (Autumn, 1977), p. 175.

over, the references in these texts to the vision of God are often accompanied by
other references to aspects of the esoteric tradition, including the Shiur Komah.
The evidence thus seems to converge and point to the probability (though not
certainty) that, by the late third century, leading Palestinian rabbis knew some
form of Merkabah mysticism and consciously shaped their midrashim on Sinai
in its light.

Reviewing both the tannaitic and amoraic midrashim studied here, we find a
number of plausible models for reconstructing the process of historical development. It may be that Merkabah mysticism was developed within the rabbinic
academies, with the midrash on Sinai being developed concurrently in those same
academies; this would be the simplest explanation for the many parallels which we
have found. Or it may be that Merkabah mysticism was developed outside the
leading rabbinic circles in the first or early second centuries, with R. Akiba and his
followers responding to it by creating new traditions about *matan Torah*. Perhaps
alternatively, Merkabah mysticism was not developed until the third century, outside the academies, its imagery consciously reflecting the existing midrashic depic-
tion of revelation; in this case the third-century amoraim would be the ones who
responded to the new creation by new midrashic creation of their own concerning
Sinai. (It is hardly likely, though perhaps possible, that Merkabah mysticism was
not developed until the fourth century or later).

But regardless of which hypothetical reconstruction one chooses, certain conclusions seem to remain valid. The rabbis were aware of the formal similarities
between the newly developing esotericism and existing Gnostic traditions, and they
acted to integrate this new kind of experience into the fabric of their
religiosity, negating its potentially disruptive effects. This integration must have
occurred relatively quickly. (If one suggests that Merkabah mysticism developed
outside rabbinic circles in the first century but was not reflected in rabbinic midrash
until the third century, one would be arguing that the parallels in tannaitic midrash
are purely coincidental, which is rather far-fetched.) The midrashim on the revelation
were not merely reflections or by-products of this effort; they were crucial instru-
ments in carrying it out and ensuring its success. Given that success, Merkabah
mysticism became not a "Jewish Gnosticism" but rather a Jewish refusal to accept
the validity of Gnosticism. Through midrash, the rabbis told their community —
and themselves — that the apparent affinities between Gnosticism and Merkabah
mysticism were far less important than the basic differences in content and meaning.

We now turn to another midrashic tradition which reinforces these conclusions
and shows us more about both the meaning of Merkabah mysticism for the third-
century rabbis and the ways in which they may have used midrash to shape the
influence of that mysticism.

III. REVELATION AND INITIATORY DEATH
IN THIRD-CENTURY MIDRASH

I

One of the consistent themes in rabbinic literature is that Torah is a source of life: "As water gives life to the world, so the Torah gives life to the world."[1] As a recent writer has put it: "In the scholars' awareness, Torah was not simply a scroll or even the book of truth, but *Torat Hayyim*, a life-giving teaching, a fountain of living waters, the source through which divine energy and blessing flow to man."[2] This concept remains central in the synagogue liturgy; the Torah reading ceremony ends with the words of Proverbs 3:18: "She is a tree of life for those who grasp her, and they who hold on to her live happy lives." Given this pervasive connection of Torah and life, it seems surprising to find a tradition appearing in many of the classical midrash collections asserting that the Israelites, upon hearing the voice of God revealing the Torah to them, immediately died. Because this tradition seems so antithetic to the rabbinic stress on Torah as a source of life, it is a particularly interesting problem.

Anyone attempting an exegesis of the Biblical account of revelation would have to deal with the relationship between revelation and death, for the existence of such a relationship is clearly implied, although it remains undefined, in the Biblical text. Exodus 20:19 reports the words of the Israelites after they received the Ten Commandments: "And they said to Moses, 'You speak with us and we will hear, but let God not speak with us, lest we die.'" In Deuteronomy, too, the statement of the Ten Commandments is immediately followed by the Israelites' expression of their fear of death:

> Today we have seen that God may speak with men and they may still live. And now why should we die? For this great fire will devour us. If we hear the voice of the Lord our God any more, we shall die . . . You go near and listen to all that the Lord our God says, and you tell us all that the Lord our God says to you, and we will listen and do it. (Dt. 5:21–24)

The earliest rabbinic exegetical text on Exodus, the Mekilta, takes up the problem of Exodus 20:19. According to the Mekilta d'Rabbi Simeon b. Yohai, the text means that "if one more word had been added on for them they would have been

---

[1] Song R. 1.2.3; Sifre Dt. 48.
[2] Daniel Jeremy Silver, *A History of Judaism*, vol. 1, p. 287.

dead."[3] The Mekilta d'Rabbi Ishmael defines the meaning even more precisely: "It tells us that they did not have the power to receive more than the Ten Commandments, as it is said, 'If we hear the voice of the Lord our God any more, we shall die.'"[4] In both cases the meaning is quite straightforward. The Israelites had the capacity to receive only the Ten Commandments directly from God Himself. They were correct in their feelings that any revelation beyond this would have killed them, and thus Moses had to mediate all further revelation to them. The Mekilta d'Rabbi Ishmael finds this to be the meaning of both the Exodus and Deuteronomy texts.

This interpretation was disputed by R. Joshua b. Levi, a first generation Palestinian amora who lived in the first half of the third century:

> R. Joshua b. Levi and the rabbis: R. Joshua says: Israel heard two commandments from the mouth of the Holy One blessed be He — "I am" and "You shall not have." This is what is written: "Let him kiss me with kisses from his mouth" (Song 1:2) — but not with all the kisses. But the rabbis say that Israel heard all the commandments from the mouth of the Holy One blessed by He. R. Joshua of Siknin said in the name of R. Joshua b. Levi that the reasoning of the rabbis is that it is written, "And they said to Moses, 'You speak with us and we will hear.'" What did R. Joshua b. Levi do with this verse? He argued that there is neither earlier nor later in the Torah, so perhaps the words "You speak with us and we will hear" were only spoken after two or three commandments. R. Azariah and R. Judah b. Simon in the name of R. Joshua b. Levi followed his view; they said: It is written: "Moses commanded us a Torah" (Dt. 33:4). The entire Torah consists of 613 commandments. The word "Torah" in *gematria'* amounts to the 611 that Moses spoke to us, but "I am" and You shall not have" were not spoken to us by Moses, but we heard them from the mouth of the Holy One blessed be He.[5]

Here we find the anonymous tradition of the Mekilta d'Rabbi Ishmael confirmed as the consensus of the tannaim — the Israelites did have the power to receive all ten commandments directly from God. R. Joshua b. Levi, however, accepted the opinion of a minority of tannaim (perhaps those who followed R. Ishmael) that only two commandments were heard directly from God. The background and original meaning of this minority view are obscure.[6] However, it seems clear that R. Joshua b. Levi meant it to reflect the danger to human beings of hearing the divine voice. For we find another tradition of his recorded in the Babylonian Talmud:

> R. Joshua b. Levi said: At each and every word which came from the mouth of the Holy One blessed be He the soul of Israel expired [literally, "went out"], as it is said, "My soul failed me [literally, "went out"] when he spoke" (Song 5:6). But since

---

[3] Mek. RS 155. Note that the Ten Commandments are called "the ten words" in Hebrew.
[4] Mek. Yitro Bahodesh 9, p. 237.
[5] Song R 1.2.2; cf. PR 22.3, 111 a and Tan. Vayeleh 2.
[6] For a full citation of relevant sources, see Abraham Joshua Heschel, *Torah Min Hasha-mayim B'aspeklaryah Shel Hadorot*, vol. I, pp. 31, 32. Heschel's interpretation of the tradition seems open to question.

their soul expired after the first commandment, how did they receive the second commandment? He brought down the dew which will resurrect the dead in the future and He resurrected them, as it is said, "A bounteous rain You did pour down, O God" (Ps 68:10)[7].

Here R. Joshua b. Levi has combined several tannaitic themes into a coherent whole by adding the new idea that the Israelites actually did die at Sinai. He has re-emphasized the danger alluded to in the Mekilta and explained why the Israelites could not hear all ten commandments from God. Yet because he apparently felt bound by the tradition that they heard two commandments, he had to explain how they heard the second commandment.

Thus the two traditions of R. Joshua b. Levi cited here served to illuminate each other, and they appear to be two parts of a single theme of death and resurrection at Sinai. While the theme may have been known before R. Joshua b. Levi's time, he is the earliest figure in the extant texts to have stated it explicitly. Therefore, this is the point at which we can first justly ask the question of meaning and intent. Why would a leading rabbi of the first half of the third century in Palestine have offered an interpretation of the Sinai event such as this which clearly contradicts the plain meaning of Scripture? There seems to be no purely exegetical need;[8] i.e., R. Joshua b. Levi has not taken any ambiguous verses from the Bible and clarified them. If anything, he has taken rather univocal verses and denied their obvious meaning (p'shat) in favor of a homiletical meaning (d'rash) of his own. The source of his ideas, then, is not in the Bible itself. What might the source be? There are two possibilities which seem worth exploring.

The first is the rather striking similarity between this midrashic theme and the development of the "binding of Isaac" story in the midrash. For in the latter case, too, a Biblical story about the experience of imminent death has been transformed into a midrashic story about actual death followed by resurrection. The midrashic material on the binding of Isaac has been collected and studied by S. Spiegel in *The Last Trial*, and his exhaustive citation of the sources shows some interesting parallels with our theme. Several sources say that Isaac's soul left him.[9] There is an early tradition, going back at least to R. Joshua b. Levi's generation, that Isaac's death was caused by burning, so that only his ashes were left on the altar.[10] There is also the important detail that in some texts Isaac is said to be revived by the dew which in the future will resurrect the dead.[11] Various midrashic sources also suggest that the

---

[7] TB Shabbat 88b.

[8] On the concept of "pure exegesis" see G. Vermes, "Bible and Midrash: Early Old Testament Exegesis," in *The Cambridge History of the Bible*, vol. I.

[9] Shalom Spiegel, *The Last Trial*, ch. 4. While Spiegel takes this phrase, which is characteristic usage in the traditions on the death at Sinai, to refer to fainting, it is clearly used in the Sinai traditions to refer to death, as will be seen below. It seems most likely that this latter meaning should be read in the binding of Isaac traditions as well.

[10] *Ibid.*, ch. 5.

[11] *Ibid.*, p. 32.

binding of Isaac occurred at the time of Passover, the beginning of the year.[12] We shall see below that some sources connect the death of the Israelites at Sinai with the verse, "This month shall be for you a beginning of months" (Ex. 12:2). While many of these citations are from relatively late texts, Spiegel is at great pains to demonstrate that this material is very early, going back at least to the earliest amoraim and probably earlier.

In explaining this transformation of a Biblical story in obvious contradiction of the literal meaning of the text, Spiegel points to the historical circumstances of the mid-second century — the vicious persecution of Palestinian Jews by the Romans following the revolt of Bar Kochba. He says:

> In the light of the historical reality of the second-century persecution under the Roman Empire, it seemed almost as though something of the splendor and awe of the biblical Akedah story was diminished. Who cares about some ancient, far off in time, who was merely *thought of as a possible* sacrifice on the altar, but who was delivered from the danger, whom no misfortune overtook; when right before your eyes, in the immediate present, fathers and sons *en masse* ascend the executioner's block to be butchered and burned, literally butchered and burned.[13]

If the binding of Isaac was to continue to serve as a model of perfect faith for the Jews, it would have to become a paradigm for the acceptance of death as a "sanctification of the Name," with the assurance that there is a reward for martyrdom — resurrection to everlasting life for the martyr and a bestowal of God's mercy upon his descendants as a sort of reparation. One could not conceive of oneself or one's kin surpassing the example of father Isaac, and so the outcome of the Biblical story was changed by midrashic exegesis.

It is possible that a similar process was at work in the midrash on the revelation at Sinai? The Roman persecution of the second century clearly had a profound effect on the development of many midrashic themes besides the Isaac story.[14] We might fairly allow several decades for such a development to take shape in oral tradition before surfacing in its full-blown form in the teaching of R. Joshua b. Levi. Yet the differences between the midrashim on Isaac and the midrashim on Sinai are very striking too. The Isaac story is almost always re-told with a particular, explicitly stated purpose or "moral." This usually deals with the value of martyrdom as an act of faith or the expectation of God's mercy in the future as a result of Isaac's faithfulness. In other words, it is a legitimation of martyrdom. If the Isaac and Sinai themes were both parallel reactions to historical persecution, we would expect to find the same kind of "moral" as an essential part of the Sinai traditions. Yet such is not the case. In fact, in R. Joshua b. Levi's tradition (and in most later developments of this Sinai theme which we shall survey) there is no purpose or contemporary relevance mentioned at all. And nowhere is it suggested that this death at Sinai was a

---

[12] *Ibid.*, ch. 7.

[13] *Ibid.*, p. 15.

[14] For several examples, see Joseph Heinemann, *Aggadot V'toldotaihen.*

martyrdom or a significant act of faith on the part of the Israelites. Furthermore, the details of Isaac's experience were elaborated in many different directions and in a large number of midrashim. It seems to have been a highly popular theme among the rabbis. The theme of the death at Sinai, on the other hand, found a limited number of expressions both in number of traditions and variety of content. It does not seem to have had nearly the same popularity in public rabbinic discourse. These significant differences lead us to look for another explanation for R. Joshua b. Levi's tradition. If it was not a response to the political-historical circumstances of the times, what motives led to its formation?

One of the distinctive features of R. Joshua b. Levi's view is his use of two passages from the Song of Songs to support it. We have already seen that, according to Scholem and Lieberman, these passages formed part of the esoterica of the Bible in the third century (and perhaps earlier). It is unlikely that any rabbi, and especially one involved in esotericism as R. Joshua b. Levi seems to have been, would have cited these verses casually or by chance. This leads us to ask whether this particular midrash should be included among those which reflect a relationship between the Sinai revelation and Merkabah mysticism. In fact, much of the evidence for such a relationship which we have already examined leads to an affirmative conclusion.

It is quite probable that R. Joshua b. Levi was developing a midrashic tradition that was already known in the second century:

> R. Judah b. Ilai says: Since Israel was scorched by the heat of the fire of the upper world, the Holy One blessed be He said to the clouds of glory: Drip down the dew of life on My children, as it is said, "Earth trembled, even the heavens dripped before God," and it says, "A bounteous rain You did pour down, O God" (Ps. 68:9,10).[15]

We have already discussed this midrash and its relationship to the pervasive motif of fire in the Merkabah texts; we have also seen other evidence that R. Judah b. Ilai described the Sinai revelation in terms of esotericism. It is not certain, though, that this midrash originated with R. Judah b. Ilai, for a variant of it is cited anonymously in the Tosefta:

> The day was clear and Israel was scorched by the fire. The Holy One blessed be He said to the clouds of glory: Drip down dew on My children, as it is said, "O Lord when You went forth from Seir, when You marched from the region of Edom" (Judg. 5:4). So the Holy One blessed be He dripped down dew and rain before them, as it is said, "A bounteous rain You did pour down, O God."[16]

This variant is virtually identical with R. Judah b. Ilai's tradition, for Judg. 5:4 continues: "Earth trembled, even the heavens dripped before the Lord." So both midrashim do in fact draw on identical proof-texts as well as offering the same idea.

---

[15] Mek. Yitro Bahodesh 9, p. 236.

[16] Tos. Arakin 1.10. Some editions read "driven away" (Heb. *mishtalḥin*) in place of "scorched" (Heb. *m'shulḥabin*), but this is no doubt a change in the original wording of the text, whether accidental or intentional.

Whether the tradition originated with R. Judah b. Ilai or with an earlier anonymous rabbi, it is clear that it was known by the end of the tannaitic period. While this tradition did not assert explicitly that the Israelites died at Sinai, the reference to the "dew of life" seems to be an implicit assertion of their death, since dew in rabbinic literature is commonly the agent of resurrection of the dead.

The idea that the Israelites died at Sinai may also exist implicitly in a midrash attributed to R. Simeon b. Yohai, another disciple of R. Akiba who, as we have seen, connected the revelation with esoteric motifs: "R. Simeon b. Yohai taught: The Torah which the Holy One blessed be He gave to Israel returned their souls to them, as it is said, 'The Torah of the Lord is pure, restoring the soul' (Ps. 19:8)."[17] There is no passage in rabbinic literature attributed to R. Simeon b. Yohai which says that the Israelites lost their souls at Sinai, so we have no context in which to interpret this tradition securely. Yet R. Joshua b. Levi did describe the death of the Israelites by saying literally that "their souls went out," and a later tradition does ascribe the return of their souls to the intercession of the Torah. It is possible, of course, that the attribution to R. Simeon b. Yohai here is pseudepigraphal. It is equally possible that this enigmatic tradition does imply that the traditions of death at Sinai and resurrection by means of the Torah were already known in the second century. Unfortunately there is not enough evidence to assess the meaning of this tradition with any certainty.

Returning to R. Judah b. Ilai, we find another midrash attributed to him which reflects more explicitly a relationship between esoteric knowledge of Torah and death:

> When Israel heard "I am the Lord your God" the mastery of Torah was fixed in their hearts, and they would learn and not forget anything. They came to Moses and said: Moses our master, act as an intermediary between us, as it is said, "You speak with us and we will hear" (Ex. 20:9), "And now why should we die?" (Dt. 5:21) – What profit is there in our destruction? They then returned to the state of learning and forgetting.[18]

This midrash is one more indication of the link between Merkabah mysticism and the rabbinic interpretation of Sinai, for the Merkabah mystic was also promised that he would never forget the Torah that he learned.[19] It also indicates that all of the basic themes in R. Joshua b. Levi's midrash were already known from midrashim attributed to R. Judah b. Ilai: the direct vision of God conceived in an esoteric context, the fire phenomenon related to revelation, the need to accept death as a means for special access to the knowledge of Torah, and the dew as the agent of resurrection.

If R. Joshua b. Levi's midrash does in fact have its roots in the esoteric tradition, then each of these themes ought to have some reflection there. The first two themes

---

[17] Song R 5.16.3; cf. Num. R 10.1 (with minor variations).
[18] Song R 1.2.4.
[19] e.g., MM, par. 25.

have already appeared frequently here in citations from esoteric texts, and the last —
the dew of resurrection — is a basic concept of rabbinic Judaism which is mentioned
explicitly in mystical cosmological texts and must have been accepted in esoteric as
well as strictly exoteric circles. As for the need to accept death, the Merkabah
literature offers many examples of the need to face lethal dangers in the ascent to
the Merkabah, as we have seen. But there is now a much more exact parallel available
to R. Joshua b. Levi's midrash. In a recently discovered fragment of an esoteric text
published by I. Gruenwald (*Tarbiz* 38, p. 360), an angel offers R. Ishmael instruc-
tions on the "descent" to the Merkabah. After describing numerous fire phenomena,
the angel tells R. Ishmael that he ought to lie on the ground and stuff his bodily
orifices with cotton "so that there will be an obstruction for your soul and it will
not go out until I reach you. And when I come I will stand over you and fan
over you and return your soul, and your soul will be revived." While the meaning of the text is not unequivocal, it certainly implies that the mystic runs the
risk of having his soul "go out." If taken literally, it seems to say that the soul must
in fact leave the body and then be returned to it. This is, of course, just what our
midrashim tell us happened to the Israelites at Mount Sinai.

It seems likely, then, that R. Joshua b. Levi's midrash was related in some very
close way to the esoteric tradition, and the same conclusion may be equally valid for
the midrashim of R. Judah b. Ilai which formed its sources. Yet there is an important difference between the two rabbis, for R. Joshua b. Levi made very clear
and explicit what was only veiled and implicit in his predecessor's midrash. Why
would he have done so? We are on very tentative ground here, so I merely want to
suggest a plausible hypothesis.

We have seen that there is a distinct difference between the second and third
century midrashim on Sinai: while the former show only fragmentary allusions to
esoteric motifs, the latter seem much more willing to make those allusions clear and
consistent. We have suggested that this may reflect a natural tendency for esoteric
matters to become somewhat more public as time goes on, and this tendency may be
reflected in the difference between the midrashim of R. Judah b. Ilai and R. Joshua
b. Levi discussed here. In this particular case, the tendency toward explicitness may
have been reinforced by another consideration. According to Johann Maier,[20] the
rabbis of the late second and early third centuries were increasingly concerned about
the dangers inherent in Merkabah speculation and the ecstatic experiences it might
engender. He sees this development as a reaction to the increasing possibility of
heretical views arising out of esoteric activity. The danger would have been even
greater since, as we have seen, the Merkabah mystic might have had grounds for
claiming that he had received new revelation like the revelation at Sinai. Such claims
might well threaten the structure of rabbinic Judaism, which was based on the
rabbis' claim that new interpretations of Torah must come out of the rabbinic

---

[20] Johann Maier, *Geschichte der jüdischen Religion*, p. 202 and *Vom Kultus Zur Gnosis*,
   pp. 139, 140.

academy and its fixed procedures of study and interpretation.[21] If such threats were perceived as increasing in R. Joshua b. Levi's time, he may well have thought it advisable to speak very explicitly of the dangers of mystical experience in a revelatory context.

If this was his intention, however, a further question arises: Why did he not deny the possibility of such direct revelatory experience at all? Why not say that the Israelites heard no commandments directly from the mouth of God, rather than allowing them two? This would seem to be the most effective way to discourage any attempt to gain mystical revelation. Yet R. Joshua b. Levi did not take this approach, and it seems to me there is only one possible explanation. He believed, in fact, that such experiences were possible and that mystics in his own time or earlier did have them.[22] While he wished to discourage them, he never denied their validity. And, just as no one could conceive of himself as having greater faithfulness than Isaac, so no one could conceive of himself or his contemporaries or earlier rabbis receiving a fuller degree of revelation than the Israelites at Sinai. Thus the experience of the Israelites had to be retained as a paradigm for the mystical experience which was, to R. Joshua b. Levi, an established fact of religious life. At the same time it was a fact – perhaps established through direct mystical experience – that there was great danger in the attempt to see and hear God, a danger which involved a threat to the very existence of the mystic. In many of the Merkabah teachings we find a stress on the importance of passwords and seals which allow the mystic a safe passage through these dangers. But the traditions we have been examining here (including those on Isaac) unanimously take a different approach to the threat of annihilation. Such an annihilation of the self, they say, must be accepted as part of the mystical experience. In fact it is the culmination of the experience, for it is precisely the self-revelation of God which causes the death of the mystic. There is, of course, another and equally important point shared by the traditions: the mystic who accepts this self-annihilation will be resurrected by the dew of life which God will pour down upon him.

R. Joshua b. Levi, then, was stressing both aspects of the mystical revelatory experience. Such experience is possible – one might, at the height of mystical experience, hope to be "kissed with kisses from His mouth." "But not with all the kisses" – the most profound revelatory moment is only a limited glimpse of the fullness of divine truth. And even such a glimpse demands the ultimate sacrifice, the willingness to suffer death (perhaps by fire), although this willingness brings with it

---

[21] See, e.g. TB Babba Metziah 59b and Gershom Scholem, "Revelation and Tradition as Religious Categories in Judaism," *The Messianic Idea in Judaism and Other Essays.*

[22] This, of course, does not prejudge the historical accuracy of such a belief on R. Joshua b. Levi's part. Even David Halperin, who claims that there was no esoteric or ecstatic *Maʿaseh Merkabah* in early rabbinic times, concludes that the "Amoraim believed, and wished others to believe, that certain rabbis had possessed hidden supernatural lore." "Merkabah and Maʿaseh Merkabah, According to Rabbinic Sources," p. 334.

the assurance that the resurrecting dew will follow. But how many would have the spiritual courage to submit themselves to such an "initiatory" death? It seems likely that R. Joshua b. Levi's stress on the limitations of revelation and the death which must come with it would have effectively discouraged many who might have contemplated an attempt to see and hear God. This seems to be a plausible interpretation of R. Joshua b. Levi's tradition. One regrets that the rabbis did not leave us more evidence to confirm or deny it.

II

In the second generation of amoraim, our theme was restated by R. Johanan. The tradition as found in Song of Songs Rabbah reads:

> "His speech is sweetness itself" (Song 5:16). R. Azariah and R. Aha in the name of R. Johanan say: When Israel heard "I am" at Sinai their soul burst out. This is what is written: "If we continue to hear." This is what is written: "My soul failed when he spoke." The word returned to the Holy One blessed be He and said, "Lord of the world, You are alive and enduring and Your Torah is alive and enduring and You have sent me to the dead. They are all dead." At that moment the Holy One blessed be He went back and sweetened the word for them. This is what is written: "The voice of the Lord in power. The voice of the Lord in majesty" (Ps. 29:4).[23]

The tradition is repeated in Numbers Rabbah with only one significant difference. Numbers Rabbah reads "their soul expired" (Hebrew *napsham yaza'*), while Song of Songs Rabbah reads "their soul burst out" (Hebrew *parḥah nishmatan*). While the former expression is consistently a euphemism for death in rabbinic literature (and in the Bible; cf. Gen. 35:18), the latter expression may mean "fainted" or "passed out," rather than died.[24] In the present context, however, it seems quite clear that both expressions serve as metaphors for death. R. Johanan followed R. Joshua b. Levi both in stating the motif explicitly and in choosing a Biblical proof-text, Song of Songs 5:6. He further combined this text with the text used in the Mekilta d'Rabbi Ishmael — Deuteronomy 5:22 — to prove that the Israelites' capacity to receive God's word directly was limited. But he added a new and significant motif; the source of resurrection here is not the dew but rather the mitigation ("sweetening") of God's word. Thus, paradoxically, the word of God is the source of both death and resurrection for the Israelites. (It is possible that the latter part of this pericope, beginning with "The word returned," is a later addition. But R. Johanan would have had to provide some explanation for Israel's resurrection, and since the tradition drawn on in this passage to explain the resurrection must have been known to him, it is altogether plausible that the attribution of the entire pericope to R. Johanan is genuine.)

---

[23] Song R 5.16.3; Num. R 10.1.
[24] See Abraham Eben-Shoshan, *Hamilon Hehadash*, pp. 1736, 1737, 2149.

R. Johanan, like R. Joshua b. Levi, drew on a tannaitic tradition and gave it a new meaning. For the Mekilta d'Rabbi Ishmael contains a comment on Exodus 20:18:

> "When all the people perceived the thunderings and the lightnings" — But how many thunderings [literally, "voices"] were there and how many lightnings were there? Rather [it means] that they caused each person to hear according to his power, as it is said, "The voice of the Lord in power."[25]

Apparently this passage means that there could not have been many different thunderings (voices) or lightnings, for there was only the one God manifesting Himself. However the plural is used to indicate that each person at Sinai had a different experience of God, depending on his individual capacity for revelatory experience. The meaning of this passage is explicated in a pericope in Exodus Rabbah which seems to be attributed to R. Judah Ha-nasi, of the last generation of tannaim. Although the attribution is uncertain, the passage does accurately reflect a common rabbinic tradition which stems from the Mekilta passage:

> The Holy One blessed be He does not become burdensome to his creatures. He only comes to them according to their power. You find that when the Holy One blessed be He gave the Torah to Israel, if He had come to them in the fullness of His power they would not have been able to withstand it, as it is said, "If we hear the voice of the Lord our God any more, we shall die." But He only came to them according to their power, as it said, "The voice of the Lord in power." It does not say "in His power" but "in power" — according to the power of each and every one.[26]

(It is perhaps worth noting that a nearly identical concept appears in the writings of Philo. He says, for example, "Or do you fail to notice that even God imparts divine communication not in a way corresponding to the greatness of His own perfection but to the ever-varying capacity of those whom He would benefit."[27] While it can not be proven that the tannaim were drawing directly on Philo, the similarities seem too great to be merely coincidental.)

By combining this tannaitic tradition with R. Joshua b. Levi's tradition, R. Johanan was able to make his own point about the experience of revelation. He distinguished between two kinds of revelations. The first, in which God's word is revealed directly and in its totality, is lethal to human beings. The second, in which God's word is mitigated ("sweetened") and tempered to fit the capabilities of each individual, is not lethal, and in fact it is said implicitly to be an agent of resurrection. The word of God, then, offers both death and life, depending on the degree of "power" in which it is experienced. But if, as we have suggested, the tradition on which R. Johanan was drawing here was an esoteric one, how are we to explain his transformation of that tradition?

---

[25] Mek. Yitro Bahodesh 9, p. 235.
[26] Ex. R 34.1.
[27] Philo, De Posteritii Caini, 43, 143; cf. Philo, De Somniis, I, 142–143.

The basic change introduced by R. Johanan was the deletion of the dew of resurrection and the substitution of God's word itself as the agent of resurrection. This also implies the assumption that the fire as the source of death is unnecessary. In other words, it seems that R. Johanan made a special effort to take the tradition out of the esoteric realm. Yet he retained the essential point that a direct revelation — if it is a revelation of God in His full power — is lethal. Thus in effect he attempted a synthesis of the views of R. Joshua b. Levi and the consensus of tannaim; the Israelites did die at Sinai, and yet they did hear all of the commandments from the mouth of God directly. What was the purpose of such a synthesis? Again, it may reflect the history of rabbinic esotericism. Scholem has noted that in the third century there was a tendency among some rabbis to re-interpret the esoteric tradition along more "ethical" lines.[28] This meant an attempt to divest the tradition of some of its less conventional or "orthodox"elements; perhaps it was motivated by a fear that the community might split into esoteric and non-esoteric camps. In any event, it would have represented an attempt to synthesize traditional and esoteric views. Although the evidence here is slim, it seems plausible to suggest this as the historical context for R. Johanan's tradition. In offering this interpretation, R. Johanan implied that the reception of God's word need not be a mystical experience of fiery death and resurrection, for God can communicate with everyone "according to his power." Yet he also implied that this "exoteric" revelation to the entire community would be a limited one; the recipient would not have a direct, immediate experience of God in all His power. Thus he retained the essence of R. Joshua b. Levi's admonition that a direct revelation of God Himself necessarily involves an "initiatory" death. The community as a whole must be satisfied with a safe but partial revelation of the fullness of God, while a full revelation of God Himself is still available to a few courageous mystics willing to suffer the requisite death. Only by maintaining that the word of God is a source of both life and death, depending on its "power," could R. Johanan impart both these messages simultaneously.

In the third generation of amoraim, students of both R. Joshua b. Levi and R. Johanan developed our theme in new ways. R. Simon b. Pazi, who is known as a frequent tradent of R. Joshua's traditions,[29] restated his master's theme but gave it a new conclusion. According to Exodus Rabbah, he said:

> When the Holy One blessed be He was revealed to give the Torah to Israel they heard His voice and died, as it is said, "My soul failed when he spoke." If this is true of Israel, how much more so is it true of the idolatrous nations?[30]

R. Simon seems to have been unconcerned with the problem of resurrection, and in fact his tradition shows little concern with the esoteric dimensions of the theme at

---

[28] Gershom Scholem, *Major Trends in Jewish Mysticism,* pp. 78, 79.
[29] Wilhelm Bacher, PA, I, p. 130, II, p. 437.
[30] Ex. R 29.9.

all. Rather he was interested in the fate of the other nations, and thus he logically extended the lethal effects of the revelatory word to include them as well. Yet he implied that there was some significant difference between Israel and the nations. This nationalistic reinterpretation of the tradition is not surprising, for by R. Simon's time Palestinian Jewry had passed through a renewed period of political and economic repression which resulted in increased bitterness toward foreign rule on the part of the rabbis.[31] It would seem that these political dimensions were more important than esoteric meanings to R. Simon.

Among R. Johanan's students, R. Levi was an outstanding master of the midrash. His development of our theme is found in a pericope in Exodus Rabbah which presents a complex set of problems. The tradition is stated as follows:

(1) "I am the Lord your God" (Ex 20:2) . . . R. Levi said: Israel asked two things of the Holy One blessed be He — that they might see His glory and hear His voice. And they did see His glory and hear His voice, as it is said, "And you said, 'Behold the Lord our God has shown us His glory and greatness, and we have heard His voice out of the midst of the fire.'" (Dt. 5:21).

(2) But they did not have the power to withstand it, for as soon as they came to Sinai and He was revealed to them their soul burst out because He spoke with them, as it is said, "My soul failed me when he spoke."

(3) But the Torah sought mercy for them from the Holy One blessed be He: "Is there a king who marries off his daughter and murders the members of his household? The entire world is rejoicing and Your children are dead." Immediately their soul returned, as it is said, "The Torah of the Lord is pure, restoring the soul."

(4) R. Levi said: But wasn't it apparent to God that if He showed Israel His glory and let them hear His voice they would not be able to withstand it?

(5) However the Holy One blessed be He foresaw that they would worship idols in the future, and [He did it] so that they would not be able to say, "If He had shown us His glory and His greatness and let us hear His voice we would not have worshipped idols." Therefore it is said, "Hear, my people, and I will speak" (Ps. 50:7).[32]

Of the five component traditions in this pericope, the first and last are quite definitely from R. Levi, as they appear elsewhere in his name in nearly identical forms.[33] Tradition (1) is itself a restatement of a tannaitic tradition. R. Levi often appears in midrashic literature as a transmitter of earlier traditions, and these are sometimes attributed to him because he transmitted and elaborated on them.[34] In this case he

---

[31] Michael Avi-Yonah, *The Jews of Palestine*, chs. 4, 5, especially pp. 127–132.

[32] Ex. R 29.4. The pericope appears in the text as one continuous paragraph; I have broken it into its five component units for purposes of analysis.

[33] In Song R 1.2.3, R. Pinhas b. Hama transmits tradition (5) in R. Levi's name. In Ex. R 41.3, both the first and last traditions appear in the name of R. Pinhas b. Hama alone; however R. Pinhas b. Hama is a frequent transmitter of R. Levi's traditions, and the appearance of these traditions in R. Levi's name in Ex. R 29.4 makes it almost certain that in all their versions they go back to R. Levi. Cf. Bacher, PA, II, pp. 302, 372, III, p. 312.

[34] Cf. Bacher, PA, II, pp. 301, 302.

took two traditions which appear consecutively in the Mekilta d'Rabbi Ishmael[35] and combined them. We have already seen that the former of the two — the request to see the "glory" of God — also appears in R. Simeon b. Yohai's name and is definitely part of the esoteric tradition. Now R. Levi himself is known to have been involved in esoteric circles, and moreover his master R. Johanan frequently transmitted traditions of R. Simeon b. Yohai.[36] Thus there is every reason to believe that such an esoteric midrash would have been known to him. But R. Levi has changed the meaning of this tannaitic tradition by adding his own comment to it in tradition (5). We can see the significance of this change if we examine the other two appearances of these traditions.

In Exodus Rabbah we find our tradition (1) followed by the question: "But do you listen to a fool when he requests something?" A variant on our tradition (5) is then offered as the explanation for God's granting a "fool's" request.[37] In Song of Songs Rabbah the order of the passage may have been disarranged, but the basic point is the same:

> But do you listen to a baby when he requests something? . . . R. Simeon b. Yohai taught: This is what they asked — they said, "Our wish is to see the glory of our King." R. Pinhas in the name of R. Levi: The Holy One blessed be He foresaw that Israel would exchange His glory for another in the future . . .[38]

In this tradition, whose esoteric import we have already seen above, we again find our tradition (1) described as an unwise request, but one which God must grant for the reason given in tradition (5). It is clear in all the appearances of the tradition (1)/ tradition (5) sequence that R. Levi saw a danger in Israel's desire to see and hear God directly; only a fool or a baby would make such a request. If the attribution of our tradition (4) to R. Levi is genuine, it explains his understanding of the danger quite clearly. If tradition (4) was not actually uttered by R. Levi — a good likelihood, since it does not appear with traditions (1) and (5) elsewhere — it must nevertheless accurately express his viewpoint. For we know that as a student of R. Johanan, R. Levi knew the tradition about the lethal power of God's word. And it seems probable that he understood it as a reference to the danger inherent in Merkabah speculations. If he labelled those who sought mystical revelations as "fools," he must have meant that they would not be able to endure such an experience. Thus it is highly possible that tradition (4) is the product of a later tradent who spelled out explicitly what R. Levi had left implicit and transmitted his words in R. Levi's name. This raises the interesting possibility that R. Levi assumed that his listeners would know R. Johanan's tradition and its implications without the need to have them stated ex-

---

[35] Mek. Yitro Bahodesh 2 end.
[36] Cf. Bacher, PA, I, p. 206.
[37] Ex. R 41.3. Note that this version of the tradition uses Song of Songs 1:2, whose esoteric import we have seen above, as a proof-text for our tradition (1).
[38] Song R 1.2.3. The English translator in *Song of Songs Rabbah* seems to have misunderstood the significance of the first part of the passage.

plicitly. Alternatively, it is possible that tradition (4) is genuinely from R. Levi but has been omitted in the other two versions of the tradition (1)/tradition (5) sequence in favor of an elliptical euphemism. This could have been done by R. Pinhas b. Hama or some later tradent, at a time when for some reason it was desired to obscure the true intent of R. Levi's words.

The implication of the foregoing discussion is that R. Levi knew and accepted R. Johanan's tradition on the death and resurrection at Sinai. This gives us reason to hypothesize that the attribution of tradition (2) to R. Levi is genuine as well, although this tradition appears nowhere else in his name. Furthermore, both the linguistic usage and the proof-text show direct affinities with R. Johanan's expression of the theme. Yet again we find that tradition (2) does not appear elsewhere with tradition (1) and (5), so the possibilities discussed in connection with tradition (4) also hold for tradition (2). Either a later tradent supplied the reference implicitly assumed by R. Levi, or a later tradent omitted an explicit reference to obscure the point.

But R. Levi, like his teacher, developed the theme in his own distinctive way. He stressed explicitly what was implicit in his master's tradition: no one has sufficient capability to experience safely the unmediated word of God in its full power. Again it seems likely that there is an element of warning about the dangers of mystical speculation here. R. Levi's principal concern, however, and his principal contribution to the development of the theme, was to ask and answer the question of why God would permit the Israelites to have this lethal experience. Why would R. Levi have raised this problem? Several explanations seem possible. It may have been a matter of theoretical elaboration on a tradition which had already become well established in his day. If one reads R. Johanan's tradition quite literally, it implies that God did not know beforehand that His word would kill the Israelites; the word itself had to return and inform Him of its effects. R. Levi, in tradition (4), may have responded directly to that implication: "But wasn't it apparent to God . . . that they would not be able to withstand it?" In other words, the theme must not be expressed in a way which compromises God's omniscience. If God is omniscient (and omnipotent), however, the problem of theodicy immediately arises. Why would God grant a request, knowing in advance its lethal effects and being capable of preventing it? Tradition (5) supplies an answer which, whatever its theological merits or defects, can be understood as an attempt to solve a problem in philosophical theology. The pursuit of such abstract questions has always been of interest to the theologically inclined for its own sake, and there seems no reason to deny such a possibility in this case.

Alternatively, it is possible that R. Levi was following the lead of his master in trying to bridge the gap between esoteric and non-esoteric interpretations of the Biblical text. If he wanted to make the idea of Israel's death at Sinai meaningful to those outside the esoteric community, he would have to find an interpretation which spoke to their own concerns in a frame of reference familiar to them. Now what R. Levi said, in essence, is that the Israelites had to die because of their future idolatry, which God in His omniscience could foresee. This could be accepted by all members of the community, for it was a variant of the well-known idea that Israel, beginning with the golden calf episode, had entered a period of religious backsliding for which they suffered justified punishment right up to the present day. In effect, the request to see and hear God could be viewed as merely one in the long series of unwise religious acts on Israel's part which brought suffering as their result. This would tend to make the tradition more acceptable to a broader segment of the populace. Moreover, if R. Levi's intention was to popularize the tradition in this manner, it may have led directly to the problem of theodicy. That is, those who knew the esoteric meaning of the tradition might not have asked the question about theodicy; they understood that this danger was a necessary element of mystical activity. Outside these circles, however, such a concept might not have been assumed, and a more "rational" explanation for God's action would have been necessary. Yet it is also possible that R. Levi was speaking within the esoteric community alone when he offered his interpretation of the theme. In this case, he might have been alluding to those who unwisely sought mystical revelations and explaining why God allows them to have such experiences. We noted earlier the increasing danger that esoteric pursuits might lead some to "break the bounds" of orthodox belief; perhaps the reference to Israel's future idolatry here is a veiled allusion to those mystics whose activities led them in this direction. Unfortunately all of these suggestions to explain R. Levi's tradition are speculative, as there is no clear evidence to support or deny them conclusively. Perhaps his motive was some mixture of all of them.

Finally, the problem of tradition (3) remains. The question of attribution is most serious here, for if tradition (3) is genuinely from R. Levi, why does tradition (4) begin with a repetition of the attribution, "R. Levi said"? Such a repetition makes it unlikely that the whole pericope has been handed down in a single piece, and it seems to indicate that what precedes the attribution is not from R. Levi. Furthermore, we have no grounds to assume that tradition (3) — which deals with the means of resurrection — was necessarily implicit in R. Levi's view, as tradition (2) seems to have been. So we can not really say anything definite about the validity of the attribution. But the problem becomes more complex when we recall that the nucleus of tradition (3) appears in the tradition attributed to R. Simeon b. Yohai: "The Torah which the Holy One blessed be He gave to Israel returned their souls to them." We have already noted the likelihood that R. Levi would know and transmit authentic traditions of R. Simeon b. Yohai, and we have seen that they both participated in the esoteric tradition. (We also saw an esoteric saying of R. Simeon b. Yohai inserted into one version of R. Levi's tradition in Song of Songs Rabbah). All of this makes it quite possible that R. Levi was the author of the whole pericope under discussion here but inserted into it a tradition he had received in R. Simeon's name. If this is the case, it raises the possibility that the whole pericope is an expansion on material that R. Levi had received, perhaps orginating with R. Simeon b. Yohai or in his time. Alternatively, it is possible that the tradition found in R. Simeon b. Yohai's name was attributed to him pseudepigraphically and actually originated with R. Levi or elsewhere. As we saw earlier, the question of attribution is important, for if the tradition did genuinely come from R. Simeon b. Yohai it would definitely indicate a tannaitic origin for the whole theme of the death at Sinai. Unfortunately the evidence here is just too sketchy to draw any firm conclusion. Moreover, it is hard to see what the meaning of tradition (3) might have been in any age. It seems to imply a distinction between the Torah and God's word experienced directly; while the latter takes away life, the former restores it. Is this an attempt to distinguish between dangerous mystical experience and the safety of more conventional Torah study? We shall explore this possibility below.

It seems fitting, though, that the one element in this pericope whose attribution is most uncertain is the means of resurrection. For we have seen that the rabbis who dealt with our theme varied significantly on this question, offering different views (or no views at all) on the means of resurrection. The one element which remained constant, being asserted by four leading rabbis whose careers spanned the entire third century, is that the Israelites, upon hearing God's word revealed directly to them, did die.

III

In conclusion: we have seen that two of the outstanding rabbis of third century Palestine affirmed that the Israelites at Sinai did die upon hearing the word of God and that each had least one disciple who repeated and elaborated upon this affirmation. We have suggested the possibility that R. Pinhas b. Hama, in handing on R. Levi's midrash, intentionally deleted the explicit reference to the death at Sinai, though this is by no means certain. Though we shall see further on that there may have been one or two other rabbis of the late fourth century, or later, who denied the Israelites' death, such a denial was, on the evidence of the extant texts, unknown in the third century and very uncommon thereafter. In other words, virtually no rabbi seems to have found this tradition offensive or wrong. Yet, as we noted at the outset, the idea of Torah as a source of life is intrinsic to all rabbinic thought. Thus we must understand the death at Sinai as being in consonance, not in conflict, with this latter idea. We have suggested that the tradition of the death at Sinai should be interpreted in light of the esoteric teachings of Merkabah mysticism, and it is in that light that we must look for the integration of these two apparently conflicting motifs.

Before exploring this problem, however, we should take note of some other rabbinic traditions, perhaps going back to the first century, which connect fire and its mortal danger with the knowledge of Torah. It seems evident from the exoteric rabbinic texts that there was a tradition of Torah study and exegesis as an esoteric phenomenon, one which concerned perhaps principally, but not solely, the first

chapter of Ezekiel. And the one consistent theme throughout all the relevant
texts is that understanding of Torah in this context is accompanied by manifestations
of fire. The *locus classicus* here is the famous story of R. Elazar b. Arak, who
expounded on the Merkabah before his master, R. Johanan b. Zakkai, causing fire
to burn in the sky around them.[39] Regardless of the historical value of this story, it
does indicate that by the late second century the association of fire with esoteric
exegeses was current. That such fire might be dangerous is suggested in the story of
the child who was studying the first chapter of Ezekiel and was burned by a
heavenly fire; this story also may well have been current in the late second century.[40]

But it was not only study concerning the Merkabah which was linked to fire.
This point is made explicit in the story of R. Akiba and Ben Azzai, two of the four
who "entered Paradise":

> "Your neck with strings of jewels" (Song 1:10) — When they were stringing together
> words of the Torah, and from words of the Torah to the Prophets and from the Prophets
> to the Writings, and the fire was burning around them and the words were rejoicing as at
> their revelation at Sinai. For when they were originally given at Mount Sinai, were they
> not given in fire, as it is said, "And the mountain burned with fire unto the heart of
> heaven" (Dt. 4:11). Ben Azzai was sitting and expounding and the fire burned around
> him . . . [R. Akiba] said to him, "Perhaps you were involved with the sections of the
> chariot?" He said to him, "No, rather I was sitting and stringing together words
> of the Torah, and from the Torah to the Prophets and from the Prophets to the Writ-
> ings, and the words were rejoicing as at their revelation at Sinai, and they were as sweet
> as at their original revelation. And when they were originally given at Sinai, were they not
> given in fire, as it is said, 'And the mountain burned with fire.'"[41]

Similarly, rabbinic legend reports about Jonathan b. Uzziel that "when he would
sit and study Torah, any bird that flew above him was immediately burned up."[42]
This connection of fire with Torah study is reflected in the common aphorism,
found in several tannaitic collections, that "the words of the Torah are likened to
fire: just as fire was given from heaven, so the words of the Torah were given from
heaven."[43] But this abstract conception was also used to express the danger involved
in any Torah study: "Just as with fire, if a man comes close he is burned but if he
stays far away he is cold, so with the words of the Torah, if a man comes close he
is burned but if he stays far away he is cold."[44] "R. Eliezer says . . . Warm yourself

[39] Tos. Hagigah 2.1; Mek. RS 158; TP Hagigah 2.1, 77a; TB Hagigah 13a. This story has
been discussed by a number of contemporary scholars; cf. the citations and summary
of Halperin, "Merkabah and Ma'aseh Merkabah," p. 206–210.
[40] TB Hagigah 13a. The dating is discussed by Halperin, *ibid.*, pp. 287–289.
[41] Song R 1.10.2; cf. Lev. R 16.4 and TP Hagigah 2.1, 77b.
[42] TB Sukkah 28a.
[43] Mek. Yitro Bahodesh 4, p. 215; Mek. RS 143; Sifre Dt. 343, p. 399 and parallels cited
there.
[44] Mek. RS 143.

by the light of the sages but be careful of their coals, lest you be burned . . . for all their words are like coals of fire."[45] It seems clear that these midrashim form the tradition within which R. Judah b. Ilai formed his own midrash about the Israelites at Sinai being burned by heavenly fire, and it is likely, though not absolutely certain, that they reflect a tradition of esoteric Torah study, one of whose chief foci was the Biblical accounts of the Merkabah.[46]

In other words, it seems likely that the dangerous aspects of Torah study represent some kind of esoteric tradition, while the concept of Torah as a source of life was shared by the exoteric majority as well. One might be tempted to discuss the relationship between the two in terms of this dichotomy; i. e., assigning the life-giving aspects of Torah to the exoteric tradition and the mortal danger of Torah to the esoteric. But it hardly seems likely that rabbis such as R. Joshua b. Levi or R. Johanan would have affirmed Torah as a source of life merely in giving exoteric teaching to the masses, while denying the validity of this affirmation in their own inner circles. Thus, if we want to understand the religious experience of these rabbis themselves and their disciples, we must still deal with the apparent contradiction, which yet was not a contradiction for them: the divinely revealed word was held to be source of both life and death.

I would suggest that a helpful theoretical framework within which to interpret this phenomenon is that of "initiatory death," as it has been developed by (among others) Mircea Eliade. Eliade has examined experiences of actual and symbolic death among a wide range of cultures and has claimed to find ubiquitous evidence of "Man's eternal longing to find a positive meaning in death, to accept death as a transition rite to a higher mode of being."[47]

> From one religion to another the immemorial theme of the second birth is enriched with new values, which sometimes profoundly change the content of the experience. Nevertheless, a common element, an invariable, remains. It could be defined as follows: access to spiritual life always entails death to the profane condition, followed by a new birth . . . One does not become a complete man until one has passed beyond, and in some sense abolished, "natural" humanity, for initiation is reducible to a paradoxical, supernatural experience of death and resurrection or of second birth.[48]

Very often, Eliade finds, the rite of initiatory death is said to be a repetition of the death of a primordial being who is seen as the founder of the ritual: "By dying ritually, the initiate shares in the supernatural condition of the founder of the

---

[45] M. Abot 2.10.
[46] This is also the conclusion reached by Halperin, "Merkabah and Ma'aseh Merkabah," pp. 221–228, in a discussion specifically directed against the conclusions of E. E. Urbach, "Hamasoret al Torat Hasod Bit'kufat Hatannaim."
[47] Mircea Eliade, *Rites and Symbols of Initiation: The Mysteries of Birth and Rebirth*, p. 136.
[48] Mircea Eliade, *The Sacred and the Profane*, pp. 201, 187.

mystery . . . Initiatory death becomes the *sine qua non* for all spiritual regeneration."[49]

It seems fair to suggest that the midrashim we have been examining here represent a rabbinic version of this initiatory death schema. For the death of the Israelites at Sinai is never said to be final; in every version of this tradition they are said to be resurrected. And this resurrection is the beginning of a new mode of life, one which is founded upon and imbued with a newly revealed mode of spirituality – the life of Torah. The revelation of these new spiritual values is itself the initiatory rite, for it is the source of both death and re-birth (particularly in those versions of the midrash which call the Torah itself the source of resurrection). Within this explanatory framework we can understand why the Torah could be said to be, at one and the same time, a source of both death and life for those who accept it.

Yet this rabbinic view of initiatory death contains not only the "common element," but also "new values" which "profoundly change the content of the experience." First, we should note that in most of the instances studied by Eliade the founder of the mystery – the first to die – is a "Supernatural Being." Such a concept would, of course, have been impossible in rabbinic Judaism, and so the people of Israel in the "generation of Sinai" take the place of the supernatural founder as the paradigm for all later initiatory death. However here again the ancient paradigm was depicted as more extreme thatn the contemporary experience. While the Merkabah mystic would face suffering, and possibly death, if he were not sufficiently qualified, the Israelites at Sinai all experienced death as a necessary concomitant of the direct revelation of God. In other words, the experience at Sinai was said to be more intense and more profound, both in its positive and negative aspects, than that of the Merkabah mystics in the present. This would tend to increase the prestige of the "generation of Sinai," and it would reinforce the sense of God as "wholly other" and radically transcendent to human beings, a sense which seems to have been basic in Merkabah mysticism. This, in turn, would probably have facilitated the adoption of the Sinai revelation as a paradigm for the Merkabah mystics.

More germane to our discussion is another feature which is peculiarly characteristic of this rabbinic version of initiatory death: it seems to be the product of a long process of accretion whose history our study has already suggested. The concept of Torah as the fundamental source and structure of spiritual values was, of course, a basic inheritance of rabbinic Judaism from the Biblical era. The concept of literal death and resurrection was well-rooted in the earliest stages of exoteric rabbinic Judaism. When the esoteric tradition added the idea of the death at Sinai, rabbinic Judaism could absorb it with little difficulty by linking it to the "new spiritual life" offered by the divine revelation and assimilating it to the well-known pattern of death and new life through resurrection. The principal point to be stressed

---

[49] Eliade, *Rites and Symbols*, p. 131.

here is that the initiatory death schema as found in rabbinic midrash represents a synthesis of esoteric and exoteric traditions; neither tradition in itself seems to have had the resources to create this particular pattern of religious experience. We recall, too, the widespread tradition which claims that the Israelites at Sinai received immortality as a consequence of their acceptance of Torah. This is also an important part of Eliade's understanding of initiatory death:

> Death ceases to present itself as a cessation and becomes a rite of passage . . . If one knows death already here below, if one is continually dying countless deaths in order to be reborn to something else . . . then one is living, we may say, a beginning of immortality, or growing more and more into immortality.[50]

If the death at Sinai was in fact paradigmatic for rabbinic esotericism, then each experience within the esoteric realm might represent a sort of symbolic death and thus a further "growing into immortality." Yet we have noted that the assertion of the Israelites' immortality at Sinai does not seem to have roots in any esoteric tradition, nor is there any reason why it should; the connection between acceptance of Torah and immortality was a fundamental (perhaps the fundamental) element of exoteric Judaism throughout the rabbinic era. So, whether we stress the new spiritual life in this world offered by Torah or the "life which is eternal" in the world to come which was the reward of Torah, we find that the initiatory scenario of the Sinai revelation is a blend of esoteric and exoteric traditions, a blend which seems to have been quite harmonious. This leads us to a further observation: It would appear that the ultimate good obtained by both esoteric and exoteric rabbinic Jews was fundamentally the same; only the means to the end differed. We must assume, of course, that there was a richness or complexity or depth in the religious experience of the esotericist which was unavailable to his exoteric co-religionist. But when each came to identify the ultimate or highest good which was available to him, both the nature and source of that highest good would have been the same. In the sequel we shall explore this observation and ask whether the evidence of the rabbinic texts bears it out. If it does, then we shall have further evidence of the difference between rabbinic esotericism and Gnosticism, for the Gnostic was set apart from his uninitiated contemporaries not only by his initiatory deaths (both symbolic and literal) but by the distinctive nature of the ultimate beneficence to which he attained after death.

There is one last point of basic importance in which rabbinic Judaism seems to differ from the general pattern of initiatory death which Eliade has outlined. In his view, initiatory death is necessary to end the old mode of existence; only after this is accomplished can the "newborn" neophyte begin to learn and live by the new spiritual values which he is taught during his symbolic childhood: "Initiatory death provides the clean slate on which will be written the successive revelations whose end is the formation of a new man."[51] In rabbinic midrash, however, the initiatory

---

[50] Mircea Eliade, *Myths, Dreams and Mysteries*, pp. 226, 227.
[51] Eliade, *Rites and Symbols*, p. xiii.

death is not the prerequisite for the reception of revelation, because the reception of revelation is itself the cause of death. In other words, the spiritual value of the death and the new life are in some sense ultimately equivalent, since both are the result of direct revelation and are therefore only two different aspects of the experience of one and the same God. Here we find a profound confirmation of a radical monotheism whose roots go back at least to the Biblical prophet of the exile: "The maker of well-being and the creator of evil, I the Lord do all these things." (Isa. 45:7) But this particular representation of the omnipotence of God could not have been developed except through the synthesis of exoteric and esoteric religious experience. And the unique contribution of the esoteric tradition seems to be the teaching that those who are willing to risk the initiatory death will in return be capable of experiencing a richer and fuller life, one which is enhanced by a more complete experience of God and/or His Torah than would otherwise be possible. Those who do not take this risk, on the other hand, will be able to experience only part of the totality of divinity and only a limited or mitigated Torah.

This apparent distinction between limited and unlimited revelation raises another set of problems, the significance of which has been pointed to by Gershom Scholem. In writing about the relationship of "revelation" and "tradition," Scholem describes the basic assumptions of the rabbinic view:

> The quintessence of Revelation does not lie in the importance of the sentences conveyed in it, but in the infinite number of interpretations to which it is open. The character of the absolute is recognizable by the innumerable possible ways of interpreting it . . . The infinite meaning of Revelation, which cannot be grasped in the one-time immediacy of its reception, will only unfold in the continual relation to time, in the tradition.[52]

This gradual unfolding of meanings through interpretation is the task of the rabbi, who thus becomes the mediator between the absolute revealed word of God and the living Jewish community:

> In Judaism, tradition becomes the reflective impulse that intervenes between the absoluteness of the divine word — revelation — and its receiver . . . Can the divine word confront us without mediation? . . . Does the divine word rather not require just such mediation by tradition in order to be apprehensible and therefore fulfillable? For rabbinic Judaism, the answer is in the affirmative. Every religious experience after revelation is a mediated one. It is the experience of the voice of God rather than the experience of God.[53]

It seems as though Scholem is suggesting a rather simple distinction: "revelation" is absolute, immediate, and unlimited, while "tradition" is contingent, mediated, and limited. Yet the texts we have examined here indicate that for some rabbis, at least, (and perhaps for all) such a distinction is too simple. These texts

---

[52] Gershom Scholem, "Jewish Theology Today," in *The Jewish Tradition and its Relevance to Contemporary Life,* p. 4.
[53] Scholem, "Revelation and Tradition," *Messianic Idea,* p. 292.

express the idea that there was, at Sinai, both an unlimited revelation of the word of God, which Moses alone could endure, and a partial revelation, in which the word was "sweetened" — i. e., limited — for the people as a whole. In some traditions, Moses is quite clearly said to be the mediator who provides the people with their mediated revelation. It may be more helpful, then, to think of three basic categories: unlimited revelation, limited revelation, and tradition (which is by definition limited at any given time, since there is always more to come in the future). As bearers of the tradition, the rabbis' view of their relationship to the Sinai revelation must have been ambivalent. On the one hand, they were mediating the word of God to their community, and in that sense were imitating the paradigmatic act of Moses "our rabbi." But on the other hand, any given rabbi could only claim to possess and transmit a part of the totality of God's word, and therefore found himself in the same situation as the Israelites at the foot of Sinai with a limited revelation.

Scholem goes on to discuss later developments of the relationship between revelation and tradition in Judaism. In the Kabbalah, he points out, the distinction between limited and unlimited revelation is still basic, but the Kabbalists extended the former category to include even the Torah which Moses had received at Sinai:

> Thus, the very words that we read in the Written Torah and that constitute the audible "word of God" and communicate a comprehensible message, are in reality mediations through which the absolute word, incomprehensible to us, is offered. This absolute word is originally communicated in its limitless fullness, but — and this is the key point — this communication is incomprehensible! It is not a communication which provides comprehension; being basically nothing but the expression of essence, it becomes a comprehensible communication only when it is mediated.[54]

While Scholem dates this view to the medieval era, the texts presented here make it possible to suggest that there was a rabbinic precedent for it. For these midrashim clearly imply that the Israelites at Sinai did receive, initially, a direct revelation of God Himself, which we may call an "expression of essence . . . in its limitless fullness," and which was, if not precisely incomprehensible, at least unendurable. The Torah which Moses mediated to the Israelites appears in this light to be a sort of compromise, in which limitations are accepted for the sake of survival. In the life of the community, only such a limited revelation is meaningful and useful. Yet if we are correct in hypothesizing that these midrashim reflect the influence of Merkabah mysticism, then the experience of Sinai as paradigmatic for the rabbis takes on further meaning. It may be that the rabbis saw themselves as repeating the experience of the Israelites at Sinai not only in possessing a limited, comprehensible verbal revelation, but also in having experiences of "essence . . . in its limitless fullness;" i. e., having visions of God and His Merkabah.

---

[54] *Ibid.*, p. 294.

There is an ambivalence toward limitless total revelation inherent in the Jewish tradition as Scholem depicts it, and that same ambivalence is expressed in the midrashim we have studied here. On the one hand, the rabbis surely wanted to have as full and immediate an experience of God as possible. On the other hand, this full and immediate revelation turns out to be too much for the community as a whole to bear, and therefore it is not useful in enriching and guiding the ongoing life of that community. The rabbis who developed these midrashim may well have been concerned primarily with this paradox. Saying that the Israelites at Sinai had to choose between a full but lethal revelation and a limited but endurable revelation, they were perhaps saying that their own community had to make a similar choice — that they themselves in fact had to make this choice. If some rabbis were in fact having ecstatic experiences of the Merkabah and of God Himself, they must have been tempted to make that the center and primary concern of their religious life. This might have meant relegating their communal role as teachers and judges of law to a secondary place. Yet all of the available evidence indicates that this potential development never occurred; the study and application of the limited but comprehensible verbal Torah remained the principal occupation of the rabbis.

One might suggest several explanations for this choice. Perhaps the rabbis saw ecstatic experience as truly of secondary concern — a sort of diversion which was permissible as long as it did not interfere with the primary task of Torah study. But the midrashim on Sinai make this approach questionable, for they seem to imply that the unlimited revelation of the divine word would have been preferable, from both the human and divine points of view, had it been endurable. In that sense it does seem to have a superior status, and the superior status of Moses is confirmed (and perhaps in part derived) through his unique ability to accept unlimited revelation. Perhaps, then, the explanation of the rabbis' choice is to be found in the particular historical situation. The rabbis may have had before them concrete examples of movements which enthroned esoteric inner experiences of illumination or gnosis as the primary religious value. But these movements, as we have seen, also tended to question the basic values of Judaism itself: the goodness of the Creator, His world and its history, His laws, etc. It may be that some rabbis really did value direct experience of God over the mediated experience of the Torah, but feared to put this value change into practice because they saw no way to do it but to head into some kind of Gnosticism. And it may be that the midrashim telling of the death at Sinai served in part to warn against any movement in such a direction.

This understanding of the historical situation seems to be a plausible explanation for the rabbis' stress on the limited and mediated revelation rather than the unlimited immediate one. Our discussion of revelation and initiatory death in the midrash may allow us to understand this choice in a wider context, however, for the rabbis were rejecting not merely the specific tenets of Gnosticism but a whole range of implicit values that went along with it. They were affirming that focussing one's attention and energies on the world of ordinary day-to-day reality is more important than focussing on the extraordinary "upper worlds," and thus saying implicitly that the world in which inter-personal and social processes occur is more important than the world in which each individual has isolated private spiritual experiences. This may be merely another way of saying that esoteric concerns, while important, were never allowed to eclipse exoteric responsibilites. But perhaps the rabbis were saying more than this. Perhaps they were suggesting that the fundamental natures of those two realms are quite different. If they were in fact describing an initiatory death at Sinai, and if this death served as a paradigm for ecstatic experiences in the esoteric circles of their own day, then they were implying that the "upper worlds" in which one could experience the fullness of God Himself were marked by a coincidence of contraries: one experienced both death and new life simultaneously, because one experienced the one God who "makes well-being and creates evil." In a sense, the esotericist knew that he could go "beyond good and evil," beyond the absolute opposition of life and death, of suffering and well-being. And thus he could go beyond the realm in which order and reason rule, into a realm which gave great scope for paradox and disorder. Here the "fullness" of unlimited revelation seems to imply a total revelation; i. e., a revelation of both the positive and negative aspects of the divine.

But this attitude, and the experiences which engendered it, were esoteric, which is to say that they were unavailable to the majority of the community and therefore fell outside the scope of most people's lives. This would seem to be true of any society, for the ordinary experience of day-to-day life in any community is governed precisely by those antinomies which the esotericist may have temporarily transcended. The ordinary processes of society, and the ordinary lives of individuals, intend to preserve life and stave off death as long as possible, whether it be the physical life-and-death of this world or the spiritual life-and-death of the next world which is of primary concern. In this attempt, society develops laws which sacralize the rigid dichotomy between right and wrong or good and evil. Law then becomes the basis for life, order, and well-being, while disobedience generates death, disorder, and suffering. The ordinary world, then, is one in which these antinomies, and the logical causal connection between them, are of primary value. From this perspective, the Torah which serves as the guide for communal life is a limited one because it insists on these dichotomies as the basis for life and therefore denies or ignores the paradoxical esoteric view − the "coincidence of opposites." On the other hand, without such "limitation" it seems as though ordinary life in society would be impossible. This perspective may help us to understand the ambivalence of the rabbis toward unlimited revelation. They may have believed it to be "in principle" superior to limited revelation, but they knew that it could not be the basis of the community's life; its inherent paradoxicality was inimical to meaningful social order, and its demand of initiatory death was too great for most members of the community to accept. But the genius of the rabbis allowed them to preserve unlimited revelation as an important, if esoteric, element which was integrated into the fabric of communal life, thereby enriching that life without disrupting it. And a central vehicle of this integration, it would seem, was the midrash.

If these conclusions suggest some important dimensions of rabbinic Judaism that may be seen in a new light (and hopefully some hypotheses that will be tested in further research), we will want to know how broad a segment of the rabbinic community they represent. We shall now turn to an examination of some midrashim of an apparently later date which deal with this theme, and we shall ask whether there are midrashim which seem to deny or contradict the death at Sinai.

IV. REVELATION AND INITIATORY DEATH
AFTER THE THIRD-CENTURY

The death of the Israelites at Sinai continued to be a topic of interest for the creators and redactors of midrash. In a number of anonymous midrashim we find this theme dealt with in contexts that show close connections with esoteric traditions; their anonymity, and their apparent reliance on third century midrash, make it probable that they are post-third century creations. We shall also examine some rare midrashim which seem to repudiate this theme.

In Pesikta Rabbati we find:

(1) The Holy One blessed be He opened the seven heavens and was revealed to them face to face in His beauty and in His glory and in His stature and with His crown and His throne of glory.

(2) As soon as they heard "I am the Lord your God" the soul of the righteous immediately expired. (Thereupon the Holy One blessed be He made descend the dew which at the resurrection will quicken the souls of the righteous) and He resurrected them, as it is said, "A bounteous rain You did pour down, O God" (Ps. 68:10).

(3) What did the Holy One blessed be He do? He brought down to them 1,200,000 ministering angels; each and every Israelite had two ministering angels holding him. One laid his hand upon his heart (that his soul should not leave him), and one raised his neck so that he could look at the Holy One blessed be He face to face. And why was He revealed to them face to face? He said to them: See that I was revealed to you in My glory and My splendor, so that if there be a generation which leads you astray and says: Come let us go and worship other gods, you will say to it: We have a God whom we serve. When we do not serve Him He sends us down to Gehinnom.[1]

We have here at least three separate traditions concerning the Sinai revelation which have been combined by a redactor to form the conclusion of a lengthy pericope dealing with Moses' ascent to heaven from Mount Sinai. The story of Moses' ascent incorporates a large amount of material which is obviously related to Merkabah mysticism. We have already suggested that tradition (2) here is also to be understood in terms of the esoteric tradition. It is a virtually exact repetition of R. Joshua b. Levi's tradition about the Israelites' death; the only interesting variation is the substitution of the term "righteous" for "Israel." This may very well have been under the influence of the common use of the term "righteous" to denote all those

---

[1] PR 20.4, 98b, The words in parentheses are supplied on the basis of manuscript readings in the English translation of W. G. Braude, *Pesikta Rabbati*, vol. I, p. 411.

who will enter paradise after their resurrection in the world to come. Thus, just as the righteous will be resurrected by dew in the future, so the righteous were resurrected by dew in the past.

Tradition (1) also seems to be quite certainly a reflection of esotericism. Scholem has pointed out that it is strikingly similar to a passage in Heikalot Rabbati:

> From His beauty the deeps were enkindled / and from His stature the Heavens are sparkling / His stature sends out the lofty / and His crown blazes out the mighty / and His garment flows with the precious . . . And His words shall drop as perfumes / Flowing forth in flames of fire.[2]

Even if such a parallel did not exist in the extant esoteric texts, we might well deduce the Merkabah background of tradition (1) from the key terms "glory" (*kabod*) and "stature" (*to'ar*); Scholem says: "I think it is obvious that the term *To'ar* (stature) here has the same meaning as *Komah* in *Shiur Komah*."[3] Tradition (3) makes it apparent that the essential point of tradition (1) and (2), at least to the redactor, was that the Israelites had in fact seen God Himself at Sinai; he took this to be a guarantee that they would be able to avoid the post-mortem punishment of Gehinnom. Such a vision or the *"komah"* or *"to'ar"* — what Scholem has called the "mystical form"[4] — of God was the essence of the Shiur Komah tradition, and the text Shiur Komah asserts that "everyone who knows this esoteric mystery may be assured that he is a participant in the world to come and is saved from the judgment of Gehinnom."[5] Thus it seems quite certain that the redactor of this pericope was consciously drawing on material from Merkabah mysticism. (He probably knew, too, that tradition (1), in its Heikalot Rabbati version, and tradition (2) both connected the divine revelation with a manifestation of fire. And he knew the tradition of the 1,200,000 angels, which we have seen repeated quite often in esoteric midrashim on Sinai.) Furthermore, it seems probable that he was bringing R. Joshua b. Levi's midrash quite consciously into the context of the Shiur Komah tradition, linking the vision of the "mystical form" to the initiatory death and asserting that this death would bring eternal life.

There may be further evidence elsewhere in Pesikta Rabbati that the death at Sinai was linked to the Shiur Komah:

> "This month shall be for you [the beginning of months]" (Ex. 12:2) . . . "My head is filled with dew" (Song 5:2). "Even the heavens dropped" (Judg. 5:4). "My locks with the drops of night" (Song 5:2). "Even the clouds also dropped water" (Judg. 5:4). When was all this? In "this month [which] shall be for you [the beginning of months.]"[6]

---

[2] HR 24.3, cited in Gershom Scholem, *Jewish Gnosticism, Merkabah Mysticism, and Talmudic Tradition*, pp. 61, 62.

[3] Scholem, *Gnosticism*, p. 62.

[4] Gershom Scholem, "Schi'ur Koma; die mystische Gestalt der Gottheit," *Von der Mystischen Gestalt der Gottheit.*

[5] Merkabah Shelemah 34 b; cf. *ibid.* 38 b.

[6] PR 15.6, 70 b.

While the pericope in which this passage appears deals with all the events of the first month, Nissan, including the Exodus, desert wandering, and revelation at Sinai, it seems reasonable to conclude that this passage refers specifically to Sinai.[7] The many midrashic texts relating the Sinai revelation to thunderstorms and rain form the natural background for it, and the sequel to Judg. 5:4 includes a specific reference to Sinai. Moreover, the reference to Judg. 5:4 may very well reflect the influence of R. Judah b. Ilai's midrash, asserting that the Israelites were "scorched" at Sinai, which we examined above. While the version attributed to him cites Ps. 68:9, we noted that the anonymous version in the Tosefta cites the parallel text, Judg. 5:4. The interesting feature of this pericope in Pesikta Rabbati is that, while ostensibly a midrash on Ex. 12:2, it is in fact a lengthy midrash on Song 5:2; the same pericope appears in Pesikta d'Rab Kahana explicitly as a midrash on the Song of Songs verse.[8] Thus it seems quite likely that the author of this pericope was combining an exegetical tradition on the Sinai revelation (perhaps some version of R. Judah b. Ilai's midrash) with an exegetical tradition on Song 5:2.

This is significant because Song 5:2 may very well have played a role in the Shiur Komah tradition. Chapter 5 of Song of Songs, particularly verses 10–16, seems to have been the Biblical *locus classicus* of the Shiur Komah.[9] In the Idra Rabbah, a section of the Zohar which incorporates Shiur Komah material, we find: "Dew from the white head drips into this skull, which is always filled by it. And from this dew, which he shakes down from his head, the dead will be resurrected in the future."[10] We know that this particular tradition was known at least as early as the eighth century, for it also appears in a discussion of the dew of resurrection in Pirkei d'Rabbi Eliezer, where it is specifically linked with Song 5:2:

> From what place does it descend? From the head of the Holy One blessed be He. And in the time to come He will shake the hair of His head and bring down the resurrecting dew and resurrect the dead, as it is said, "I slept, but my heart was awake . . . My head is filled with dew."[11]

If the death at Sinai was directly linked with the Shiur Komah in the anonymous midrashim of late rabbinic times, it would explain the comment of the Midrash T'hillim to Ps. 68:9:

> "The earth trembled" — All the living in the land of Israel instantly died, but the dead came back to life, for the Holy One blessed be He dripped the dew of the resurrection of the dead on them, as it is said, "Even the heavens dripped down."[12]

---

[7] This interpretation is followed in the English translation of W. G. Braude, *Pesikta Rabbati*, vol. I, p. 314.

[8] PRK 5.6, p. 88; cf. Song R 5.2.2.

[9] Scholem, *Mystischen Gestalt*, p. 15; *idem.*, *Major Trends in Jewish Mysticism*, p. 63.

[10] Zohar III, 135b; cf. Gershom Scholem, *Kabbalah*, pp. 104, 113.

[11] PRE ch. 34 end, 81a.

[12] MT 68.5.

The reference to "the living in the land of Israel" may be an intentional re-interpretation of R. Joshua b. Levi's midrash or, as seems more likely, an erroneous restatement of it. In either event, this is the only midrash which explicitly asserts the death of the Israelites as a comment on Ps. 68:9. R. Judah b. Ilai's midrash was a comment on this verse, but it did not claim explicitly that the Israelites died. R. Joshua b. Levi's midrash, as we have it, uses only verse 10 of the psalm.[13] It is possible that we have here an independent development of R. Judah b. Ilai's midrash which was unrelated to R. Joshua b. Levi's, but it seems more likely that it is a restatement of the latter's midrash which has been intentionally linked to a different proof-text. One possible explanation for the change in proof-texts is that the author of this variant knew of the connection between this motif and Song 5:2 and wanted to allude to it in his own midrash. While Ps. 68:9 (identical to Judg. 5:4) would make this allusion quite obvious, Ps. 68:10 would not do so at all. Thus, if the author of this passage in Midrash T'hillim knew of the link between the death at Sinai and the Shiur Komah tradition, it would explain quite well his use of a proof-text which until his time had not been used in this way (as far as the extant texts are concerned).

This midrash is followed by another, commenting on the sequel in Ps. 68:9 (identical with Judg. 5:5):

> "Yon Sinai" — The word "yon" [zeh] means nothing but fire and conflagration, as it says, "It was wont to burn [mezyeh]" (Dan. 3:19). As it is said, "And the mountain was burning with fire unto the heart of heaven" (Dt. 4:11).[14]

This is rather tortuous exegesis of a Hebrew word, taking great pains to stress the fire phenomenon as part of the revelation and to relate the fire to the descending dew, although fire is not mentioned in the Biblical proof-text, Ps. 68:9. If fire and dew are particularly significant elements in the esoteric tradition as it was applied to Sinai, then this passage should be connected with that tradition. The relevant part of this pericope then concludes with a comment on Ps. 68:10:

> "A bounteous rain" — As soon as the ministering angels saw that the soul of Israel had burst out they said to the Holy One blessed be He: To whom are You giving the Torah, to the dead or to the living? The Holy One blessed be He immediately waved the rains of life

---

[13] While the texts of both R. Judah b. Ilai's midrash and the anonymous Tos. version of that midrash as we have them refer to both Ps. 68:9 and 10, it seems likely that the reference to verse 10 is the work of later redactors, perhaps under the influence of R. Joshua b. Levi's midrash. In the Tos. version the last line: "So the Holy One blessed be He dripped down dew and rain before them, as it said, 'A bounteous rain You did pour down, O God' (Ps. 68:10)" is redundant, and the reference to rain makes it likely that this phrase was added specifically to work Ps. 68:10 into the midrash. The reference to Ps. 68:10 in R. Judah b. Ilai's midrash also seems to be a secondary proof-text which is unnecessary, and thus probably a later addition.

[14] MT 68.5.

upon Israel so that they might receive the Torah with a bounteous spirit. And the ministering angels waved it upon them with fans, as it is said, "You did pour down, O God."[15]

This midrash is principally an exercise in paronomasia. The phrase "a bounteous
spirit" *(ruaḥ n'dibot)* echoes the proof-text's "bounteous rain" *(geshem n'dabot)*,
while the image of the angels waving the rain down with fans *(manipin lahem
b'manipot)* echoes the proof-text's "You did pour" *(tanip)*. Beyond this, it is essentially a re-working of R. Joshua b. Levi's midrash, adding from R. Johanan's
midrash the motif of a divine agent informing God of the death, thus instigating the
resurrection. (We should note here that R. Johanan's midrash was a comment on
Song 5:16, an essential source of the Shiur Komah tradition.) The one novel substantive element which is added is the role assigned to the angels.

The connection between the angels and our theme appears again in the Midrash
T'hillim in an anonymous comment on Ps. 68:13: "Hosts of angels did move them,
did move them."[16] For the compiler of the Midrash T'hillim inserted R. Judah b.
Ilai's tradition into his text as a comment on this verse, not on verses 9 and 10 as we
might expect. There are two possible reasons for this. The Midrash T'hillim to 68:13
is largely a repetition of a comment in the Mekilta d'Rabbi Ishmael.[17] In the Mekilta
this comment is followed immediately by R. Judah b. Ilai's tradition, although there
is no evident connection between the two. It is possible that the compiler of the
Midrash T'hillim (or some earlier tradent who was his source) took both traditions
in the Mekilta to be a single unit commenting on Psalm 68:13 and thus included
both in the collection. On the other hand, it is possible that the two traditions in the
Mekilta may have had some thematic relationship which is no longer clear to us. If
so, this relationship would probably have been part of the early esoteric tradition.
The Mekilta tradition on the angels' role at Sinai is repeated in the name of R. Joshua
b. Levi in the Talmud immediately following his midrash on the death and resurrection at Sinai. Pesikta Rabbati, immediately after repeating R. Joshua b. Levi's
tradition, mentions the role of the angels at Sinai as well (although not following the
Mekilta tradition). We know that angelology was an important part of the esoteric
tradition; unfortunately it is particularly difficult to know exactly what role it played: "As long as our knowledge is confined to the meager fragmentary material
scattered across the different parts of the Talmud and Midrashim we shall probably
be unable to say how much of this was mystical and theosophical speculation in the
strict sense."[18] If the connection between the angels and the death at Sinai is a
substantive one, as appears probable from the frequency with which it appears, it

---

[15] *Ibid.* In a Merkabah text cited in Chap. III above, an angel restores a mystic's soul by
"waving."

[16] MT 68.7. Ps. 68:13 is translated here as the midrashic commentators understood it,
although this differs significantly from the modern translations.

[17] Mek. Yitro Bahodesh 9, p. 236.

[18] Scholem, *Major Trends*, p. 42; cf. *idem., Kabbalah*, pp. 19, 20.

strengthens our impression that the Midrash T'hillim has drawn on esoteric circles for its versions of the traditions under study here. But the interpretation of that connection must await further investigation.

The citation of R. Judah b. Ilai's tradition in the Midrash T'hillim involves another very different kind of problem, however. The majority of the extant manuscripts offer a reading which is significantly different from the reading we have cited from the Mekilta:

> R. Judah b. Ilai says: Since Israel was ravaged among the nations by the heat of the fire, the Holy One blessed be He said to the clouds of glory, "Drip down the dew of life on My children." Therefore it is said, "A bounteous rain You did pour down, O God."[19]

At least one manuscript, however, renders: "Since Israel was scorched among the nations by the heat of the fire . . ."[20] In the Yalkut Makiri on Psalms, which apparently was based on an older version of this latter manuscript,[21] the reading is exactly the same as that of the Mekilta: "Since Israel was scorched by the heat of the fire of the upper world . . ."[22] In attempting to make sense out of this problem, Buber suggests (in his note ad loc.) that the reading "scorched" (m'shulhabin) is an erroneous conflation of the two words "ravaged among" (m'shul'lah bein). Such a scribal error is possible, of course. But it seems more likely that the process worked in reverse; at some point the word "m'shulhabin" was broken up by an exegete into the two words "m'shul'lah bein"; by then adding the one word "nations" the exegete could change the meaning of the passage entirely.[23] The variant manuscript cited by Buber seems to be an attempt to include both versions of the tradition side by side in a single tradition. Because variant manuscripts can circulate side by side for centuries, it seems impossible to date the point at which the new, more nationalistic version of the tradition first arose. This is unfortunate, for the change is a most significant one and it would be helpful to know where and when it first occured. It is not likely that this change could have been accidental, since it involves not only the division of one word into two but the addition of the word "nations" and the deletion of the words "of the upper world." If, then, this alternation was intentional, what was its purpose? R. Judah b. Ilai's tradition pertained to the relationship between God and Israel and to some harm which befell Israel because of that relationship. The new version of the tradition pertains to the relationship between Israel and the nations and the harm which the nations caused Israel. Thus the point of this latter version is that God is only a source of good and never a source of harm for Israel. However the author was apparently unwilling to deny the validity of R.

---

[19] MT 68.7.

[20] Cited by Buber in MT 68.7, n. 19.

[21] This is Buber's view in his introduction to MT, p. 64.

[22] W. G. Braude, in his English translation, accepts this as the authentic reading: *The Midrash on Psalms*, vol. I, p. 541.

[23] The splitting of words and adding or subtracting of letters is a standard device in the "creative philology" of the midrash. See I. Heinemann, *Darkei Ha' aggadah*, p. 103.

Judah b. Ilai's tradition directly, so he changed the subject of the tradition completely, eliminating any reference to revelation and the direct experience of God. We have seen that a similarly oblique denial of the harmful effects of revelation may have caused the variation in R. Levi's tradition when it was repeated by R. Pinhas b. Hama or some later tradent.[24]

In addition to these two possible attempts to deny the validity of the "death at Sinai" theme indirectly, there is one and only one tradition in rabbinic literature which states directly that the Israelites at Sinai heard God's word directly and yet were not harmed:

> R. Johanan said: The voice would go forth and be split into seven voices and from seven voices into seventy languages so that all the nations would hear, and each and every nation would hear in the language of that nation and their souls would expire, but Israel would hear and not be harmed. How did the voice go forth? R. Tanhuma said: It was two-faced, and it would go forth and murder the nations who did not accept the Torah, but it would give life to Israel who accepted the Torah. This is what Moses said to them after forty years: "For who is there of all flesh that has heard the voice of the living God as we have speaking out of the midst of the fire and has lived?" (Dt. 5:23). You heard His voice and remained alive, but the nations would hear it and die. Come and see how the voice would go forth in Israel's case — to each and every one according to his power. The old men would hear the voice according to their power and the young men according to their power and the boys according to their power and the little children according to their power and the infants according to their power and the women according to their power and even Moses according to his power, as it is said, "Moses spoke and God answered him in thunder [literally, "in a voice"]" (Ex. 19:19). In a voice that Moses would be able to endure. And so it says, "The voice of the Lord in power." It does not say "in His power" but "in power" — so that each and every one would be able to endure it. And even the pregnant women according to their power; so you must say, each and every one according to his power. R. Jose b. Hanina said: If it surprises you, look at the example of the manna which only fell for Israel according to the power of each and every one of them. The young men would eat it as if it were bread . . . and the old men as a wafer with honey . . . and the infants as milk from their mothers' breasts . . . and the sick as fine flour mixed with honey . . . but to the nations it would taste as bitter as coriander . . . R. Jose b. Hanina said: If the manna, which was of one species, was transformed for them into many species according to the needs of each and every one, how much more so was it true of the voice which went forth and had power that it was transformed for each and every one according to his power so that it would not harm him?[25]

The pericope seems to fall into five distinct units; we shall now examine each of the units individually to determine its antecedent development and its place in the pericope as a whole.

---

[24] In Ex. R 41.3, R. Levi's tradition — attributed to R. Pinhas b. Hama — forms part of a larger pericope, the conclusion of which is that "the Torah was given to them from God's mouth"; there is no mention of any injurious effects at all.

[25] Tan. Sh'mot 25; Ex. R 5.9; Tan. B Sh'mot 22 (with some variations).

(1) R. Johanan said: The voice would go forth and be split . . . so that all the nations would hear, and each and every nation would hear in the language of that nation.

(2) and their souls would expire, but Israel would hear and would not be harmed.

Tradition (1) is a well-known saying of R. Johanan.[26] Nowhere else, however, is tradition (2) found with it. Tradition (2), of course, directly contradicts R. Johanan's tradition cited above that the Israelites died at Sinai. Thus it seems quite likely that tradition (2) has been added on to tradition (1) by a later tradent to give the impression that it is an integral part of R. Johanan's tradition. Is it possible, however, that the other appearances of tradition (1) are truncated, while we have here in traditions (1) and (2) together the original saying of R. Johanan? There is a tradition reported in R. Johanan's name: "'For the nations and kingdom that will not serve you shall perish; those nations shall be utterly laid waste [ḥarob yeḥeribu]' (Isa. 60:12) – From Horeb they were laid waste; they received their death sentence."[27] However this tradition is quite different from our traditions (1) and (2). It does not use the characteristic phrase "their souls expired." Neither does it necessarily carry the same meaning. There is a common rabbinic tradition that the nations were offered the Torah at Sinai (Horeb) and refused it; thus they are responsible for their own punishment for failing to live by Torah.[28] This does not mean, however, that the nations actually died upon hearing the revelation from Sinai, as our tradition (2) implies. Thus R. Johanan's explanation of "*ḥarob*" does not imply his acceptance of tradition (2). And certainly his statement that the Israelites died at Sinai directly contradicts tradition (2). Thus it is most likely that tradition (2) is an addition to R. Johanan's original tradition (1), perhaps based on the words of R. Tanhuma in tradition (3):

(3) How did the voice go forth? R. Tanhuma said: It was two-faced, and it would go forth and murder the nations who did not accept the Torah but it would give life to Israel who accepted the Torah . . .

It seems most likely that tradition (2) is a bridge passage, inserted to provide a transition between traditions (1) and (3), as well as to re-interpret the meaning of tradition (1). It is also possible, of course, that R. Tanhuma knew traditions (1) and (2) as a unit – i.e., that tradition (2) existed before tradition (3) – and that he was merely expanding on this preexisting tradition. Furthermore, R. Tanhuma is one of the most popular names for pseudepigraphs in the midrash, especially in the collections which bear his name, so it is possible that we have a later anonymous source at work in both traditions (2) and (3). Yet the attribution to R. Tanhuma in this particular case seems most probably to be genuine, for it occurs in the middle of the pericope and seems to relate only to that small part of the pericope found in tradition (3). Pseudepigraphal attributions to R. Tanhuma, on the other hand, generally

---

[26] Tan. Yitro 11; Ex. R 28.6; TB Shabbat 88b.

[27] Song R 4.4.1; TP Sotah 21d.

[28] Mek. Yitro Bahodesh 5, p. 221 and parallels cited there.

refer to entire pericopes;[29] if the author of our pericope wanted to use R. Tanhuma's name to lend prestige to his composition, he surely would have invoked that
name at the beginning of the pericope.

In any event, one fact is clear: the author of tradition (3), whether R. Tanhuma
or not, drew directly on a tradition of R. Simon b. Pazi but changed its meaning by
placing it in a new context. R. Simon commented on a tradition of his master, R.
Joshua b. Levi,[30] that before the Tent of Meeting was established the word of God
speaking to the Israelites frightened the other nations:

> R. Simon said: The word would go forth in a two-faced way. It was a life-giving drug for
> Israel, but a death-dealing drug for the nations of the world. A life-giving drug for Israel:
> "As you have heard and lived" − you heard and remained alive. But a death-dealing drug
> for the nations of the world − they heard and died.[31]

R. Simon's strongly nationalistic bent is in evidence here, for R. Joshua b. Levi's
tradition made no reference to the death of the nations. We have seen this same
motif in R. Simon's development of the tradition on the death of the Israelites at
Sinai. It is also apparent if we compare R. Simon's use of the metaphor of Torah as a
drug with its original source, a tradition which is also found in R. Joshua b. Levi's
name:

> R. Joshua b. Levi said: Why is it written, "And this is the Torah which Moses put" (Dt.
> 4:44)? [The Hebrew words for "put" and "drug" sound the same, although spelled dif-
> ferently.] If he is worthy it becomes a life-giving drug for him; if he is not worthy it be-
> comes a death-dealing drug for him.[32]

Similar traditions appear elsewhere in the Talmud under other names,[33] but in no
case is there any question of a difference between Israel and the nations. The
meaning of the tradition is always that the Torah can be a source of life or death for
the Jews, depending on their fidelity or lack of fidelity to it. Only in R. Simon's case
is there the nationalistic dimension of Israel's superiority to the nations. Thus, given
R. Simon's consistent nationalistic attitude, we might not be surprised to find him
asserting that God's word at Sinai killed the nations but not Israel, as is asserted in
tradition (3). However we have already seen that R. Simon asserted that God's word
did kill both the nations and Israel at Sinai. It is clear that the author of tradition (3)
took a tradition originally referring to the post-Sinaitic situation and made it apply
to Sinai.[34] It may be fair to say that he adopted the spirit of R. Simon's teaching but

---

[29] See L. Zunz, Had'rashot B'yisrael, pp. 112−115.

[30] Wilhelm Bacher, PA, I, p. 130, II, p. 437.

[31] Lev. R 1.11; Song R 2.3.5.

[32] TB Yoma 72b.

[33] TB Ta'anit 7a, Shabbat 88b, Yoma 72a.

[34] In Song R, R. Simon's tradition concludes with the words: "Therefore it says, 'Under the
apple tree I awakened you' (Song 8:5)." Some of the traditional commentaries suggest that
this is a reference to Sinai; if so, its meaning is unclear. However R. Simon's tradition
appears in Lev. R, the older of the two texts, without this reference to Song of Songs. Thus

extended it to a new situation and thereby violated the letter of R. Simon's own viewpoint. The author of the entire pericope adopted tradition (3) to expand on the meaning of traditions (1) and (2), emphasizing the different fates of Israel and the nations at Sinai.

> (4) Come and see how the voice would go forth in Israel's case — to each and every one according to his power.

This unit has the most complex background of any part of the pericope and thus must be examined in some detail. In the tannaitic period, when the tradition about Israel's death at Sinai was not expressed (at least according to the evidence of the extant texts), this tradition of "each according to his power" served to explain how the Israelites could have heard the Ten Commandments directly from God.[35] A passage in Exodus Rabbah attributed to R. Judah Ha-nasi says:

> The Holy One blessed be He does not become burdensome to His creatures. He only comes to them according to their power. You find that when the Holy One blessed be He gave the Torah to Israel, if He had come to them in the fullness of His power they would not have been able to withstand it, as it is said, "If we hear the voice of the Lord our God any more, we shall die." But He only came to them according to their power, as it said, "The voice of the Lord in power." It does not say "in His power" but "in power" — according to the power of each and every one.[36]

While the attribution of this passage may be questioned, it does accurately reflect a widespread rabbinic tradition (which may in fact go back to Philo).[37] R. Johanan combined this tradition with his assertion that the Israelites died at Sinai. For after making that assertion he went on to say that "the Holy One blessed be He went back and sweetened the word for them. This is what is written: 'The voice of the Lord in power. The voice of the Lord in majesty' (Ps. 29:4)."[38] In this way R. Johanan could explain how the Israelites, having died and then been resurrected, could receive further revelation.

Apparently R. Johanan learned this tradition in the school of his master, R. Hanina b. Hama,[39] for other members of that school knew the tradition as well. But the point to be stressed here is that, unlike the tannaim, the amoraim never used the tradition to prove that the Israelites did not die at Sinai. One version of the tradition is found only as a conclusion to R. Johanan's tradition just cited; apparently a redactor felt that R. Johanan's cryptic allusion needed to be made more explicit:

---

it seems likely that the reference is a later addition and did not form part of the original tradition. Its insertion may reflect an attempt by some later author to connect it with Sinai, as in our tradition (3) here.

[35] Mek. Yitro Bahodesh 9, p. 235.

[36] Ex. R 34.1.

[37] Cf. Chapter III, n. 27 above.

[38] Song R 5.16.3; Num. R 10.1.

[39] On the relations among the members of R. Hanina b. Hama's school referred to here, cf. Bacher, PA, I, pp. 6, 58, 208, 447.

"'The voice of the Lord in power. The voice of the Lord in majesty.' R. Hama b. Hanina said: To the [strong] young men, 'The voice of the Lord in power,' to the weak ones, 'The voice of the Lord in majesty.'"[40] R. Hama b. Hanina's saying may have been originally intended to complement R. Johanan's tradition, or it may have circulated independently; in the latter case, we have no way to determine what its original meaning might have been. Another student of R. Hanina b. Hama offered a different version of this tradition:

> R. Samuel b. Nahman said: R. Jonathan said: What is the meaning of "The voice of the Lord in power?" For is it possible to say this, since no creature can withstand the power of even a single angel, as it is said, "His body was like beryl, his face like the appearance of lightning, his eyes like flaming torches, his arms and legs like the gleam of burnished bronze, and the sound of his words like the noise of a multitude" (Dan. 10:6). And the Holy One blessed be He − of whom it is written, "Do I not fill heaven and earth?" (Jer. 23:24) − how much more is this true of Him? Does He have to speak with power? Rather [it means] with a voice that Moses was able to endure.[41]

The author of our pericope may very well have drawn on R. Jonathan's tradition when he included a specific reference to Moses hearing God's word according to his power. While this tradition differs from the other versions cited in that it refers to Moses, not the people as a whole, it points up one fact common to all the versions: all are meant to stress that God's word, when heard directly and in its fullness, is unendurable for humans. And there is no evidence that in the third century this tradition was used as proof for the claim that Israel heard all ten commandments directly from God.

The one other rabbi known to have transmitted this tradition on Psalm 29:4 is R. Levi. His version of the tradition must be studied in its context:

> (A) "I am the Lord your God." "Has any people heard the voice of God." The sectarians asked R. Simlai, "Are there many gods in the world?" He said to them, "Why do you ask?" They said to him, "Because you see that it is written, 'Has any people heard the voice of God ['Elohim, a plural form].'" He said to them, "Then is it written [immediately afterwards] 'speaking' in the plural? No, rather it is written 'speaking' in the singular." His students said to him, "Rabbi, you have put them off with a broken reed, but what will you answer to us?"
>
> (B) R. Levi rejoined and explained it. He said to them, "Has any people heard the voice of God." What does it mean? If it were written "The voice of the Lord in His power" the world would not be able to withstand it. But [it is written] "The voice of the Lord in power" − in the power of each and every one. The young men according to their power, and the old men according to their power, and the children according to their power.

---

40 Song R 5.16.3; Num. R 10.1.
41 Tan. Yitro 11; cf. Ex. R 28.6 end.

(C) The Holy One blessed be He said to Israel: "Do not think because you heard many voices that there are many gods. But know that I alone am the Lord your God, as it is said, 'I am the Lord your God.'"[42]

There is a curious circumstance concerning the pericope as a whole. It is strikingly similar to three other pericopes in which sectarians are said to ask R. Simlai about the use of the plural form "'*Elohim k'doshim*" ("the holy God") in Joshua 24:19. In each of those three pericopes, the students demand an answer to satisfy them, and in each case a different rabbi (never R. Simlai himself) is cited as offering the response, although in no case is the response the same as R. Levi's.[43] Thus it is possible that later redactors have taken the same tradition (A) concerning R. Simlai and attached different independent traditions to it which in their eyes formed fitting responses.

While this circumstance might tend to cast some doubt on the authenticity of any of these attributions, it seems quite likely that traditions (B) and (C) are genuinely from R. Levi, for they are part of a larger complex of traditions in which R. Levi's name is often mentioned.[44] Among these traditions are the following:

"I am the Lord your God." R. Hanina b. Pappa said: The Holy One blessed be He appeared to them with an angry face, with a neutral face, with a friendly face, with a joyous face . . . The Holy One blessed be He appeared to them like this statue which has faces on every side. A thousand people look at it and it looks at all of them. Thus the Israelites would say, "The word is speaking to me." It does not say "I am the Lord your God ['*Eloheikem*, a plural form]" but "I am the Lord your God ['*Eloheka*, a singular form]."[45]

R. Levi said: The Holy One blessed be He appeared to them at Sinai with many faces: with an angry face, with a repelling face, with a defiant face, with a joyous face, with a laughing face, with a kind and friendly face . . . R. Hiyya b. Aba said: If a heretic says to you, "There are two different gods," answer him: It is not written "The gods ['*Elohim*] have spoken face after face," but 'the Lord [*YHWH*] has spoken with you face after face." (Dt. 5:4)[46]

R. Johanan said: Just as with a statue, a thousand people look at it and each and every one says, "It is looking at me," so the Holy One blessed be He made each and every Israelite feel that He was looking at him, as it is said, "I am the Lord your God." . . . R. Levi said: . . . A single sound can enter ten ears at once, but can ten sounds enter one ear at once? Yes. God can hear the prayers of every creature at one and the same time . . . If He has such power, how much more so can He look at each and every Israelite, as it is said, "I am the Lord your God."[47]

---

[42] Ex. R 29.1. The pericope appears in the text as one continuous paragraph; I have broken it into its three component units for purposes of analysis.

[43] TP Berakot 12d; Tan. K'doshim 4; Tan. B B'reshit 7.

[44] The component traditions of this complex have been collected in PRK 2.24 and 12.25; PR 21.6; Tan. B Yitro 17.

[45] PRK 12.25; Tan. B Yitro 17. Buber, in his note *ad loc.*, suggests that this passage was originally a part of the pericope from Ex. R 29.1 under discussion here.

[46] PR 21.6, 101a.

[47] PR 21.6, 100b.

In this complex of traditions we find one overriding theme: although each Israelite had a different experience of God at Sinai, and Israel as a whole experienced God differently in different situations, yet it is always the same one God who is being experienced. Of the four names attached to this complex of traditions, three — R. Johanan, R. Levi, and R. Hiyya b. Aba — were the members of the same school.[48] At the same time, we know that the theme of "each according to his power" was known in this school in connection with the Israelites' death at Sinai, for R. Johanan himself had made that connection. Thus the reply to R. Simlai's students given in tradition (B) and (C) above consists of material all of which was well known to R. Levi, and there is probably no reason to deny the authenticity of the attribution.

The complex of traditions we have just surveyed also allows us to ascertain R. Levi's intention in tradition (B). His point, of course, was to refute the sectarians by proving the unity of God from Scripture, and in particular from the same verse the sectarians had quoted: "Has any people heard the voice of God speaking from the midst of the fire as you have heard and lived?" He drew on the tannaitic interpretation of the verse — i. e., that they lived because God spoke "to each according to his power" — but changed the meaning of the interpretation by adding tradition (C). Only traditions (B) and (C) together could directly refute the sectarians, by admitting a plurality of voices and yet denying a plurality of gods. R. Levi did not use tradition (B) in its tannaitic sense, to prove that the Israelites survived a direct experience of God's word (which would be irrelevant in this context). In fact, as we have seen, R. Levi elsewhere asserted that the Israelites died upon hearing God's word at Sinai. Thus tradition (B) must refer to the Israelites' experience after being resurrected at Sinai; we have already seen that R. Levi's teacher, R. Johanan, drew on the same "each according to his power" theme in a similar way. Thus it seems most likely that R. Levi was drawing on his master's teaching but incorporating it into the complex of traditions centering on the unity of God.

We can conclude, then, that none of the amoraim who repeated the "each according to his power" theme meant it to prove the survival of Israel at Sinai in contradistinction to the nations. Yet the author of our pericope in the Midrash Tanhuma has employed this tradition — our tradition (4) — to make precisely that point. In doing so he has repeated a tradition which was stated by both R. Johanan and R. Levi, but he has completely ignored the contexts in which they used the tradition and in fact created a wholly new context. He has gone beyond even the tannaitic context, for the tannaim never introduced the question of the nations' death at Sinai.

> (5) R. Jose b. Hanina said: If it surprises you, look at the example of the manna which only fell for Israel according to the power of each and every one of them . . .

This tradition in all of its appearances is part of the "each according to his power" theme. In fact, judging on the basis of frequency of citation, it is the most

---

[48] Cf. Bacher, PA, II, pp. 174, 175, 296, 300.

popular of all the traditions on that theme.[49] It is susceptible to many different interpretations; in some of its appearances it is part of the complex discussed above concerning the plurality of voices and singularity of God[50] — just as many different tastes come from the same food, so many different experiences of revelation come from the same one God. The one distinctive note in the version given in tradition (5) here is the reference to the nations; it does not appear in many of the versions and thus may very well be a later addition. If so, it is in line with the author's tendency throughout this pericope to take earlier traditions and give them a nationalistic interpretation, so that Israel is seen to prosper in some way while the nations suffer.

Having examined each of the component traditions, what can we say about the pericope as a whole? Certainly it demonstrates the literary skill of the author; he has taken a group of disparate traditions, each with a more or less complicated history of its own, and molded them into an apparently simple and straightforward unity. His ability is seen both in his choice of traditions and the way he combines them and gives them new contexts in order to communicate his own message with the apparent support of earlier authorities. In fact, the only one of these earlier rabbis who actually supported the author's point was R. Tanhuma (assuming the attribution in tradition (3) to be genuine). We might speculate that the author began his work with tradition (3) as a nucleus. He might have joined tradition (1) to tradition (3) by creating tradition (2) as a bridge passage himself, or he might have received traditions (1) and (2) as a pre-existing unit. In either event, he has forged traditions (1), (2), and (3) into an harmonious unit himself. He certainly knew traditions (4) and (5) as a single unit, and could easily add them on as an explanation for the survival of the Israelites which the first three traditions merely assert without explanation.

Our author also followed R. Tanhuma's lead in making traditions seem to contradict the views of their original authors. R. Tanhuma, as we saw, took a tradition of R. Simon originally unrelated to Sinai and made it apply to Sinai, thus contradicting R. Simon's assertion of the death of Israel. Our author took R. Johanan's tradition (1) and did the same thing. He also used the tradition (4) and (5) unit to contradict the view of R. Johanan and R. Levi, who already had asserted tradition (4) in different forms. Moreover, he denied the original intention of tradition (4) in its tannaitic expression. The tannaim had ignored the fate of the nations but asserted that the Israelites were in mortal fear at Sinai and demanded Moses' mediation.[51] Yet our author ignored the Israelites' fear while stressing the death of the nations. His purpose, clearly, was to point up the superiority of Israel among the nations, for only Israel, he claimed, could receive God's word in such safety and security. While the author's point and the skill he used to make that point are clear,

---

[49] It also appears in PRK 2.25; Ex. R 5.9; Tan. B Sh'mot 22 and Yitro 17; Midrash Hagadol Yitro 19.16; TB Yoma 75b.

[50] PRK 2.25; Tan. B Yitro 17.

[51] Mek. Yitro Bahodesh 9, p. 237; Mek. RS 155.

two questions remain. First, did he intentionally choose traditions which he knew had been asserted by R. Johanan, R. Levi, and R. Simon, all proponents of the idea that Israel died at Sinai? Was he trying to prove that they could not have actually asserted the Israelites' death, since here were other traditions of theirs which seemed to prove the opposite? Of course the use of these particular traditions could be coincidental. Furthermore, R. Joshua b. Levi, who also asserted the death at Sinai, is not represented in the pericope. And traditions (4) and (5), at least, were known in the name of rabbis unconnected with the death at Sinai idea. Yet it remains a highly intriguing fact that, out of all the traditions he could have chosen, the author used preponderantly traditions related to R. Johanan, R. Levi, and R. Simon.

The second question concerns the purpose of this literary composition. We have already seen that it was intended to glorify Israel at the expense of the other nations. To say anything more specific, we would have to know the time of its composition, and this appears to be an insoluble problem. Even the date of the final redaction of the Midrash Tanhuma is extremely difficult to set.[52] And there is no reason to believe that our author was necessarily connected with or contemporary with the final redaction. We can fix a *terminus post quem* for the author's work, since he was dependent on R. Tanhuma who lived toward the end of the fourth century. We should most likely look for a period in which nationalistic feeling and antagonism toward the gentiles was intense among the Jews. In fact, R. Tanhuma's generation in Palestine was such a time, largely as a result of increased oppression of the Jews following the accession of the Emperor Theodosius I in 383. M. Avi-Yonah has labelled this period "The Great Assault on the Jews and Judaism."[53] It is possible that our author did his work in the same period. Alternatively, he may have worked in some similar period of persecution (of which, in the following centuries, there was surely no lack). Beyond this, we can not really say anything about the time in which our author lived, nor about the author himself. He must remain one of the many anonymous figures who transmitted the teachings of the classical rabbis and shaped those teachings into the form in which we have received them.

Looking back at the work of these anonymous creators as they dealt with the Israelites at Sinai, we may make two summary statements. Those who continued to assert that the Israelites had died seem to have been quite conscious of a link between this assertion and some aspect of the esoteric tradition concerning the Merkabah. Those who denied the death of the Israelites may very well have done so because of specific historical circumstances which led them to stress the superiority of Israel above all other considerations. Thus these few instances of denial need not

---

[52] For a summary of the present state of the problem and the various attempts to solve it, see M. D. Herr, art. "Tanhuma" in *Encyclopedia Judaica*, xv, col. 795, and the sources cited there. Herr's own evaluation largely follows the discussion of Albeck in Zunz, *Had'rashot B'yisrael*; Herr assigns the final redaction to the ninth century. Joseph Heinemann, in *Aggadot V'toldotaihen*, Appendix, assigns it to the sixth or seventh century.

[53] Michael Avi-Yonah, *The Jews of Palestine*, ch. 9.

necessarily represent a denial of the basic attitudes underlying the "initiatory death" midrashim; rather they may represent a situation in which those attitudes were relegated to secondary importance in the interests of other attitudes seen as more pressing in a particular historical hour. It seems fair to conclude, then, that the message of the midrashim telling of the death at Sinai was shared by virtually all the rabbis from the third century on. If there were objections voiced to this message, they have been omitted by the redactors of the midrash collections and therefore are lost to us.

V. "NOURISHED BY THE SPLENDOR OF THE SHEKINAH:" A MYSTICAL MOTIF IN RABBINIC MIDRASH

Having examined some of the relationships between esotericism and *matan Torah* which appear to be reflected in rabbinic midrash, we shall now turn our inquiry to the relationships between esotericism and eschatology. In particular, we shall look at the reward promised to the righteous in rabbinic Judaism and ask whether it is related to Merkabah mysticism in any way. We have already noted that this question is important, in part, because of its bearing on the problem of "Jewish Gnosticism." The Gnostic thought himself destined for a post-mortem bliss achieved through esoteric knowledge and ecstatic experience of supra-terrestrial realms. If there was a "Jewish Gnosticism" among the rabbis, it might well have centered on similar claims of special eschatological privilege. In fact, Gershom Scholem, in discussing Merkabah mysticism as "Jewish Gnosticism," has defined Gnosticism as the acquisition of "knowledge of an esoteric and at the same time soteric (redeeming) character."[1] The implication of Scholem's view is that the rabbis would have been led into esoteric pursuits in order to gain the redemption which such esoteric knowledge could bring.

If this were the case, the ecstatic experience of the Merkabah might have been considered a sort of "preview" of the realm which awaited the righteous after death. K. Schubert has endorsed this view, asserting that "the rabbinic 'gnostic' wants to achieve in his lifetime what the righteous will know collectively after their resurrection."[2] His student, J. Maier, limited the soteriological aspect of Merkabah mysticism to its concern with "the will of the creator God, the Lord of history who is also the covenant God, thus above all with questions of law and *Heilsgeschichte*,"[3] and at the same time he spoke of the "completely non-soteriological character of this ascent."[4] I. Gruenwald has agreed that "the ascension of the soul in this literature has nothing to do with soteriology,"[5] and he has found the texts of Merkabah

---

[1] Gershom Scholem, *Jewish Gnosticism, Merkabah Mysticism and Talmudic Judaism*, p. 1.
[2] Kurt Schubert, "Jüdischer Hellenismus und jüdische Gnosis," *Wort and Warheit* 6/7 (1963), p. 459. Anthony J. Saldarini, "Apocalypses and 'Apocalyptic' in Rabbinic Literature and Mysticism," *Semeia* 14 (1979), has recently suggested that there is a strong eschatological element implicit (and sometimes explicit) in several Merkabah texts.
[3] Johann Maier, *Vom Kultus zur Gnosis*, p. 16.
[4] *Ibid.*, p. 25; cf. chapter I, n. 84 above.
[5] Ithamar Gruenwald, "Knowledge and Vision," *Israel Oriental Studies* 3 (1973), p. 106.

mysticism to be "quite neutral from the eschatological point of view."⁶ Most recently, P.S. Alexander has flatly asserted that "rabbinic 'Gnosis' is not soteric" and that it is "premature" to categorize the Merkabah mysticism as Gnostic.⁷ The trend in scholarship has thus been increasingly to minimize the soteric significance of esoteric knowledge. These judgments have been made principally on the basis of the specifically mystical texts, especially the Heikalot texts. Yet the question must also be pursued by a study of the predominantly exoteric rabbinic literature, since this can show us what aspects of the esoteric teachings were accepted in the wider rabbinic community. I want to offer here one small example of how the Talmud and midrash texts can illuminate the problem of Merkabah mysticism's role in rabbinic Judaism.

One of the best known rabbinic comments on the nature of redemption is that of Rav, a leading first generation Babylonian amora:

> Rav was in the habit of saying: The coming aeon is not like this aeon. In the coming aeon there is neither eating nor drinking nor procreation nor trade and commerce, nor is there jealousy or hatred or competition; rather the righteous sit with their crowns on their heads and feed upon the splendor of the Shekinah [*nehenim meziv hashekinah*], as it is said, "And they beheld God and ate and drank" (Ex. 24:11).⁸

There is a great deal of evidence connecting Rav with esoteric concerns,⁹ and therefore we might justly hypothesize that Rav's "habitual saying" about redemption might have some connection with esotericism. In fact, this hypothesis can be substantiated from the literature of the Merkabah mystics.

"The splendor of the Shekinah" [*ziv hashekinah*] is a phrase which occurs repeatedly in this literature, and the ability to "gaze" at the splendor of the Shekinah was apparently one of the culminations of mystical experience. In the text Maʿaseh Merkabah (which is "most characteristic of this material"¹⁰) we find, after a series of theurgic prayers: "R. Ishmael said: R. Nehuniah b. Hakanah said to me: Everyone who prays this prayer with all his strength is able to gaze upon [*l'ẓapot*] the splendor of the Shekinah and the Shekinah is beloved to him."¹¹ This possibility may have been conceived as a repetition of the paradigmatic act of the Primal Adam, for we find in III Enoch: "The Primal Adam and his generation would sit at the gate of the Garden of Eden to gaze upon [*l'histakel*] the image of the stature of the splendor of

---

⁶ *Ibid.*

⁷ P. S. Alexander, "The Historical Setting of the Hebrew Book of Enoch," *Journal of Jewish Studies* 28 (Autumn, 1977), pp. 179, 180.

⁸ TB Berakot 17 a.

⁹ The evidence has been summarized by Jacob Neusner in *A History of the Jews in Babylonia*, vol. II, pp. 180–187.

¹⁰ Scholem, *Gnosticism*, p. 76.

¹¹ MM par. 31 end. *l'ẓapot* is a *terminus technicus* for mystical experience according to Gershom Scholem in *Kabbalah*, p. 13.

the Shekinah."[12] More specifically, we find in Heikalot Rabbati that such a vision of the splendor of the Shekinah is referred to in gastronomic terms: "Happy is the eye which is nourished [*nizonet*] and which gazes upon [*mistakelet*] this wondrous light of God's throne, this wondrous and marvellous vision [*r'iyah*]."[13] In Heikalot Zutarti we find a similar term employed on a less positive note: "Be very careful about the glory of your Master, and do not descend to Him. But if you have descended to Him, do not feed upon Him. For if you have fed upon Him [*'im neheneita mimenu*] you will end up being eliminated from the world."[14] Rav may well have agreed with this last text that the vision of the splendor of the Shekinah was only possible after death. The possibility of such a post-mortem reward is indicated indirectly in another passage in III Enoch: "Za'afiel is appointed over the souls of the wicked, in order to bring them away from the presence of the Holy One blessed be He, from the splendor of the Shekinah, down to Gehinnom."[15]

Moreover, there is also a precise parallel between Rav's saying and the esoteric texts concerning the kind of world which was left behind in such experiences. The aspirant to the ascent to the Merkabah was told to refrain from eating and drinking (and, implicitly, sexuality, since he was sequestered).[16] In the world of the Merkabah he would find an environment in which there was "neither jealousy nor hatred nor competition"; Heikalot Rabbati, in describing the angel Dumiel, has God say: "Qazpiel the prince is with him, but he does not feel any enmity or hatred or jealousy or competition toward him, since the one is there for My glory and the other is there for My glory."[17] The same text elsewhere asserts that God "rejects hatred and jealousy and despises enmity and competition."[18] These precise parallels make it obvious that Rav's saying is part of the esoteric teaching which was incorporated into exoteric rabbinic teaching. It seems to indicate a close relationship between Merkabah mysticism and soteric experience as understood by the rabbis.

Yet Rav's view, while widely quoted in modern scholarship, seems to have had few echoes in rabbinic literature itself. In fact it appears only one other time in the extant texts, in an anonymous pericope in Abot d'Rabbi Nathan (ARN). The pericope forms the conclusion of a list of the psalms for each day of the week which

---

[12] III Enoch 5.3. "*l'histakel*" is also a *terminus technicus* for mystical experience according to Scholem, *ibid*. On the esoteric significance of "stature" see Scholem, *Gnosticism*, p. 62. On Rav's special interest in the Primal Adam see Neusner, *A History*, II, p. 156–158, 185–186.

[13] HR 8.3, p. 90. The term "*r'iyyah*" may have been a *terminus technicus*, since the earliest of the Merkabah texts, elaborating on the *locus classicus* of this tradition in Ezek. 1, was titled "Re'uyyot Yehezkiel;" cf. the remarks of I. Gruenwald in his edition of this text in *Temirin* 1 (1972).

[14] Heikalot Zutarti par. 1, as cited by Scholem, *Gnosticism*, p. 77, n. 6.

[15] III Enoch 44.3. Some mss. read "the judgment" instead of "the splendor."

[16] MM pars. 11, 14, 19.

[17] HR 18.6, p. 97.

[18] HR 26.1 p. 102; cf. 12.2 p. 92 and Sifre Dt. 47.

were sung by the Levites in the Temple; to understand it we must examine it in its component parts:

(1) On the seventh day what is recited? "A psalm, a song for the Sabbath day:" a day which is entirely rest [ŠBT]
(2) for on that day there is neither eating nor drinking nor trade and commerce; rather the righteous sit with their crowns on their heads and are nourished [nizonin] by the splendor of the Shekinah, as it is said, "And they beheld God and ate and drank" –
(3) like the ministering angels.[19]

Part (1) is the conclusion of a series of midrashic glosses on the seven daily psalms attributed to R. Akiba.[20] The meaning of R. Akiba's midrash is not certain. Rashi took it to mean that "in the future the world will be desolate and there will be no human beings and all work shall cease."[21] Other Talmudic authorities, however, took it to refer to a more positive concept of the coming aeon: "'A psalm, a song for the Sabbath day': for the future to come, a day which is entirely rest and tranquility for the life which is eternal."[22] Whoever first combined parts (1) and (2) in our ARN pericope clearly meant to give the same positive eschatological interpretation. However part (1) in itself does not show any particular esoteric concerns, and it is possible (though perhaps not likely) that parts (1) and (2) circulated as a unit without any intentional esoteric reference.

The addition of part (3) (whether simultaneous with or occurring after the combination of (1) and (2)) does, however, betray an explicit esoteric interest. It reflects an esoteric theme whose earliest attributed evidence in the extant texts comes from the school of R. Abbahu, a third generation Palestinian amora:

R. Abbahu says . . . The creatures of the upper world and the creatures of the lower world were created in the same instant, but the creatures of the upper world are nourished by the splendor of the Shekinah while the creatures of the lower world do not eat unless they exert themselves.[23]

Another member of the same school elaborated on this point:[24]

R. Isaac says: It is written, "My sacrificial offerings, my food" (Num. 28:2). But is there any eating or drinking for Me? If you say that there is any eating or drinking for Me, learn from My angels, learn from My ministers, as it is written, "His ministers are burning fire" (Ps. 104:4). From whence are they nourished? R. Judah in the name of R. Isaac says: From the splendor of the Shekinah, as it is written, "In the light of a king's face there is life" (Prov. 16:15).[25]

---

[19] ARN version A ch. 1, 3a.
[20] TB Rosh Hashanah 31a.
[21] Ibid., Rashi ad loc.
[22] TB Tamid end; cf. TB Sof'rim 18; MT 92.2.
[23] Gen. R 2.2, p. 15.
[24] Wilhelm Bacher, PA, II, p. 209.
[25] PR 16.2, 80a; PRK 6.1, p. 110; Tan. Pinhas 12; Num. R 21.16; Y Ps. 761, Prov. 955, Neh. 1071.

R. Haggai in the name of R. Isaac says: It is written . . . "You sustain [*m'ḥayeh*] all of
them" (Neh. 9:6) — you are the sustenance [*miḥyeh*] of all of them.[26] The angels do not eat
or drink or taste death. Why? Because they see the image of My glory and they are nourished by the splendor of the Shekinah. For even though I have said that they do not see My
glory, as R. Isaac said, they see as though through a veil. "In the light of a king's face there
is life." "You alone are God . . . and You sustain all of them."[27]

The central role of R. Isaac Nappaha in this tradition suggests an esoteric *Sitz im
Leben*, for R. Isaac is known to have been "deeply steeped in Merkabah
mysticism."[28] The content of these traditions confirms this suggestion. The theme
of the angels seeing the splendor of the Shekinah appears several times in the
literature of the Merkabah mystics. In Heikalot Rabbati we find:

Those angels who serve Him one day do not serve Him the next day, and those who serve
Him the next day do not serve Him again, because their strength is exhausted and their
faces are blackened, they are thrown into confusion and their eyes are darkened, because
of the brilliance of the splendor of the beauty of their king, as it is said, "Holy, Holy,
Holy."[29]

In III Enoch both the angel Kerubiel and the "living creatures" supporting the
divine throne are described as having "the splendor of the Shekinah upon their
faces."[30] More specifically, we find the question raised in Maseket Heikalot whether
the angels can be "nourished" by the divine splendor:

He spread over the throne something like the likeness of a candle of splendor and illumination and brilliance . . . so that even the holy living creatures which are in the chariot
and the guardian cherubim and the offanim of the Shekinah can not gaze upon the splendor
of the glory because it is spread over it. And from the splendor, His throne is encircled by
what looks like brilliance all around His throne. Therefore the Holy One blessed be He
encircled Himself with darkness and cloud all around, as it is said, "He made darkness His
hiding place" — His surrounding and His covering, so that the ministering angels can not
be nourished by the splender of the Shekinah nor by the splendor of His throne nor by the
splendor of His glory nor by the splendor of His kingship, as it is said, "The Lord is
exalted above all nations, His glory above the heavens."[31]

In this passage we seem to have just the situation to which R. Isaac responded
by claiming that the angels can be nourished by the splendor of the Shekinah
because they see as through a veil.[32] Both the problem and the solution reflect

---

[26] PR *loc. cit.* and PRK *loc. cit.*

[27] PR 48.3, 194 a.

[28] Scholem, *Gnosticism*, p. 27; cf. pp. 24—26. R. Abbahu's involvement in Merkabah mysticism is also apparent in TB Hagigah 13 a.

[29] HR 8.2, p. 89.

[30] III Enoch 22.7,13.

[31] Maseket Heikalot 3, p. 41.

[32] The significance of the "veil" in Merkabah mysticism has been discussed by Gershom
Scholem, *Major Trends in Jewish Mysticism*, p. 72.

the ambivalence of *tremendum* and *fascinans* inherent in the numinous quality of the Merkabah texts.[33]

Having seen that each of the three parts of our ARN pericope is known from attributed rabbinic sources, it is tempting to conclude that the author of the pericope was merely redacting traditions created by others. However, we can not demonstrate that he drew directly on these attributed sources, nor that his work necessarily post-dated them.[34] All that we can conclude with certainty is that this ARN peri-

---

[33] This aspect of the Merkabah mystics' literature has been noted by Scholem, *Major Trends*, p. 57, and by G. A. Wewers, *Geheimnis und Geheimhaltung im rabbinischen Judentum*, pp. 235, 251.

[34] The midrashic comments attributed to R. Akiba in TB Rosh Hashanah are significantly different from the comments on the seven daily psalms in ARN; this may reflect erroneous oral transmission or independent variants, perhaps stemming from an unknown common source pre-dating R. Akiba. Part (2) poses the same problem: the variant readings make it possible that Rav drew on the ARN tradition, as well as vice versa, or that both represent variants of a tradition pre-dating Rav. A. M. Goldberg, in *Untersuchungen über die Vorstellung von der Schekhinah in der Frühen rabbinischen Literatur* (1969), p. 286, has argued the priority of Rav's tradition on the basis of his translation of "*nehenim*" as "enjoy" ("*geniessen*"). However if "*nehenim*" here actually means "to feed upon" (or "to feast upon" as translated by Maurice Simon in *Berakoth* and accepted by Neusner, *A History*, II, p. 56), then it is actually synonymous with the ARN reading.

In support of the translation of "*nehenim*" as "feed upon" we may cite the proof-text offered by Rav: "And they beheld God and ate and drank." Clearly he meant that there is no normal eating and drinking because the "splendor of the Shekinah" was to be conceived as an eschatological food; the term "*nehenim*" is a substitute for, not an opposite to, "eating and drinking." Moreover, in TB Sanhedrin 98b we find:

R. Gidal said: Rav said: Israel is destined in the future to enjoy ["*d'akli*," literally "to eat"] the days of the Messiah . . . This was said in opposition to R. Hillel, who maintained that there will be no Messiah for Israel since they enjoyed him in the reign of Hezekiah.

One must translate "'*KL*'" here as "enjoy" (as does G. F. Moore in *Judaism*, vol. II, p. 347, n. 2) since it would make little sense to ascribe to R. Hillel the view that Israel "ate" the Messiah. Thus Rav was not contradicting his tradition in Berakot — not saying literally that Israel would "eat" in the days of the Messiah — but he was drawing on the synonymity between the concepts of "eating" and "enjoying" in both Talmudic passages. A similar use of the term "'*KL*'" as "enjoy" occurs in the sequel to the passage from Maseket Heikalot quoted in n. 31 above; it says that the angels surrounding God's throne "enjoy ['*oklim*] greatness and royalty because of His glory." We should also note that while Schechter's edition of ARN reads "*nizonin*," he cites (3a, n. 70) the alternate reading of "*nehenin*" in the Epstein ms. A similar alternation in readings apparently existed in M. Middot 4.5, where we read that when work was done on the Temple, precautions were taken with the workmen "so that their eyes would not be nourished by the Holy of Holies." However the version of the Mishnah used by Obadiah of Bertinoro in his commentary apparently read "so that their eyes would not feed upon the Holy of Holies." (Incidentally, in light of the thesis of J. Maier that Merkabah mysticism had its roots in the Temple

cope and Rav's tradition are the only two assertions in our texts that the future reward of the righteous will include being "nourished by the splendor of the Shekinah," and that the latter statement stems from the first half of the third century while the former comes from that time or the century or so following.[35]

There are a few other midrashim which ought to be mentioned here as possibly relevant to our theme, although their precise meaning seems very difficult to fix. The first is attributed to a fourth generation Babylonian amora:

> "When I awake I shall be satisfied with beholding Your form" (Ps. 17:15). R. Nahman b. Isaac said: These are the scholars who keep their eyes from sleeping in this aeon, and in the coming aeon the Holy One blessed be He will satisfy [masbi'an] them from the splendor of the Shekinah.[36]

The same motif appears in an anonymous text:

> "For the choirmaster; upon lilies" (Ps. 45:1). This is what Scripture says: "I will be as dew to Israel; he will blossom like the lily" (Hos. 14:6). This verse refers to the coming aeon: just as the dew does not harm any creature, so the righteous in the future are destined to be satisfied [lisboa'] from the splendor of the Shekinah and they will not be injured, as it is said, "In Your presence is the fullness of joy; the pleasures of eternity are at Your right hand" (Ps. 16:11).[37]

If the term "satisfy" [SB'] here refers to satiety from eating, then we would have evidence for a continuation of our theme. But there seems no way to determine with any certainty whether this is the meaning intended. It seems probable that "satisfy" here might refer to some aspect of esoteric experience, for we do find the term used in an apparently esoteric context:

> R. Judah b. Hiyya said: Any scholar who studies Torah in pressing circumstances has his prayer heard, as it is said . . . "And the Lord will give you the bread of adversity and the water of affliction" (Isa. 30:20), R. Abbahu says: They satisfy him from the splendor of the Shekinah, as it is said, "And your eyes will see your master" (ibid.).

---

cult, one might well speculate that this concept of the vision of God as "nourishment" has its origins in the terminology of the Temple as well.)

Part (3) seems to reflect a tradition unknown in tannaitic times; cf. the discussions on whether the angels eat at all in TB Yoma 75b, Gen R 48:11, 14, and Ex R. 47:5, in which no reference to our theme appears. The fact that the first attributed mention of the theme stems from third generation amoraim does not exclude the possibility that our ARN pericope reflects an earlier version of the tradition. The absence of part (3) in Rav's tradition makes it perhaps likely, but no means necessary, that the tradition about the angels first developed after Rav's time. In any event, the inclusion of part (3) surely represents the ARN author's (or redactor's) attempt to link his pericope even more firmly with the esoteric tradition, and it is probable evidence for post-tannaitic dating.

[35] On the dating of ARN, see Judah Goldin, *The Fathers According to Rabbi Nathan*, p. xxi, and Anthony J. Saldarini, *The Fathers According to Rabbi Nathan Version B*, pp. 12–16.

[36] TB Babba Batra 10a.

[37] MT 45.3.

R. Aba b. Hanina said: It is even the case that the curtain is not closed before him, as it is said, "And your master will no longer hide himself" (*ibid.*).[38]

Having seen R. Abbahu's interest in esoteric matters, it is not surprising that he picked up R. Judah b. Hiyya's reference to Isaiah 30:20 and interpreted it in esoteric fashion, implying that the splendor of the Shekinah is the "bread and water" with which the scholar will be "satisfied." R. Aba b. Hanina certainly viewed the same Biblical verse as an esoteric reference, for we know that the "curtain" (*pargod*) was an important element in rabbinic esoteric speculations.[39] But it is not at all clear that these midrashim refer to an eschatological or post-mortem reward; they might equally well refer to ecstatic visions in this life, especially since they are comments on a midrash of R. Judah b. Hiyya which is not eschatological. A similar problem surrounds another relevant midrash: "R. Yohai b. Yoshaiah said . . . Whoever puts himself near to sin but does not do it is nourished by the splendor of the Shekinah like the ministering angels, as it is said, 'And they beheld God and ate and drank.'"[40] Like the other three midrashim just cited, this text may reflect a confluence of esoteric and soteric interests, but on the other hand it may be using an esoteric motif in a non-soteric context. The difficulty of interpreting all four of these texts leads to the conclusion that, if they were intending to communicate the same esoteric and soteric message as Rav's tradition, they were surely reticent about stating it as plainly as did Rav.

All of the material reviewed here thus far indicates that at least some members of the rabbinic community could have conceived the experience of the redeemed to be analogous to the experience of the "descenders" to the Merkabah, at least in this particular detail. Therefore they could (following Schubert's view) have seen the experience of the "descenders" as foreshadowing the redemptive experience of the righteous. I want to argue, however, that the important thing about the traditions just discussed is the extent to which many other rabbis did not share this view and, quite possibly, explicitly rejected it. I want to show that the concept of being nourished by the splendor of the Shekinah was well known in rabbinic circles as an esoteric motif but was not applied to the experience of redemption except in these few cases. Based on the evidence of our extant texts, it appears that a majority of the rabbis (particularly in the third century) did not want to use this motif to indicate that the experience of the Merkabah pre-figured the redemption of the righteous. They did, however, want to indicate that the experience of the Merkabah was in some way closely linked to the revelation of the Torah at Mount Sinai.

---

[38] TB Sotah 49a.

[39] Scholem, *Major Trends*, p. 72, and *Kabbalah*, p. 18.

[40] TB Kallah. I can not share Goldberg's confidence that this midrash refers to the "blessed deceased" (*Untersuchungen*, p. 273).

The first rabbinic evidence of this view[41] is a midrash on Exodus 24:10 in the Mekilta d'Rabbi Simeon b. Yohai:

> "And they saw the God of Israel" It teaches that their eyes were nourished by the splendor of the Shekinah. "And beneath His feet" It teaches that they became arrogant and made the upper equal to the lower. "A pavement of sapphire" — and it says elsewhere "like the gleaming of chrysolite" (Ez. 1:16); just as it refers there to the "wheel" so it refers here to the "wheel" ['ofan]. But it might mean a real pavement of sapphire; that is why it says, "as it were," and further on it says, "the four of them full of eyes all around" (Ez. 1:18).[42]

The reference to Ezekiel 1 makes it clear that Exodus 24:10 is being interpreted here in the context of the ma'aseh Merkabah. The vision of God is explicitly called being "nourished," and this term carries no pejorative meaning, if the first sentence of the passage is taken alone. The second sentence clearly is pejorative, but its meaning is not clear, nor is it clear whether it is meant to be read in direct conjunction with the first sentence. It might mean that the elders perceived themselves to be in some way equal to the heavenly beings, or that they perceived the heavenly beings "beneath His feet" to be equal to God himself;[43] neither of these interpretations, however, demands that the "nourishing" vision of the Shekinah in itself be seen as negative. It is the response of the elders which is being indicted here.

This possibility of ambivalent responses to the vision of God was clearly articulated in the first generation of amoraim by R. Hoshaiah Rabbah.[44] One of his midrashim has been set in the context of a discussion of the sin of Nadab and Abihu, although it may have originally applied to all the elders:

---

[41] The earliest evidence in any Jewish literature is apparently in Philo, Quaest. in Ex. 2:39 (following the translation of Ralph Marcus, *Questions and Answers on Exodus*, p. 82):

> They see the Master in a lofty and clear manner, envisioning God with the keen-sighted eyes of the mind. But this vision is the food of the soul and true partaking is the cause of a life of immortality. Wherefore it is said indeed "they ate and drank" (Ex. 24:11). For those who are indeed very hungry and thirsty did not fail to see God become clearly visible, but like those who, being famished, find an abundance of food, they satisfied their great desire.

The proof-text here was, as we shall see, also a central text for amoraic midrash reflecting this motif.

[42] Mek. RS 221. On the dating of the Mekilta, see Chap. I, n. 45 above.

[43] The latter interpretation has been suggested by Goldberg, *Untersuchungen*, p. 275, as a "very subtle interpretation."

[44] It is likely that R. Hoshaiah would have been knowledgeable in esoteric matters, since his principle teachers, R. Hiyya and Bar Kappara (cf. Bacher, PA, I, p. 91), were both very active in esotericism, according to Scholem, *Kabbalah*, p. 34 and Wewers, *Geheimnis*, p. 212.

R. Hoshaiah said: But did they take food up on Sinai with them, since it says, "And they beheld God and ate and drank"? Rather, it means that they feasted [zanu] their eyes upon the Shekinah like a man who looks at his friend while eating and drinking.[45]

Here, as Goldberg points out,[46] the meaning of "feasted their eyes" is clearly negative; it implies undue familiarity which amounts to the sort of transgression of God's glory which is strictly forbidden in the Mishnah.[47] In another version of this midrash R. Hoshaiah contrasted the action of Nadab and Abihu with the action of Moses in the same situation:

R. Hoshaiah Rabbah said: Moses acted very respectfully when he hid his face from God. But Nadab and Abihu uncovered their heads and feasted their eyes upon the Shekinah, as it is said, "But upon the elders of the children of Israel He did not lay His hand, and they beheld God and ate and drank."[48]

Yet another version of R. Hoshaiah's understanding of this incident reflects even more precisely the difference between Moses and Nadab and Abihu:

R. Hoshaiah Rabbah said: He did a good thing when he hid his face. The Holy One blessed be He said to him: I came to show you My face, and you honored Me and hid your face. By your life! You will be with Me on the mountain for forty days and forty nights without eating and without drinking, for you will feed ['atid leihanot] upon the splendor of the Shekinah, as it is said, "And Moses did not know that the skin of his face shone because he had been talking with God" (Ex. 34:29). But Nadab and Abihu uncovered their heads and feasted their eyes upon the splendor of the Shekinah.[49]

Here we see quite clearly R. Hoshaiah's view that being fed or nourished by the splendor of the Shekinah is in itself a positive good; only when one fails to show the proper respect for God does it become negative. While we cannot say that R. Hoshaiah's midrash shows any linguistic affinity with the Mekilta passage cited above, there certainly does seem to be affinity in theme and context. This may well reflect the attempt on the part of the rabbis to limit esoteric speculation on the Merkabah by emphasizing its dangers. Such an attempt, according to J. Maier,[50] was stressed by the last tannaim and first amoraim but grew even stronger as the third century progressed.

---

[45] Num. R. 2.25; PRK 26.9, p. 396; Y Lev. 524; also with minor differences in Lev. R 20.10; Tan. Aharei 6; Tan. B Aharei 7 (where the attribution is erroneous).

[46] Goldberg, *Untersuchungen*, p. 276

[47] M. Hagigah 2.1. It is perhaps significant that the term used here for "feasted upon" is "*zanu*," an active *kal* verb, while the term previously rendered as "feed upon" is "*nizonim*," a passive *nif'al*. The implication may be that such an experience is legitimate if undergone passively but illegitimate if initiated actively. As we shall see, R. Hoshaiah used the passive *nif'al* "*neheneh*" in a positive sense in this context. But cf. Maier, *Vom Kultus*, p. 17.

[48] Ex. R 45.5.

[49] Ex. R 3.1.

[50] Cf. Chap. III, n. 20 above.

In fact we do find that this tradition stemming from the Mekilta and R. Hoshaiah
was passed on and repeated in various ways in each generation of the Palestinian
amoraim. Taken as an aggregate, these midrashim reveal a continuing ambivalence:
the vision of God in the context of revelation was seen to be positive and expressed
in images of "feeding," but the danger of overstepping one's bounds was always
present. In the second generation of amoraim, R. Johanan, "the most important of
Hoshaiah's disciples,"[51] added a comment which has been attached by redactors to
his master's midrash on Exodus 24:11 in nearly all of its appearances:

> R. Hoshaiah said: But did they take food up on Sinai with them, since it says, "And they
> beheld God and ate and drank"? . . . R. Johanan said: It actually was eating, as it is said,
> "In the light of a king's face there is life" (Prov. 16:15).[52]

Here, as in R. Hoshaiah's midrash on Exodus 34:29, the divine light accompanying
revelation is said to be a form of food. However R. Johanan was apparently not
concerned about proper or improper ways of receiving this light; rather he was
concerned that the link between light and food not be taken as a mere metaphor.
Given R. Johanan's deep involvement in esoteric interests, it seems likely that this
literal interpretation reflects the tradition of Merkabah mysticism which we
surveyed earlier.

In the next generation R. Levi, a leading student of R. Johanan, showed that the
warning implicit in R. Hoshaiah's midrash was still well remembered:

> R. Joshua of Siknin in the name of R. Levi said: Moses did not feast his eyes upon the
> Shekinah and he fed upon the Shekinah. He did not feast his eyes upon the Shekinah,
> as it is said, "And Moses hid his face" (Ex. 3:6). And he fed upon the Shekinah. What is
> the evidence? As it is written, "And Moses did not know that the skin of his face shone"
> . . . Nadab and Abihu feasted their eyes upon the Shekinah and did not feed upon it.[53]

---

[51] Bacher, PA, I, p. 93.

[52] Cf. references in n. 45 above.

[53] Lev. R 20.10; Num. R 2.25; PRK 26.9, p. 396 (cf. the reading of the Carmoly ms. cited in
the critical apparatus); also with some differences in Tan. Aharei 6 and Tan. B Aharei 7
(and cf. Buber's n. 115 *ad loc.*). The ellipsis in the text as cited here represents an inter-
polated tradition about Moses which is attributed to R. Jonathan in TB Berakot 7a; Goldberg says: "Since the inserted gloss is from another author, the possibility always exists
that the second part of the midrash (Nadab and Abihu) was introduced later. The parallel
between the two midrashim does not necessarily contradict this, since this juxtaposition
was very popular and widespread" (*Untersuchungen*, p. 277). However, even if we omit
this second part as a later addition, R. Levi's midrash still reflects the substance of R.
Hoshaiah's tradition. Goldberg says: "R. Levi represents the view that all gazing upon
the Shekinah — i.e., even that which is possible and basically permissible — shows a
lack of respect." (*ibid.*) However, his view again is based upon his translation of "*neheneh*"
as "enjoy" rather than "feed upon", the implication being that Moses never gazed upon
or "fed upon" the Shekinah at all. However the thrust of all the traditions examined here
(and especially R. Hoshaiah's) is that Moses was enabled to gaze or "feed" upon the

In the last generation of amoraim, R. Tanhuma offered a midrash on Exodus 24:11 which seems to be a conflation of R. Hoshaiah's tradition and the anonymous Mekilta midrash: "R. Tanhuma said: It teaches that they became arrogant and stood upon their feet and feasted their eyes upon the Shekinah."[54] If in fact the Mekilta tradition did precede R. Hoshaiah's tradition, it is interesting to note that the phrase "became arrogant"[55] resurfaced here after being omitted in all the third century versions of the theme. This may indicate that the Mekilta tradition circulated independently of R. Hoshaiah's midrash. If so, then the phrase "to be nourished [nizon] by the splendor of the Shekinah" may have continued to be used in a positive sense in connection with the revelation at Sinai as well as in angelogical and eschatological contexts.

Such a positive sense of the term "nizon" does appear in an anonymous (and therefore perhaps late) midrash:

> "And he was there with the Lord . . . He neither ate bread nor drank water" (Ex. 34:28) . . . But what did he eat? From the splendor of the Shekinah he was nourished. And do not be surprised at this — the living creatures who hold up the throne are nourished by the splendor of the Shekinah.[56]

The connection of Moses' "nourishment" with the theme of the angels being nourished by the splendor of the Shekinah is also implicit in another anonymous midrash:

> It was a good thing for Moses that he fasted one hundred and twenty days when he received the Torah. From what did Moses eat? From the splendor of the Shekinah, as it is said, "And you provide sustenance for all of them."[57]

We have seen Nehemiah 9:6, the proof-text here, as an important verse in midrashim concerning the angels, so we may suspect that the angelogical motif has had an influence here. While the connection of the angelogical motif with the traditions concerning Moses is probably a late phenomenon, it is interesting to note that such a connection could be made, just as the angelogical motif could be

---

splendor of the Shekinah precisely because he did not seek this privilege in a disrespectful manner.

[54] Tan. Aharei 6; Tan. B Aharei 7; Num. R 2.25; PRK 26.9, p. 396; cf. Lev. R 20.10, which has a reading similar to R. Hoshaiah's midrash in Ex. R 3.1 and the Carmoly ms. of PRK cited in n. 53 above.

[55] The reading is "higisu da'atam" in the Mekilta and "higisu libam" in R. Tanhuma's midrash.

[56] Ex. R 47.5; Tan. B Ki tissa 19; Y Ex. 406. The reference to the angels may not have been part of the original midrash since it is only found in one of the mss. used by Buber, the one which in his view served as the basis for Ex. R (see n. 139 ad loc.). However, it is obvious that at some point the two motifs of Moses and the angels were linked together.

[57] Ex. R 47.7.

connected to Rav's eschatological motif. But at no time in our extant texts is there a connection (either explicit or implicit) between the experience at Sinai and the eschatological experience of the righteous. Although the angelological theme could have formed a link between the two (if such a *tertium quid* were deemed necessary), it was never used in such a way. This leads us to make some summary remarks about the significance of the material reviewed here.

We have examined a limited midrashic theme here in hopes of suggesting a larger point about the role of Merkabah mysticism in rabbinic Judaism. The point, briefly, is this: Several leading amoraim deliberately used a motif found in Merkabah mysticism to describe the experience of Moses and the elders at Sinai. They also apparently wanted to make a point about the proper attitude necessary for the Merkabah mystic in approaching and experiencing the vision of the Shekinah. In other words, they used a particular detail of the revelation at Sinai as a paradigm for the Merkabah mystical experience. At the same time, a tradition existed which postulated a very similar (perhaps identical) experience as an essential part of the eschatological reward of the righteous. I think we must assume that this tradition was known to rabbis such as Hoshaiah, Johanan, Levi, and Tanhuma. Yet those rabbis never, as far as our texts indicate, made any connection between the Sinai paradigm and the eschatological motif.[58] Of course there is danger in argument from silence. But given the large corpus of texts which has been preserved, it seems striking that this image of the vision of God as nourishment plays such a small role in describing the final reward of the righteous (especially in light of the rabbis' readiness to draw parallels between Sinai and the coming aeon in other respects.[59]) I think we must conclude that the rabbinic community as a whole showed a tendency to keep the revelation and the final reward quite distinct when using this "nourishment" motif, and that it was generally reticent to use the motif in the eschatological context.

This conclusion gives added support to those scholars who have denied the importance of the soteric element in rabbinic esotericism. At this point, however, we must still see this opinion as an hypothesis which needs further testing with other relevant midrashim. Moreover, on the basis of the material studied here, we can not endorse the unqualified denial of any soteric significance to the esoteric traditions. Rather we must suggest that a minority of the rabbis did see Merkabah mysticism as a pre-figuring of the destiny of the righteous. This suggests the further hypothesis that there may have been two distinct schools of thought on this question.[60] If such an hypothesis can be sustained, then we must ask why the

---

[58] There is a possible exception in the midrash attributed to R. Levi in MT 68.10 and PRK 12.22, p. 220, but it seems very tangential to our theme.

[59] For a survey of these parallels, see Ira Chernus, "Redemption and Chaos: A study in the Symbolism of the Rabbinic Aggada," Ch. VI, sec. 1.

[60] P. S. Alexander, "Hebrew Book of Enoch," has recently suggested that the extant literature of Merkabah mysticism may represent an attempt to synthesize traditions stemming from

rabbis opposing soteric significance would have placed such stress on the esoteric interpretation of the revelation at Sinai. Here I can only offer an educated guess. If there were rabbis who saw the ecstatic experience of the Merkabah as pre-figuring their own post-mortem redemption, it would not be a large step to see the ecstatic experience as redemptive in itself. However those who took such a step might easily be led to take the further step of denying the traditional rabbinic soteriology, which centered on Torah and covenant, in favor of a thoroughly esoteric view, allowing redemption only for those few who have the necessary esoteric knowledge. At this point one would have crossed the line from rabbinic Judaism into some kind of true Gnosticism.

To prevent this, the rabbinic majority might well have denied the soteric significance of esoteric or mystical experience and, at the same time, re-affirmed the centrality of Sinai (i. e., Torah, covenant, and community) in any interpretation of Jewish soteriology. By separating revelation from redemption in the esoteric tradition, and by emphasizing the former while ignoring the latter, the rabbis could bring these esoteric experiences into their community without endangering the foundations of their religiosity.

This relationship between esotericism and revelation is one more example of the rabbinic ambivalence to esoteric pursuits which has been noted by most recent writers on the subject. Most of the rabbis were willing to allow such a dimension in Judaism, but only if it were limited by subordination to the exoteric fundamentals. This ambivalence is also apparent in the substance of the midrashim we have surveyed: it is not esoteric experience itself which is condemned, but rather the claim of personal privilege because of that experience. And the greatest such privilege, of course, would be the privilege of personal salvation. From another point of view, however, the ambivalence existed not in the rabbinic attitude toward esotericism but in the nature of the esoteric tradition itself. That is, rabbinic esotericism, as evidenced in Merkabah mysticism, was not intrinsically either Gnostic or anti-Gnostic; rather it could incorporate (or exclude) Gnostic elements and tendencies in varying degrees, depending on its context in the religious life of the community. And a crucial — perhaps the crucial — factor in determining that context was the relationship of such experience to redemption. Thus, while a majority of the rabbis excluded the soteric dimension from their esoteric pursuits, there may well have been a minority who admitted it, with its consequent Gnosticizing tendency, in varying measure. How these different approaches might have related to each other, and how they might have been harmonized, are questions which remain to be answered.

---

groups which engaged in esoteric pursuits quite separately from each other. It seems likely that if such separate groups existed, they would have developed differing interpretations of their experiences.

VI. MERKABAH MYSTICISM AND ESCHATOLOGY IN MIDRASH

We have established as an hypothesis that a majority of the rabbis consciously separated the experience of the realm of the Merkabah from the experience of the paradise of the world to come. If this hypothesis can be sustained, it would indicate that this rabbinic majority did not hold the experience of the Merkabah to be a foreshadowing or foretaste of the ultimate reward of the righteous after death. In order to test this hypothesis, we must examine the general conception of the eschatological reward in rabbinic Judaism to see what elements it might have in common with the literature of Merkabah mysticism. Elsewhere I have surveyed the descriptions of the eschatological paradise in rabbinic literature;[1] this survey yielded a number of basic motifs which seem to be most prevalent: The righteous receive their reward in the garden of Eden, in proximity to the tree of life in the center of the garden. This paradise has fabulous fertility. It is crossed by rivers, among which rivers of wine and spice are particularly noted. It is an environment which is always light. The light comes in part from the enormously increased size of the heavenly bodies; in part it comes from the many jewels and precious metals which abound there. The phenomenon of fire is also a feature of this paradise. There are various phenomena of height and ascension, particularly mountains. This paradise is a world-kingdom, with Jerusalem as its capital, ruled by God and the righteous. It includes an academy in which God Himself teaches the true meaning of the Torah. Every aspect of it is marked by enormous dimensions and sizes, indicative of infinitude. Perhaps most importantly, there is an infinitude of life and time; i. e., immortality. Thus the life of the world to come is timeless and changeless, a world which is "entirely rest and tranquility for the life which is eternal."

---

[1] Ira Chernus, "Redemption and Chaos: A Study in the Symbolism of Rabbinic Aggada," ch. II. In studying the eschatological material in terms of symbolic motifs, it has appeared to me that the distinction between "Messianic age" and the "world to come" is not of primary importance. The exact meaning of these two terms, and their relationship to the even more common term "in the future" (l'atid labo), is not at all precise in rabbinic literature, as has been noted by several leading scholars: Joseph Klausner, *The Messianic Idea in Israel*, p. 408; Salo W. Baron, *A Social and Religious History of the Jews,* Vol. V, pp. 147, 148; George F. Moore, *Judaism*, Vol. II, pp. 323, 378; Gershom G. Scholem, *The Messianic Idea in Judaism and Other Essays*, p. 8. In the present study I have only alluded to the difference between these terms in the few places where it seems to have a substantive importance.

If we compare these motifs with the basic themes of the Merkabah literature, we can distinguish three groups: those motifs which do not appear in Merkabah texts at all, those which play a marginal role in them, and those which are frequent and important in the Merkabah texts. Within the first group we may place the garden of Eden and all of the traditions about fertility, luxuriant foliage, and abundant crops. None of this seems to play any role in the experience of the Merkabah mystics. The closest one might come to suggesting a relationship is the well-known Talmudic passage[2] which asserts that the souls of the (deceased) righteous are in the seventh heaven, Arabot. But it is not at all clear that this is intended to be understood as the garden of Eden or any kind of celestial paradise; in fact, the rabbinic texts are extraordinarily vague on the location of the eschatological paradise.[3] Even if we conjecture that the Talmud is placing the paradise in Arabot, we find that it immediately[4] goes on to say that Arabot is dwarfed by the immense size of the "living creatures," which are in turn dwarfed by the throne of glory above them. The same tradition is repeated in the Merkabah texts themselves: verbatim in Maseket Heikalot[5] and in an allusion in Heikalot Rabbati[6] which says that the throne of glory supported by the living creatures flutters above Arabot, so that their feet just barely touch it. Re'uyot Yehezkiel repeats the Talmudic tradition about the souls of the righteous in Arabot, but it adds the throne of glory as a separate heaven above Arabot, one which contains the living creatures and the throne and God Himself.[7] The point of all these traditions seems to be that the "descenders" to the Merkabah were not particularly interested in Arabot, even if it did contain the celestial paradise. Their interest as reflected in all the Merkabah texts was in the phenomena above Arabot. The only specific mention of the Garden of Eden in the Merkabah literature is in III Enoch,[8] which says that before the time of Enoch the Shekinah did dwell in the garden of Eden, but because of the sins of his generation the Shekinah left the garden and rose up to Arabot.[9] Here there is clearly a distinction between the paradise and Arabot, and again the interest of the Merkabah mystics would not be in the paradise. In general we may say that the vegetative imagery which is so important in rabbinic eschatological texts is completely absent from the Merkabah literature.

The same may be said for the water — i. e., the rivers — which are the complement to this vegetation motif. There are many references to rivers in the realm of the Merkabah, of course, but they are always rivers of fire. In III Enoch[10] these

---

[2] TB Hagigah 12b.
[3] Gen. R 15.2, p. 136; TB Berakot 34b; TB Sanhedrin 99a; etc.
[4] TB Hagigah 13a.
[5] Ch. 4, p. 43.
[6] 2.2
[7] pp. 135–139.
[8] See also MM, par. 27.
[9] III Enoch 5.3–14; cf. 23.18, 43.2, 44.7, 48a.3.
[10] III Enoch 18.19.

rivers are said to come from the throne of glory, just as the eschatological rivers are said to come the Holy of Holies.[11] The only exception in the Merkabah texts is in Heikalot Rabbati,[12] which describes "rivers of happiness, rivers of joy, etc." which come from the throne of glory, but this too is quite different from the eschatological rivers of the exoteric texts. Wine, which is an important symbol of the paradise of the future world in exoteric texts, seems to play no role at all in Merkabah mysticism. Neither do mountains play any role, since the Merkabah mystic's experience takes place totally detached from the earth.

In addition to these graphic symbols of the future redemption, we also find that the more abstract conceptual motif of tranquility and rest seems to be absent from the Merkabah texts. This is extremely important, since "*shabbat*" is perhaps the most important feature which distinguishes the world to come from this world; in addition to the specific texts which mention it, "*shabbat*" is a pervading feature in the background of all rabbinic discussions of the world to come. Yet it is hardly conceivable that one would use this term to describe the experiences reflected in the Merkabah texts. Several writers on Merkabah mysticism have referred to Rudolph Otto's concept of the "numinous," with its distinguishing feature of "*mysterium tremendum,*" to characterize these texts. As Scholem puts it: "It is entirely characteristic of the outlook of these believers that the theurgist, in adjuring the 'Prince of the Divine Presence,' summons the archons as 'Princes of Majesty, Fear and Trembling.' Majesty, Fear and Trembling are indeed the key-words to this Open Sesame of Religion."[13] It is possible, of course, that the Merkabah mystics experienced some kind of spiritual tranquility at the culmination or completion of their mystical experiences, but if so, this tranquility is not reported in their texts. Terms like "fear," "agitation," "excitation," and "trembling," on the other hand, recur over and over again as a dominant motif. It seems, therefore, that the rabbinic Jew looked forward to the world to come as a release from the tensions of this world. But if he were a Merkabah mystic it was not the prospect of such a release which attracted him to the realm of the Merkabah.

Among those eschatological motifs which are mentioned tangentially in the Merkabah texts we may mention first the spices. An explicit reference to this motif occurs in III Enoch,[14] which describes the winds carrying the fragrance from the garden of Eden as a reward for the righteous; this passage seems to be unique in the Merkabah literature.[15] The Merkabah mystic is said to experience fragrance

---

[11] TB Sanhedrin 100b; Andre Neher, "Le Voyage Mystique des Quatres," *Revue de l'Histoire des Religions* 140 (1951), pp. 59–82.

[12] 8.4.

[13] Gershom Scholem, *Major Trends in Jewish Mysticism*, pp. 56, 57.

[14] III Enoch 23.18.

[15] Ithamar Gruenwald, in "Knowledge and Vision", *Israel Oriental Studies* 3 (1973), p. 99, n. 45, has noted that III Enoch generally tends to include much more eschatological material than is found in other Merkabah texts.

directly when he hears God's words which "drop as spices,"[16] and the prayer of
the descender to the Merkabah is said to be like a "pleasing fragrance" before
God.[17] Another motif which, surprisingly, occurs infrequently is that of jewels
and precious metals. Given the importance of brilliant shining lights in the
Merkabah traditions, and the association of such lights with jewels in exoteric
eschatological texts, we might well expect this to be a point of close contact
between the two. Yet the few brief references in the Merkabah texts[18] are hardly
characteristic of this material in general. Similarly, it is surprising that there is
virtually no reference to the heavenly bodies in the Merkabah texts, for they too
might easily have been stressed as a source of visions of light. Yet apart from one
brief allusion to the "lights of the firmament"[19] there seems to be no interest in the
heavenly lights at all. Again we may well have evidence that the Merkabah mystic
was not interested in the heavens of exoteric cosmology but rather in what was
above them.

Finally, there is occasional allusion in the Merkabah literature to the more
abstract theme of immortality. The possessor of a given esoteric secret "may be
assured that he is a participant in the world to come."[20] However, the possession of
this secret may not necessarily entail an experience of the realm of the Merkabah
itself. There is apparently a reference to the time when the descender to the
Merkabah will "take refuge under the wings" of the Shekinah, though the text is
somewhat confused,[21] but this occurs in the future and not during the mystical
experience. One of the mystical hymns praises God as He who "resurrects the
dead and raises the dead from the dust,"[22] but this is merely a common exoteric
phrase which has been introduced into an esoteric text. In fact all of these few
references to immortality can best be understood as reflections of the "orthodoxy"
of the Merkabah mystics[23] – they were rabbinic Jews who expected to gain
immortality as members of the Torah observant community. Their mystical
experience did not lead them to give up this expectation, but there is little evidence
that the expectation of immortality was related to their experience of the Merkabah.

We may now turn to those motifs in the descriptions of the redeemed world
which also play a major role in descriptions of the realm of the Merkabah. One such
theme is the singing of hymns in the presence of God. This is an essential and

---

[16] HR 24.3 as cited in Scholem, *Gnosticism*, p. 62.

[17] HR 9.2, p. 90; the Hebrew is *"reyaḥ niḥoaḥ,"* a term which is drawn from the language
of the Biblical Temple cultus.

[18] HR 9.5, p. 91; Maseket Heikalot 4, p. 42; III Enoch 22.14 and 25.6.

[19] HR 19.3, p. 98.

[20] MM par. 4 (Cf. *ibid* par. 24); Shiur Komah in Merkabah Shelemah 38b.

[21] HR 2.4 p. 84; cf. HR ed. Wertheimer 2.5 and Merkabah Rabbah in Merkabah Shelemah 5a.

[22] MM end.

[23] See Gershom Scholem, *Jewish Gnosticism, Merkabah Mysticism, and Talmudic Tradition*,
pp. 9–13, and P. S. Alexander, "The Historical Setting of the Hebrew Book of Enoch,"
Journal of Jewish Studies 28 (Autumn, 1977), pp. 173–174.

pervasive aspect of the Merkabah literature, but as an element of exoteric eschatology it seems to be relatively uncommon and unimportant. We do find:

> The rabbis say: In the future the generations gather in the presence of the Holy One blessed be He and say to Him: Master of the Universe, who shall sing a song in Your presence first? And He says to them: In the past none sang a song in My presence but the generation of Moses, and now none shall sing a song in My presence but that generation. What is the reason? Because it is said, "Sing unto the Lord a new song, His praise from the end of the earth, those who go down to the sea" (Isa. 42:10).[24]

This particular midrash, which describes a scene reminiscent of those in the Merkabah texts, is not repeated anywhere else in rabbinic literature. There are more general allusions to the singing of a hymn before God in the world to come, and this idea was apparently known in the third century.[25] However its rarity as an element of rabbinic eschatology would seem to indicate that the rabbis did not choose to make it a significant part of their eschatological midrash. This may suggest that they consciously avoided the use of motifs likely to suggest esoteric implications.

The theme of divine light, on the other hand, plays an important role in both eschatology and esotericism. But in general it seems safe to say that this is developed quite differently in each of these contexts. It is often said in rabbinic texts that there is no darkness or night in the world to come.[26] Some texts speak of the greatly intensified light that will be given off by the sun and moon;[27] more common is the notion that God Himself will be the source of light:

> R. Samuel b. Nahmani said: In this world Israel used the light of the sun in the daytime and the light of the moon at night, because they were necessary for illumination, but in the world to come they will not be necessary for them, as it is said, "The sun will no longer be your light by day, nor for brightness shall the moon give light to you" (Isa. 60:19). Then who will give them light? The Holy One blessed be He, as it is written, "But the Lord will be your everlasting light" (*ibid.*)[28].

Another well known tradition identifies the eschatological light with the light created on the first day of creation:

> It is taught: The light which was created during the six days of creation to illuminate during the day can not do so, for it would eclipse the sphere of the sun, and it can not do so at night because it was not created to illuminate at night but only during the day. Then where is it? It is hidden away for the righteous in the future.[29]

---

[24] Ecc. R 1.9.

[25] Mek. B'shalah Shirta 1, p. 118; Song R. 1.5.3, which seems to attribute the idea to R. Joshua b. Levi, R. Samuel b. Nahman, and R. Berakiah.

[26] Gen. R 91.10, p. 1134; TB Pesahim 2b; MT 23.7; PRE ch. 19, 44b; Ex. R 18.11.

[27] Ex. R 15.21; Ecc. R 11.7, PRE ch. 51, 123b; the proof-text in each case is Isa. 30:26.

[28] MT 36.6; cf. PRK 21.5, p. 322; Gen. R 59.5, p. 634; Ex. R 15.21; Song R 2.6.1.

[29] Gen. R 3.6, p. 21 and parallels cited there; cf. Louis Ginzberg, *Legends of the Jews*, vol. V, p. 8, n. 19.

All of these eschatological traditions imply, in one way or another, an environment of continuous intense light which may be understood by analogy from extremely bright sunlight. This is quite different from the light imagery in Merkabah texts, which most commonly refer to brilliant, sparkling points of light emanating from specific sources, on the analogy of lightning flashes or flaming torches. These latter are so bright that it is difficult for anyone to endure them; they are part of an extraordinary environment which human beings enter only for short periods of time. The eschatological light, on the other hand, is one that can be enjoyed indefinitely. There are exceptions to this generalization,[30] but on the whole it seems to be valid. Of course there would inevitably be some similarity in the use of light imagery in any two sets of religious texts from the Hellenistic world, for light played such a central role in all depictions of spirituality and divinity.[31] But the mere fact that both traditions used light imagery extensively would not be evidence of direct relationship between them. In the same way, both the Merkabah texts and rabbinic eschatological midrash employ enormous numbers to indicate the transcendent, supramundane character of the experience which they attempt to describe. But the use of huge dimensions to indicate the transcendence of finitude is such a common feature of all religious traditions that one can hardly claim here any evidence of mutual influence between esotericism and eschatology.

Another feature held in common by both the eschatological and esoteric texts is the ability to learn something about Torah which is not available through normal exoteric study. But this theme too is developed in two quite separate ways. In the world to come, the learning occurs in a replica of the rabbinic academy, with God as the master, and it centers on the reasons for various laws.[32] A similar scene is not depicted in the Merkabah texts. Rather the individual initiate learns the "secrets of the Torah" privately, in a manner which is not at all clear; however it is rarely if ever said that God instructs the initiate in the same way that a rabbi instructs his students. Moreover, the content of the "secrets of the Torah" is not at all clear either,[33] but it is not stated that this content consists of halakic matters or the reasons behind the halakot (though this may in fact have been the case). The one exception to this rule is found in the apparently late addition to Heikalot

---

[30] In the Merkabah texts parallels to eschatological themes can be found in HR 19.3, p. 98 and 26.2, p. 102, and in Maseket Heikalot 3, 4, pp. 41, 42. TB Berakot 17a and ARN version A ch. 1, p. 3a show Merkabah-type imagery in eschatological texts.

[31] See, e.g., Rudolph Bultmann, "Zur Geschichte der Lichtsymbolik im Altertum," *Philologus* 97 (1948), pp. 1–36.

[32] Tan. B Vayigash 12, I, 211 and Balak 23, IV, 145; Num. R 20.20; Gen. R 95.3, p. 1190; ARN version B ch. 43, p. 120; TP Shabbat 8d, etc. Among these texts only TB Baba Metzia 85b shows a relationship with Merkabah mysticism.

[33] G. A. Wewers, *Geheimnis und Geheimhaltung im rabbinischen Judentum*, has argued that in fact the "secrets of the Torah" refers fundamentally to a process or type of learning rather than to any particular content.

Rabbati known as Sar Torah.[34] The exoteric and esoteric texts do share one interesting detail in common: that which is learned in the eschatological academy or in the realm of the Merkabah is never forgotten, while ordinary Torah study may soon be forgotten. However, while this detail does appear in several Merkabah texts,[35] it is apparently late and quite uncommon as an exoteric idea.[36]

Some sources, in mentioning the heavenly academy, add the detail that the angels are excluded from it and must ask the righteous what they have learned from God.[37] This is particularly interesting because it represents a rare allusion to the angels in an eschatological context; normally they do not play any role at all. Here we find that when the angels are introduced they are relegated to a secondary role.[38] In the Merkabah literature, on the other hand, angels and heavenly beings play a primary role throughout and generally have a status equal to or higher than human beings in the realm of the Merkabah. So once again we have a theme common to both the esoteric and eschatological texts playing a very minor role in the latter. A similar situation exists with regard to the motif of ascension through the heavens, which is fundamental to all the Merkabah texts. We noted above the Talmudic assertion that the souls of the righteous are in the highest heaven, Arabot. Some texts state that they are hidden beneath the throne of glory.[39] However this location for the souls of the deceased is by no means unanimous; some texts refer to the "storehouse" of deceased souls[40] or to the "courtyard" of the dead.[41] Yet even if we assume that there was widespread acceptance of the divine throne as the place of the souls of the righteous, it seems that the rabbis had little if anything to say about a journey of the soul to its place in Arabot; I have been unable to find any references in the literature to such a journey. Moreover, all these references to the location of the souls are quite secondary in rabbinic eschatology; they are mentioned but never described or discussed in any detail. The major focus of eschatological interest was

---

[34] HR chs. 27–30; cf. Gershom Scholem, *Kabbalah*, p. 374.

[35] e.g., MM par. 25.

[36] Y Isa. 479 reads: "The Holy One blessed be He said: In this world Israel learned Torah from flesh and blood; therefore they forgot it, since it was given by Moses who was flesh and blood, and just as flesh and blood is transitory so his teaching is transitory. But in the future Israel will learn Torah from no one but the Holy One blessed be He Himself, as it is said, "All your sons shall be taught by the Lord" (Isa. 54:13), and it also says, "No longer shall each man teach his neighbor and each his brother" (Jer. 31:33). For just as God lives eternally, so will be their learning – they will never forget what they learn from Him." This may be a later rationalization of an originally esoteric idea; cf. the variants in PRK 12.21, p. 219 and Tan. B. Yitro 13, II, p. 76, both of which are juxtaposed by the redactors of the respective works with esoteric midrashim.

[37] Num. R 20.20; Tan. B Balak 23, IV, 145.

[38] Cf. Peter Schäfer, *Rivalität zwischen Engeln und Menschen*.

[39] ARN version A ch. 12, p. 50; TB Shabbat 152b.

[40] Sifre Num. 139, p. 185 and parallels cited there.

[41] MT 11.6.

rather the garden of Eden or paradise where the souls were re-joined with their re-surrected bodies.

The other place of interest described in some detail in the exoteric texts is the eschatological Jerusalem. In general, it would seem that the rabbis believed that the earthly and heavenly Jerusalems would be united at the end of time;[42] according to the Talmudic schema this place would be in the fourth heaven, Zebul. However there are some opinions in rabbinic literature that the heavenly Jerusalem was in Arabot, because that is where the throne of glory and the heavenly Temple are located.[43] This view is apparently the basis for the opinion attributed to the tanna R. Eliezer b. Jacob that "in the future Jerusalem will be elevated and it will rise until it reaches the throne of glory."[44] It is difficult to say what the original intention of this saying might have been; if it did have any link to esoteric traditions that link is obscure. However, it could easily be employed in esoteric midrash, and in fact we have one clear-cut instance of such a usage. In the Midrash Tanhuma we find:

> In the future this is what I will do for Zion: All of that population, from the First Man to the [last] of the resurrected dead, where will they all stand? They will say: "The place is too narrow for me; make room for me to dwell in' (Isa. 49:20). What will I do? I will enlarge it, as it is said, "Enlarge the place of your tent" (Isa. 54:2).[45]

As proof of God's ability to do this, the text then offers the traditions about the 22,000 chariots which descended upon Mt. Sinai, traditions which we have seen to be closely linked to the esoteric Merkabah tradition. The text then continues:

> And thus you find in the world to come, that the Holy One blessed be He will enlarge Jerusalem, as it is said, "And it was enlarged as it was surrounded and it rose story by story" (Ezek. 41:7), until it rises to the heavens . . . As soon as it arrives in the heavens it says, "The place is too narrow for me" (Isa. 49:20). Nevertheless, the Holy One blessed be He raises it from the heavens to the firmament, from the second firmament to the third, from the third to the fourth, from the fourth to the fifth, from the fifth to the sixth, from the sixth to the seventh. R. Eliezer b. Jacob said: Until it reaches the throne of glory.
>
> And how do they rise? The Holy One blessed be He brings clouds and they fly them as it is said, "Who are these who fly like clouds?" (Isa. 60:8). And each and every one of the righteous has a canopy to himself, as it is said, "Then the Lord will create over the whole site of Mount Zion and over her assemblies a cloud by day, and smoke and the shining of a flaming fire by night, for over all the glory will be a canopy" (Isa. 4:5). As soon as they reach the throne of glory the Holy One blessed be He says to them: You and I will walk together through the universe, as it is said, "And I walked among you" (Lev. 26:12). And the Holy One blessed be He sits in the middle and the righteous point at Him with their fingers, as it is said, "It will be said on that day: Behold, this is our God, we have waited for Him that He might save us" (Isa. 25:9).[46]

---

[42] This is the conclusion reached by V. Aptowitzer in "Beit Miqdash Shel Ma'aleh Al Pi Ha'aggadah," *Tarbiz* 2 (1930), pp. 137–153, 257–287.

[43] The sources are cited by Aptowitzer, *ibid.*

[44] PRK 20.7, p. 318; Y. Isa. 472; Song R 7.4.

[45] Tan. Zav. 12; Tan. B Zav 13, III, 20.   [46] *Ibid.*

The entire pericope is clearly a composite of a number of traditions which the redactor brought together in a unique way. The original element is the description of Jerusalem rising through the seven firmaments; this appears in no other rabbinic text.[47] To support this innovation, the redactor introduced the tradition attributed to R. Eliezer b. Jacob, but since he was juxtaposing a number of traditions without regard for their original intent we can not point to this text as evidence for the original intent of R. Eliezer's midrash. The freedom with which the redactor treated his material, and his lack of concern for the logic of his juxtapositions, appear most clearly immediately after his citation of R. Eliezer, where he introduced a totally separate set of traditions having nothing to do with Jerusalem *per se*. His purpose here seems to have been the suggestion of a parallel between Jerusalem and the righteous, thus implying that the latter will rise through the firmaments to the throne of glory like the former. This implication is set in a context of esoteric concerns, for it is preceded by the tradition about the 22,000 chariots and is followed by the tradition about "pointing," which may have had esoteric dimensions as well.[48] Here, then, we do have an only slightly veiled assertion that the eschatological fate of the Jewish people would resemble both the experience of the Israelites as Sinai and that of the "descenders" to the Merkabah.

But it must be stressed that this is an anonymous pericope in a relatively late text; it is certainly later than the third century, since it draws on third century material and substantially re-works it. In fact, if we look at the third century tradition on the change in size of the eschatological Jerusalem, we find that R. Eliezer's tradition, though it was probably known to the amoraim, was not used, so that it had to be introduced somewhat artificially by later redactors:

> R. Johanan said: In the future Jerusalem will reach to the gates of Damascus . . . How does R. Johanan explain the verse, "The city shall be rebuilt upon its mound" (Jer. 30:18)? Like this fig tree, which is narrow at the bottom and broad at the top, so Jerusalem is destined to widen on all sides, and the exiles will come and repose beneath it, in order to fulfill what is said, "For you will spread out to the left and to the right" (Isa. 54:3). So much for its length. How do you learn about its width? Because it says, "From the tower of Hananel to the winepresses of the king" (Zech. 14:10) . . . So much for its length and width. How do you learn about its height? Because it says, "And the side chambers were enlarged as it was surrounded and it rose story by story" (Ezek. 41:7). It is taught as a tannaitic tradition: Jerusalem is destined to enlarge and to rise and to reach the throne of glory until it says, "The place is too narrow for me."[49]

---

[47] TB Baba Batra 75b attributes to R. Johanan the opinion that the eschatological Jerusalem will rise three parasangs into the air.

[48] Cf. Song R. 2.14.3 and Ex. R 23.15 and Saul Lieberman, "Mishnat Shir Hashirim," nn. 5 and 15.

[49] Song R. 7.5.3; the parallels in PRK 20.7, p. 318 and Y. Isa. 472 attribute the tannaitic tradition to its author, R. Eliezer b. Jacob.

This indicates that the third century rabbis, and R. Johanan in particular, specifically did not want to say that Jerusalem would rise to the throne of glory as the Merkabah mystics claimed to have done.

The pericope from Tanhuma which we have just cited seems to represent a minority view in its usage of the tradition of R. Eliezer b. Jacob. We must now inquire whether the same is true of the other eschatological traditions which it cites. For example, the redactor employed a midrash on Isa. 25:9 to suggest that the righteous in the world to come will see God and be in His presence, thus repeating the experience of the "descenders" to the Merkabah. Were there other exoteric texts which make the same suggestion? In fact, the same proof-text was occasionally used to substantiate the same idea. In describing the Israelites' vision of God at Sinai, the Mekilta d'Rabbi Simeon b. Yohai says:

> In the same way, in the future Israel is destined to see the Shekinah face to face, as it is said, "For face to face they will see the return of the Lord to Zion" (Isa. 52:8), and it says, "This is our God, we have waited for Him" (Isa. 25:9).[50]

The parallel passage in the Mekilta d'Rabbi Ishmael does not contain this eschatological note,[51] indicating that it may be a later insertion; the redactional insertion of eschatological parallels to past events appears quite frequently in midrashic texts. But we can not assert anything about the date of this text with certainty. The same juxtaposition of proof-texts appears in two other places, and in both of these we also find possible indications of an esoteric context:

> "When I awake I shall be satisfied with beholding Your form" (Ps. 17:15). But is it not written: "For no man shall see me and live" (Ex. 33:20)? But it is only in this world that it is impossible. However in the future at the time of the awakening of the dead, I shall be satisfied with beholding Your form, as it is said, "For face to face, etc." (Isa. 52:8), and it is written, "This is our God, etc." (Isa. 25:9).[52] The Holy One blessed be He said: In this world, if they saw My glory they were destroyed, as it is said, "For no man shall see me and live." But in the future, when I shall return My Shekinah to Zion, I will be revealed in My glory to all Israel and they will see Me and live forever, as it is said, "For face to face they will see the return of the Lord to Zion." Moreover, they will point at Him with their fingers . . . as it is said, "This is our God, we have waited for Him."[53]

There does, then, seem to have been an exegetical tradition on Isa. 25:9 which referred to an eschatological vision of God and, in some cases, a "pointing" to Him as well. There is no evidence that this tradition was known in the third century, since it only appears in anonymous texts, all of which except one are found in late compositions.

---

[50] Mek. RS 140
[51] Mek. Yitro Bahodesh 2, pp. 210, 211.
[52] MT 17.13 end. Ps. 17:15 is used in an apparently esoteric context in TB Babba Batra 10a; cf. chap. V, n. 36 above.
[53] Tan. B'midbar 17 end; cf. Tan. B B'midbar 20, IV, 18.
[54] MT 13.2.

The texts we have just cited also indicate a continuing exegetical tradition on Isa. 52:8, which is attested in at least two other texts:

> [God said to Israel:] In this world I have withheld My presence from you, but in the world to come, "For face to face they will see the return of the Lord to Zion."[55]

Once again we have anonymous texts in late compositions, but these texts lead us to a further observation. The principal point of concern here seems to be the vision of God in the Temple; this is reflected both in the choice of Isa. 52:8 as a proof-text and in the substance of at least some of the midrashim on the text. It has been suggested that much of the language and imagery of Merkabah mysticism was drawn from that of the Temple cult.[56] If we accept even the partial validity of this suggestion, we can conclude that any description of the eschatological Temple cult in the exoteric texts would probably bear some resemblance to the descriptions in the Merkabah texts. This means that these references to an eschatological vision of God may be part of the larger exoteric theme of the re-institution of the Temple cult; if so, would expect to find it subordinated to a more general interest in the various aspects of the cult, especially the sacrifices. If, on the other hand, we have here evidence of reciprocal influence between exoteric eschatology and Merkabah mysticism, we would expect to find the vision of God, which is so central in the Merkabah tradition, to be equally central in the eschatological tradition. Even a cursory review of rabbinic eschatology, especially as reflected in the liturgy, reveals that the former is in fact true, while the latter is not. This at least suggests the possibility that the relatively uncommon tradition of the eschatological vision of God may have originated as part of the exoteric tradition, although in the extant texts it may have been linked to esoteric allusions.

The fact that virtually all of the relevant texts are apparently late makes it difficult to say anything conclusive about the origin of this theme. In fact, there seems to be only one attributed and thus datable tradition concerning the eschatological vision of God:[57]

> R. Berakiah said in the name of R. Aba b. Kahana: So long as the seed of Amalek [remains] in the world, it is as if, as it were, a wing covers the face. When the seed of Amalek vanishes from the world, the wing is removed, as it is said, "Your teacher will not hide himself any more, and your eyes will see your teacher" (Isa. 30:20).[58]

---

[55] Tan. B Vayetze 9, I, 151.

[56] This view is maintained most strongly by Johann Maier, *Vom Kultus zur Gnosis*. It has been criticized most directly by Wewers in *Geheimnis*.

[57] I follow A. M. Goldberg, *Untersuchungen über die Vorstellung von der Shekhinah in der frühen rabbinischen Literatur*, p. 330, in his analysis of Lev. R 1.14, where an assertion of the eschatological vision of God has been attached by a later redactor to an early midrash of R. Hoshaiah.

[58] Tan. B Teze 18, V, 45; Y. B'shalah 268; Tan. Teze 11; PRK 3.16, p. 53; cf. PR 12.9, 51 a and Wilhelm Bacher's note in PA, II, p. 481, n. 3.

It is difficult to interpret the original intent of this midrash. The proof-text, which is obviously an integral part of the original midrash, may indicate an esoteric allusion.[59] If so, its intent would still be unclear; the term "wing" is apparently an allusion to Isa. 6:2, which refers to the wings covering the faces of the angels, not the face of God, and the term "teacher" might be more appropriately applied to angelic teachers such as the Prince of the Torah or Metatron than to God Himself in the Merkabah tradition. Thus this midrash might be referring to a direct vision of an angel, although it is more likely that it does refer to a vision of God. If it is a vision of God which is meant, we must ask again whether this might mean primarily the experience of God in the restored Temple cult; the vision reported in Isa. 6:2 seems to have taken place in such a cultic context, and the substance of this midrash implies a "this-worldly" setting rather than one which is heavenly or paradisaical. If we grant that the midrash should be taken more literally than metaphorically, the most obvious place in "this world" where the face of God is now "covered"[60] but might later be revealed is in the Holy of Holies in the Temple. Moreover, even if there is an esoteric dimension here, the principal thrust of this midrash seems to be a political, anti-Roman one. So we can not be sure whether esoteric concerns played any significant part in the original motivation of this midrash. This may explain the puzzling fact that when later rabbis apparently did want to claim explicitly that there would be an eschatological vision of God, they specifically did not use R. Aba b. Kahana's midrash nor his proof-text; this midrash has no later development or echo in rabbinic literature at all. If these later rabbis did want to suggest that the experience of the redeemed would resemble that of the "descenders" to the Merkabah, and if this were the principal intent of R. Aba b. Kahana's midrash, it seems likely that the latter would have been known to and employed by the later rabbis. This suggests that perhaps either one tradition or the other (or both) did not originate within an esoteric framework, though this argument is, of course, not conclusive.

To recapitulate: We have suggested that, among the motifs which are of central importance in the Merkabah texts, those which also appear in exoteric rabbinic eschatology often play a relatively minor role there. In pursuing this suggestion, we have examined a pericope in the Midrash Tanhuma which is unusual precisely because its author wanted to say that the eschatological reward of the righteous would be closely akin to the experience of the Merkabah mystics. To make this point he drew on various existing eschatological traditions, such as that attributed to R. Eliezer b. Jacob, which originally may or may not have had a similar intent. One of these was the tradition about the eschatological vision of God. We are unable to say with certainty whether in this case the Tanhuma redactor was faithful to the intention of his sources, but even if he was, we can conclude that this tradition was rare,

---

[59] It appears to have an esoteric meaning in TB Sotah 49a, though I can not accept the assumption of Goldberg (*Untersuchungen*, p. 285) that in Sotah it is used eschatologically.

[60] The rabbis often spoke of the Temple and its cult in the present tense, despite its destruction and the cessation of the cult.

if known at all, in the third century. It may not have originated until the end of the
fourth century or later, and even then it became one of those motifs which is central
in Merkabah mysticism but relatively secondary in exoteric eschatology. If we
assume that this tradition, as well as that of R. Eliezer b. Jacob, was known to later
rabbis and available as a basis for further exegesis, the likelihood is that a majority of
the rabbis consciously excluded such traditions from their eschatology. This may
very well have been due to their potential or actual links to esoteric subjects. (It is
appropriate to recall here the midrashic tradition asserting that the Israelites at the
Reed Sea saw God directly, in a way denied to even the greatest of the prophets. We
found that this tradition, which originally asserted a vision of God in the context of
redemption, was taken out of that context by later tradents and made to refer rather
to the context of the Sinai revelation. This, too, may well reflect a desire to keep
mystical experience separate from the experience of redemption.)

    We now turn to the part of the Tanhuma pericope which asks:

> And how do they rise? The Holy One blessed be He brings clouds and they fly them, as it
> is said, "Who are these who fly like clouds?" (Isa. 60:8). And each and every one of the
> righteous has a canopy to himself, as it is said, "Then the Lord will create over the whole
> site of Mount Zion and over her assemblies a cloud by day, and smoke and the shining of a
> flaming fire by night, for over all the glory there will be a canopy" (Isa. 4:5).

This text is replete with potential esoteric allusions. We must now inquire as to how
they were developed in rabbinic eschatology. The tradition about the clouds, with
Isa. 60:8 as the relevant proof-text, was apparently known in the mid-third
century.[61] However the original tradition concerned the flight of the righteous to
participate in the worship service at the rebuilt Temple in Jerusalem; again we find a
tradition centering on the eschatological Temple which could be turned by a later
redactor into a source of esoteric midrash. Yet this midrash really has no precise
analogue in the esoteric texts, for while flying to the place of God's presence is
certainly a central theme in those texts, there is as far as I know no reference to
clouds carrying the descenders to the Merkabah. We should note here, too, that this
midrash, while perhaps old, is extremely uncommon in the extant texts and seems to
have been relatively unimportant in rabbinic eschatology, again indicating that the
rabbis consciously avoided it.

    The idea that the righteous have special canopies as part of their reward is one
which dates back to at least the second century and is frequently cited in rabbinic
literature. Once again, we want to ask whether the redactor of the Tanhuma pericope was following the original intention of his sources in using this motif and the
proof-text, Isa. 4:5, to tie together eschatological and esoteric material. The earliest
evidence of this idea is a midrash attributed to R. Akiba:

> "And the children of Israel journeyed from Raamses toward Sukkot" (Ex. 12:37). The
> sages say that Sukkot is nothing but the name of a place . . . R. Akiba says that Sukkot

---

[61] It was discussed by R. Reuben, a second generation amora, as recorded in PR 1.3, 2a.

means nothing but the clouds of glory, as it is said, "Then the Lord will create over the whole site of Mount Zion and over her assemblies a cloud by day, and smoke and the shining of a flaming fire by night, for over all the glory will be a canopy" (Isa. 4:5). This only tells me about the past. From where do I learn about the future? Because it says, "And there will be a *sukkah* for shade by day from the heat" (Isa. 4:6).[62]

The eschatological reference here seems to be a later addition. However R. Akiba's midrash would lose its force if it did not originally include verse 6, which contains the key term "*sukkah*," as well as verse 5 of Isaiah 4. A variant of this midrash also suggests that its main point was originally eschatological:

> R. Akiba says: From the way that I surrounded them with clouds of glory − This is what is said: "And the Lord walking before them in the day. . . . The pillar of cloud did not depart during the day (Ex. 13:21,22) − you may know what I will do for them in the final consummation, as the Scripture says, "And there will be a *sukkah* for shade by day."[63]

Of course if the eschatological note were a later addition to R. Akiba's midrash, this variant could be an abbreviated conflation of the two. Another question raised by this variant is the significance of the pillar of cloud. The substitution of Ex. 13:21, 22 for Isa. 4:5 suggests either that R. Akiba himself equated the pillar of cloud with the clouds of glory or at least that a later tradent understood him to mean this.

The principal point to be underscored is that R. Akiba, expounding Isa. 4:5, seems to have had no interest in the potential esoteric interpretations that were available. Given the prevalence of fire imagery in the esoteric tradition, he certainly could have focused on the "shining of a flaming fire by night," which has its analogue in Ex. 13:21, 22 in the pillar of fire. We know that R. Akiba identified fire as a manifestation of the glory of God when it descended on Mt. Sinai and that this identification seems to reflect his interest in esotericism.[64] Yet here he chose to avoid this line of interpretation. If the eschatological dimension of this midrash is R. Akiba's own, it would indicate that he made such a choice in order to separate esoteric and eschatological concerns. This conclusion is reinforced when we note that the term "clouds of glory" does not appear at all in the literature of the Merkabah mystics; it seems to have been reserved in rabbinic Judaism for descriptions of redemption, both past and future.[65]

Later generations followed R. Akiba's lead in their reluctance to interpret Isa. 4:5 esoterically, tending rather to concentrate on Isa. 4:6 as a source of exoteric

---

[62] Mek. Bo 14, p. 48; cf. *ibid.* B'shalah p'tihtah, p. 80; Mek. RS 47; Tan. Bo 9.

[63] Song R 1.7.3.

[64] Cf. Song R 1.12.1; Mek. Yitro Bahodesh 9, p. 238; MT 18.13; Mek. RS 154; cf. Chap. I above.

[65] Clouds are occasionally mentioned in the Merkabah texts; e. g., "clouds of fire" in MM par. 4, "clouds of consolation" in *ibid.* par. 32; "clouds of light" in Maseket Heikalot Ch. 6, p. 45, clouds surrounding the throne of glory in III Enoch 22 c. 4. The only reference to the pillar of cloud in these texts is in some mss. of III Enoch (48 b.1), but its absence in other mss. makes it unlikely that the reference is part of the original text.

eschatological midrash concerning the canopies of the righteous. We also find a tendency to divorce the pillar of cloud from these eschatologically oriented verses of Isaiah, and a virtual absence of interest in the pillar of fire. For example, one midrash which may have been developed by the tanna R. Simai (whose interest in esoteric matters we have seen previously) describes the actions of Abraham which call forth corresponding actions by God both in the wilderness wandering and in the eschatological future.

> You said: "Rest yourself under the tree" (Gen. 18:4). By your life, I shall repay your children: "He spread a cloud for a covering" (Ps. 105:37). This applies to the wilderness . . . How do we learn about the future? "And there will be a *sukkah* for shade" (Isa. 4:6).[66]

Here both Isa. 4:5 and the second half of Ps. 105:37, with their reference to fire and the pillar of fire, are avoided completely. Several variants of R. Simai's midrash (not attributed to him) in other texts show no interest at all in connecting the pillar of cloud with eschatological reward.[67] Similarly, among the amoraim we find at least two who were interested in both the pillar of cloud and Isa. 4:5 but apparently kept these two interests separate:

> "And I covered you with silk" (Ezek. 16:10). R. Judah b. R. Simon said: He surrounded them with clouds of glory; this is what is said, "The pillar of cloud did not depart during the day."[68]
> R. Judah b. R. Simon said: The Holy One blessed be he said to Israel: . . . In the world to come I will repay you for thirteen things, as it is said, "Then the Lord will create over the whole site of Mount Zion, etc."[69] R. Levi said in the name of R. Hama b. Hanina: . . . It is the custom among human beings that the pupil carries the lantern and walks before the master, but here, "The pillar of cloud did not depart during the day nor the pillar of fire during the night" (Ex. 13:22).[70] R. Levi said in the name of R. Hama b. Hanina: In the future the Holy One blessed be He is destined to make tents of canopies of glory for the righteous – each and every one according to his status [*kabod*], as Isaiah says, "Then the Lord will create over the whole site of Mount Zion . . . for over all the glory will be a canopy."[71]

---

[66] Gen. R 48.10, pp. 487, 488 and parallels cited there; cf. also the discussion of the attribution there.

[67] Mek. B'shalah p'tihtah, p. 81, and PR 14.3, 57a cite a midrash on Ex. 13:21 which appears in Gen. R 48.10, but is not connected to the part of Gen. R 48.10 which we have cited. Here it has no eschatological referrent at all. Num. R 14.2 cites Isa. 4:6 but omits any reference to the pillar of cloud. Num. R 21.22 cites Isa. 4:5 as evidence that "God will give every righteous person a canopy of clouds of glory in the future," and later in the same pericope cites Ex. 13:21, but there is no substantive link between them; they are both used merely as illustrations of the general principle that God does everything "according to His power."

[68] Song R 4.12.2.

[69] Tan. T'rumah 5; Tan. B T'rumah 4, IV, 91.

[70] PRK 11.8, p. 184; cf. Ex. R 20.11 and Tan. B B'shalah 10, II, 58.

[71] PR 31.6, p. 145a.

R. Hama b. Hanina's midrash on Ex. 13:22 was developed in later texts with an eschatological twist,[72] but in accordance with their source these texts avoid any mention of the canopies or the clouds of glory or Isaiah 4.

R. Hama b. Hanina's midrash on Isa. 4:5 may have been a development of an earlier midrash by R. Johanan,[73] for the two are found together in the Talmud:

> Rava said: R. Johanan said: In the future the Holy One blessed be He is destined to make seven canopies for each and every righteous person, as it is said, "Then the Lord will create over the whole site of Mount Zion, etc." It teaches that the Holy One blessed be He makes a canopy for each and every one according to his status.[74]

Assuming that the last sentence of this passage was not originally part of R. Johanan's midrash, we must examine the two traditions separately. R. Johanan seems to have been the first since R. Akiba to link the motif of canopies to Isa. 4:5,[75] and perhaps it is more than coincidence that these two were apparently central figures in esotericism among the rabbis. Yet, to repeat, neither the exoteric nor esoteric texts provide any evidence that the image of the canopies was part of the esoteric tradition. And R. Johanan, while not singling out the reference to the cloud in Isa. 4:5 for special attention, refrained from singling out the "shining of a flaming fire" as well. He seems to have meant that "cloud," "day," "shining," "flaming," "smoke," and "night" in the verse each referred to a separate canopy. This is an interesting example of "pure exegesis"[76] — making every word of Scripture hold its own significance — but it adds nothing substantive to the previous tradition. It does, though, carefully avoid any implication of esoteric meaning. Similarly, R. Hama b. Hanina's midrash is a literal interpretation of the last part of the verse — "for over all the glory will be a canopy" — understanding it to mean "over every *kabod* [glory, status] there will be a canopy." Such an interpretation avoids the obvious meaning of "*kabod*" as the glory of God, and thus it avoids the implication that the cloud, and more importantly the flaming fire, are to be identified with the glory of God. Such an identification is, of course, extremely common in the Merkabah literature.[77]

---

[72] Gen. R 51.2, p. 533 and Ex. R 15.18 and 19.7. There may be an eschatological meaning in Ex. R 32.3 as well.

[73] Evidence for a relationship between the two is found in Bacher, PA, I, p. 448 n. 2 and p. 449 n. 2.

[74] TB Babba Batra 75a.

[75] The R. Hanina cited in TB Babba Batra 75a and Num. R 21.22, discussing the canopies, may be R. Hanina b. Hama, the first generation amora. But since his comments seem to be based on R. Johanan's midrash, I assume that this is a later R. Hanina.

[76] This term is explained by G. Vermes in "Bible and Midrash: Early Old Testament Exegesis," *The Cambridge History of the Bible*, vol. I.

[77] For the sake of completeness we should also note the midrash attributed to R. Levi in PRK, additional chapter 2.1, p. 452, which also carefully avoids any esoteric tendency: "Of every one who fulfills the commandment of the *sukkah* in this world, the Holy One blessed be He says: He fulfilled the commandment of the *sukkah* in this world; I will spread a *sukkah* over him against the heat of the coming day [of judgment]."

The result of this discussion is clear by now. While the theme of the canopies, apparently rooted in the Biblical tradition of the pillar of cloud, and Isa. 4:5 could both easily have been employed to suggest links between esotericism and eschatology, the redactor of our Tanhuma pericope was the first and only rabbinic author to do so. We have seen how his predecessors avoided taking this step. The motive for avoiding Isa. 4:5 or giving it rather tortuous interpretation may very well have been to avoid asserting its plain meaning — that the divine glory would be manifest eschatologically in the form of fire. But we have not found a motive for the tendency to avoid the pillar of cloud as an element of eschatology after the second century. The link between the pillar of cloud and the canopies and/or clouds of glory was not a problem, since none of these themes seem to have had any importance in the esoteric texts. I would suggest as one possibility that the pillar of cloud, like Isa. 4:5, was avoided because it might easily suggest a manifestation of God as fire — in this case the pillar of fire, with which the pillar of cloud is inextricably connected in the Biblical text. This is one more instance of the persistent attempt by the majority of rabbis to keep eschatological and esoteric concerns separate. We can conclude, then, that when a redactor of rabbinic traditions wanted to prove a parallel between eschatological and esoteric motifs, he had in virtually every case to do violence to the original intent of his sources. When his sources share his intent, they tend to be both relatively late and relatively uncommon.

Fire is perhaps the most important of all the visual images in Merkabah mysticism, and yet images of fire play a relatively small role in rabbinic eschatology. The discussion thus far suggests that when fire is mentioned in eschatological contexts, the rabbis were careful to avoid suggesting parallels between the experience of the Merkabah mystics and the reward of the righteous in the future. We must now look at those texts in which fire does play a role in rabbinic eschatology, asking whether the same pattern persists. One fairly widespread tradition specifically mentions fire as an important element of the eschatological future, but it clearly refers to the sacrificial fire of the re-built Temple:

> When the Temple was destroyed the menorah was hidden, and this is one of the five things which were hidden: the ark, the menorah, the fire, the Holy Spirit, and the cherubim. And when the Holy One blessed be He returns in His mercy and builds His house and His temple, He will return them to their place and make Jerusalem joyous.[78]
> "My beloved has descended to his garden" (Song 6:2). This refers to the day that the fire descended to the sacrifice of Abel and the sacrifice of Noah . . . And it is destined to descend one more time in the future.[79]

With all the fire imagery found in the Merkabah texts, there is no indication anywhere that the Merkabah mystics linked this to the sacrificial ritual, nor that they claimed to have experienced any kind of heavenly sacrificial ritual. While there is a rabbinic tradition concerning the sacrifices offered by the angel Michael in the

---

[78] Tan. B'ha'alot'ha 6; Tan. B B'ha'alot'ha 11, IV, 50 and parallels cited there.
[79] Aggadat Shir Hashirim 6.2.

heavenly Temple,[80] this is not placed in the highest of the seven heavens and does not seem to have been a concern of the "descenders" to the Merkabah.[81]

There is more similarity to Merkabah mysticism in a small number of midrashim which suggest that the righteous in the future will be able to endure fire or will become fire:

> In this world Israel adheres to the Holy One blessed be He, as it is said, "But you that adhere to the Lord" (Dt. 4:4). But in the future they will become alike: just as the Holy One blessed be He is a devouring fire, as it is said, "For the Lord is a devouring fire" (Dt. 4:24), so they will become devouring fire, as it is written, "And the light of Israel will become a fire, and his holy one a flame" (Isa. 10:17).[82]

We may be able to establish a *terminus ad quem* for this tradition on the basis of a parallel:

> "You are today as the stars of heaven for multitude [*LRB*]" (Dt. 1:10). He said to them: Today you are like the stars, but in the future *LRB* − you are destined to be similar to your Master [*LRBKN*]. How is this? It is written here, "For the Lord your God is a devouring fire," and it is written concerning Israel in the future, "And the light of Israel will become a fire, and his holy one a flame." R. Levi b. Hama said: If one who worships idols becomes like them, as it is said, "Those who make them will become like them" (Ps. 115:8), how much more is it true of one who worships the Holy One blessed be He that he will be like Him.[83]

If the attribution to R. Levi b. Hama is genuine, and if he was in fact referring to the midrash which precedes his here, we could establish that this tradition was known in the mid-fourth century.[84] If it was known that early, we may say that it seems to have had little popularity, as it only appears in these two places in all of rabbinic literature.[85]

Of the traditions which speak of Israel enduring fire, one seems clearly unrelated to the realm of the Merkabah, for its locale is not the upper world but the lower:

> In the future Israel will enter Gehinnom together with the nations of the world, and the latter will enter into it and perish, while Israel will come out of its midst unharmed −

---

[80] TB Hagigah 12b, Menahot 110a, Zebahim 62a; cf. Scholem, *Gnosticism*, pp. 48−50.

[81] Ithamar Gruenwald, in RY pp. 128, 133, specifically distinguishes between the heavenly Jerusalem, which is a concern of rabbinic eschatology, and the realm of the Merkabah which is above it.

[82] PR 11.7, 46b. The proof-text for the immediately preceding midrash, Ps. 147:5, while quite probably unrelated to this midrash, is intriguing because of its centrality in the Shiur Komah tradition; cf. Gershom Scholem, *Von der mystischen Gestalt der Gottheit*, p. 16.

[83] Dt. R 1.12.

[84] I assume that R. Levi b. Hama is the same as R. Levi b. Haita; the same variant on the name appears in Tan. B Lek Leka 4, I, 60. The date is established on the basis of R. Levi's being a contemporary of R. Jose, who lived in the mid-fourth century (TB Sotah 21b; cf. Herman L. Strack, *Introduction to the Talmud and Midrash*, p. 130).

[85] Lieberman's edition of Dt. R, which has many comments on Dt. 1:10, does not include any version of this tradition.

"When you walk through fire you shall not be burned, and the flame shall not consume you" (Isa. 43:2). Why not? "For the Lord your God holds your right hand" (Isa. 41:13).[86]

While this midrash may reflect some influence of Merkabah mysticism, it is more closely related to a series of older midrashim which show no such influence.[87] It, in turn, may very well have formed the basis for the following midrashim:

> Eating and drinking, happiness and rejoicing for the righteous in the days of the Messiah and the world to come. How will this happen? Beds will be spread out for the righteous in the middle of the fire and they will eat and drink and be extremely happy.[88]
> In the future the righteous will walk in fire like a man who walks in the sun on a cold day and finds it pleasant.[89]

Not only the probable source traditions, but also the substance of these midrashim indicate that they are not really related to the Merkabah tradition. One can hardly imagine the experience of the Merkabah mystic described as a man pleasantly strolling out in the sun, nor as a man lying on a bed, eating and drinking and feeling happy. Again we find that the eschatology of the rabbis tends toward images of tranquil satisfaction, while feelings of *"mysterium tremendum"* are much more characteristic of Merkabah mysticism.

The last of the texts cited here is interesting too because it is set in the context of Zech. 2:9. This verse also forms the proof-text for one passage in rabbinic literature which does assert that the pillar of fire is a part of the eschatological experience:

> The pillar of fire would go before them and strike down snakes and scorpions and thorns and it would illuminate the whole camp at night . . . And in the future the Holy One blessed be He will return it to Israel, as it is said, "For I will be to her a wall of fire round about, says the Lord" (Zech. 2:9).[90]

We have seen thus far that there is very little fire imagery in the eschatological midrashim of the rabbis; what there is tends to appear as anonymous midrashim in relatively late texts. We suggested earlier that the rabbis consciously wanted to avoid speaking of eschatological fire, going so far as to avoid mentioning the pillar of cloud because it would suggest the pillar of fire, and that this may be explained by their desire to separate esoteric and eschatological discourse. The one eschatological tradition in which fire did become significant and fairly widespread is that based on Zech. 2:9, and so we want to ask whether this tradition shows any connection with esotericism.

---

[86] PR 11.5, 65b; Num. R 2.13; cf. MT 1.20.
[87] MT 1.20 — traditions attributed to "the rabbis," R. Eliezer of Modiʿim, and R. Hanina; cf. TB Erubin 19a and PRK additional chapter 2.2, p. 453.
[88] Seder Eliahu Rabbah, p. 26.
[89] PR 35.2, 160b.
[90] Midrash Hagadol, Exodus 5.4; cf. Ginzberg, *Legends,* V, p. 113.

Before doing so, though, we should briefly summarize the results of our inquiry thus far. We began by noting a number of important eschatological motifs which play either no role or a very peripheral role in the Merkabah texts. We then turned our attention to those eschatological motifs which are also important in the Merkabah texts, and we found that a large number of them are of relatively little importance in rabbinic eschatology. We also found some that are important in both traditions but are developed in quite different ways in each, including those which are especially related to the eschatological Temple cultus and therefore show a superficial resemblance to Merkabah mysticism. We noted that in a number of cases the rabbis seem to have consciously avoided potential esoteric dimensions in their eschatological midrash, thus indicating their desire to keep the two distinct. Finally, we noted some weakening of this distinction in anonymous midrashim in later collections, which may indicate that esotericism did begin to influence rabbinic eschatology increasingly as time went on. We can see what may be a culmination of this increasing interplay in the apocalyptic texts which were produced beginning in the early seventh century,[91] where many features of the redeemed world seem to correlate with features of the realm of the Merkabah. However, with respect to the formative period of rabbinic Judaism (second to fourth centuries), it seems safe to say that the evidence presented here substantiates our initial hypothesis: The large majority of rabbis must have wanted to maintain a consistent separation between their eschatology and their involvement in Merkabah mysticism.

This discussion, of course, is based on the assumption that the extant Merkabah texts reflect the substance of Merkabah mysticism as it existed in the third century and perhaps earlier. If one does not accept this assumption, however, the results of our inquiry would still be of interest. For if the mystical experience of the Merkabah did not become part of Judaism until a later date, we may conclude that when such experience did crystallize into a fixed tradition, the basic elements of rabbinic eschatology were excluded from that tradition. Thus, regardless of how one dates the beginnings of the experience reflected in the Merkabah texts, the basic conclusion remains the same: Most who engaged in and developed Merkabah mysticism did not perceive themselves as obtaining a foretaste or proleptic experience of their eschatological reward. Their motivation for involvement in Merkabah mysticism, then, is not to be found in soteriological considerations. This, as we have observed previously, sets them apart from their contemporaries, the Gnostics, for whom the journey through the heavens to the place of the divinity was in itself an experience of redemption. This conclusion, then, rules out one possible type of motivation for involvement in Merkabah mysticism, and it leads us to ask what the actual motivation of the Merkabah mystics might have been and how that motivation may be related to rabbinic Judaism as a whole. This will certainly have to be a central focus for research on Merkabah mysticism in the future.

---

[91] These texts have been collected and edited by J. Eben-Shmuel in *Midrashei Ge'ulah*.

VII. "A WALL OF FIRE ROUND ABOUT": ON THE HISTORY OF AN ESCHATOLOGICAL MOTIF IN MIDRASH

We now turn our attention to the rabbinic exegesis of Zechariah 2:9. We have cited one midrash which asserts, on the basis of this proof-text, that the pillar of fire will return in the eschatological future, and we noted that this midrash is unique in rabbinic literature. If there were rabbis who were involved in Merkabah mysticism and thought of their mystical experience as a foretaste of their eschatological reward, we would expect them to pay particular attention to this verse. Its message is obviously eschatological, and it claims quite explicitly that God will be manifest in the form of fire; we have seen how frequently this image recurs in the literature of Merkabah mysticism. If, on the other hand, we find the exegesis of this verse motivated by factors unrelated to esotericism, we would have further evidence that the rabbis wanted to keep their eschatology separate from esoteric concerns. We shall find, in fact, that a wide variety of rabbinic concerns are reflected in the history of exegesis on this verse, but none of them seem to reflect the tradition of Merkabah mysticism.

I

It is a striking fact that there is no mention of Zech. 2:9 in any of the tannaitic midrashim.[1] The verse is referred to in at least two Jewish texts which predate the third century, however. The Jewish Sybilline Oracles (III, 702–707) says:

> Then again all the sons of the great God shall live quietly around the Temple rejoicing in those gifts which He shall give them, who is the Creator and sovereign righteous Judge. For He by Himself shall shield them, standing beside them alone in His might, encircling them, as it were, with a wall of flaming fire. Free from war they shall be in city and country.

We notice here that the wall of fire has a particular function – protection from war. But we also notice the reticence of the author to take the Biblical precedent at face value; i.e., it is not at all clear that God Himself actually is the fire, and the author inserts the qualifying phrase, "as it were."

---

[1] The material presented here thus constitutes an exception to the general conclusion of G. Vermes in *Scripture and Tradition in Judaism*, p. 229, that there was "scarcely any new creation" of aggadic themes after the second century.

The other appearance of the text which is probably pre-third century is in the Targum of Pseudo-Jonathan:[2] "And My Memra shall be to her, says the Lord, as a wall of fire surrounding her all around, and in glory I will make My Shekinah dwell within her." Here we find the characteristic Targumic practice of substituting the terms "Memra" or "Shekinah" for God Himself. But this is probably not intended to deny the actual presence of God as fire.[3] Beyond this we find no change in the Targumic rendering which might constitute a significant midrashic development.

The first use of Zech. 2:9 in rabbinic midrash is an exegetical remark of R. Joshua b. Levi:

> But is not the dwelling place of the Holy One, blessed be He, only on high, as it is said, "His glory is above the heavens" (Ps. 113:4)? What then is intended by, "And I will be the glory within her?" R. Joshua b. Levi said: It was intended to make known to all the inhabitants of the world the high esteem of Israel, for on account of Israel the Holy One blessed be He brings His Shekinah[4] down from the heavens on high and causes it to dwell on the earth. Hence it is said, "And I will be to her a wall of fire round about, and I will be the glory within her."[5]

In saying that God "brings His Shekinah down," R. Joshua b. Levi may have drawn directly on the Targum of Pseudo-Jonathan. But since the latter renders the verse virtually literally, this observation does not help us to determine R. Joshua b. Levi's intention. This midrash has at least two things in common with the same rabbi's midrash on the death of the Israelites at Sinai, which we discussed earlier: it was apparently created by R. Joshua b. Levi, and it reflects an unexpected paradox. In the case of the Sinai midrash, R. Joshua b. Levi asserted a fatal danger in an event that was usually said to be wholly positive. Here he asserted a positive benefit in an event that was usually thought of as fatally dangerous — the eschatological fire. We have tried to show that the idea of the death at Sinai is rooted in the esoteric tradition, and so we might expect that this midrash, too, would show a similar influence, particularly given the nature of its Biblical proof-text. R. Joshua b. Levi could easily have asserted that the divine glory (*kabod*), which is now accessible only to the few who are esoterically initiated, will in the future be accessible to all when it descends from its transcendent heavenly throne. If the imagery of Merkabah mysticism was in fact

---

[2] Arguments for the early dating of the Palestinian Targum tradition (pre-132 A. D. and perhaps much earlier) are advanced by Vermes in *Scripture and Tradition* and in "Bible and Midrash: Early Old Testament Exegesis," *The Cambridge History of the Bible*, vol. I.

[3] In the Targumic literature the Shekinah, God's presence, serves as an equivalent for God Himself when He is manifest on earth, especially in cultic contexts. (In eschatological midrash Jerusalem and the Temple are often interchangeable terms, and thus Jerusalem has a cultic value). Cf. Arnold M. Goldberg, *Untersuchungen über die Vorstellung von der Schekhinah in der frühen rabbinischen Literatur*; E. E. Urbach, *Hazal, 'Emunot V'de'ot*, chap. 3.

[4] The term *"shekinah"* is used as an equivalent for God Himself in rabbinic literature; cf. the references cited in n. 3 above and Gershom Scholem, *Von der mystischen Gestalt der Gottheit*, pp. 135–191.

drawn largely from the Temple cultus, such an idea could be all the more easily sustained; the glory could easily be believed to return after the final redemption to its original dwelling-place (its "*shekinah*") in the Temple of Jerusalem. Yet this does not seem to be the point of this midrash at all. R. Joshua b. Levi seems to have been trying to solve a problem of pure exegesis here, an apparent contradiction which would arise if both Biblical texts were taken literally.[6] He solved the problem by attaching different meanings to the word *kabod* in the two verses. While he took it in Ps. 113:4 to refer to the divine "glory," the *kabod* as known to the Merkabah mystics, he interpreted its appearance in Zech. 2:9 to refer to the "honor" or "prestige" of Israel. Thus the essence of his midrash is the assertion that the manifestation of the wall of fire will point up the "high esteem" (*shebah*) of Israel, which is nearly synonymous with Israel's "prestige" (*kabod*). This is somewhat tortuous exegesis, contradicting what would seem to be the obvious meaning of the Biblical text. If R. Joshua b. Levi took the problem posed by the two verses as one of pure exegesis, rather than one of substantive theology, and if he chose this approach to its solution, it seems likely that he was intentionally avoiding the obvious meaning of the verse: that the divine *kabod* would in fact descend from its inaccessible throne and make itself available to all in the eschatological Jerusalem, thereby giving all the experience which in the present is reserved for the descenders to the Merkabah.

The fact that we have an example of pure exegesis here is important in another respect. We shall see that by the end of the third century exegeses of Zech. 2:9 had been transferred almost entirely into the realm of applied exegesis. Thus the attribution of this pure exegesis to a rabbi of the early third century seems quite plausible, although R. Joshua b. Levi's midrash only appears in Pesikta Rabbati, a relatively late compilation.[7] The earliest example of the transition to applied exegesis is a variation of R. Joshua b. Levi's midrash, attributed to R. Levi:

> R. Eliezer b. Jacob said: Jerusalem is destined to keep rising until it reaches the throne of glory where it will say to the Holy One, "The place is too narrow for me; make room for me to dwell in" (Isa. 49:20). R. Jose b. Jeremiah and R. Dostai, in the name of R. Levi, added: You still do not know the high esteem of Jerusalem. However from what is said, "For I will be to her a wall of fire round about, says the Lord, and I will be the glory within her," from this you may know the high esteem of Jerusalem.[8]

---

[5] PR 35.2 end.

[6] The Yalkut Shimeoni on Zech. 2:9 repeats the passage but changes the first words to read: "But is not the glory of the Holy One . . .". This emphasizes even more strongly that R. Joshua b. Levi's problem is the location of God's glory, not the meaning of the wall of fire image itself. In fact, it might be that he cites Zech. 2:9 merely because of the last phrase, which mentions the "glory"; the wall of fire image might be brought in quite accidently. Cf. Goldberg, *Schekhinah*, p. 329.

[7] On the dating of PR, see W. G. Braude, *Pesikta Rabbati*, pp. 20—26.

[8] PRK 20.7 end.

Another version of this tradition is reported in the name of R. Jose b. R. Jeremiah: "We still have not learned the high esteem of Jerusalem; from where do we learn her high esteem? From her walls, as it is said, 'And I will be to her a wall of fire round about, says the Lord.'"[9] But as R. Jose is well known as a transmitter of R. Levi's traditions,[10] it is most likely that both versions are variants of the same tradition going back to R. Levi. R. Levi does not seem to have been interested in (and perhaps was unaware of) the pure exegetical problem which R. Joshua b. Levi was trying to solve. Rather he was concerned with making a substantive point of "creative historiography": God will provide a visible sign of Jerusalem's high esteem in the future by becoming a wall of fire.

The other change introduced by R. Levi was to make the verse refer to Jerusalem, rather than to Israel. The text as we have it seems to indicate that this change occurred because R. Levi was responding to the midrash of R. Eliezer b. Jacob. We have seen previously that the latter midrash probably reflects a basic motif of Merkabah mysticism; given R. Levi's tendency to incorporate mystical tendencies into his midrashim, we might well have expected him to follow R. Eliezer b. Jacob's lead here. Having detached this midrash from its basis in pure exegesis, he certainly could have done so quite easily. Yet there is no evidence that he was making any esoteric point in this case. We have also seen that the pericope in which both these midrashim appear is a late compilation of many traditions concerning the eschatological Jerusalem. Thus the juxtaposition of R. Levi's midrash with R. Eliezer b. Jacob's may very well have been the work of a later redactor rather than a reflection of R. Levi's intent. If so, the reference to Jerusalem may be explained as a result of the transition to applied exegesis. The contradiction that R. Joshua b. Levi attempted to solve was one between the "dwelling" of God in heaven and His "dwelling" on earth. Thus the earliest version merely says that God will make His Shekinah dwell "on earth." No more specific location was needed. R. Levi, however, lived at a time when a concretization of the eschatological expectation was taking place among the aggadists of Palestine; he himself was among the leading forces in this process.[11] Given the centrality of Jerusalem in these eschatological expectations, it is not surprising that he wanted to emphasize a visible manifestation of God in Jerusalem, which would also serve implicitly to vindicate the "high esteem" of Jerusalem vis-à-vis her archrival, Rome. To make this essentially political point, in an atmosphere motivated by changed political conditions, R. Levi introduced the requisite change into the exegetical remark of R. Joshua b. Levi, and he could do so because the problem which the latter wanted to solve was no longer the focus of interest.

We can date this turning from purely exegetical to applied eschatological concerns more precisely, however. Zech. 2:9 was also the subject of a midrash of

---

[9] Song R 7.10 end.
[10] See Wilhelm Bacher, PA, III, p. 729.
[11] Michael Avi-Yonah, *The Jews of Palestine*, pp. 128–132.

R. Simeon b. Lakish, whose career fell precisely between the generations of
R. Joshua b. Levi and R. Levi:

> "For I will be to her a wall of fire round about, says the Lord, and I will be the glory
> within her"; this is what the Holy One blessed be He said: I and all of My family will
> become a wall for Jerusalem in the future, and I will command the angels to guard her.[12]

Here again there is some problem concerning the attribution, for it is based on a
manuscript of Pesikta Rabbati and on the Yalkut Shimeoni, a very late collection.
However the attribution seems reasonable based on these two readings and the
fact that the motivation is partially in the realm of pure exegesis. There is a tradition
cited frequently in rabbinic literature that "wherever it is said 'V'YHWH' ['and the
Lord' or 'for the Lord'] it means the Lord and His court."[13] Though the attribution
of this tradition is not certain (a R. Elazar or R. Eliezer), it cannot be much later
than a younger contemporary of R. Simeon b. Lakish and may well be older. Thus
it looks very much as though R. Simeon B. Lakish, in this passage, was drawing
directly on this exegetical rule (as both the "court" and the "family" of God refer to
the angels). In the words of R. Simeon b. Lakish, however, the pure exegetical
motive is not given precedence, as it is in the tradition ascribed to R. Joshua b. Levi;
in fact, it is not even mentioned explicitly and must be hypothetically reconstructed.
One might be tempted to see in the reference to the angels a link to Merkabah
mysticism. But this reference is seen to be of secondary concern here, just because
it is a reflection of the pure exegesis involved. The absence of an explicit reference to
this "creative philology" underscores the primary intention of the midrash, which
is in the realm of "creative historiography":[14] the promise of divine protection for
Jerusalem in the future. Thus, in addition to marking a transitional stage between
pure and applied exegesis on Zech. 2:9, this tradition initiates a second motif, which
we shall call the "protection" motif. And once again we find that a rabbi whose
midrashim have appeared to be linked to esotericism chose to avoid such a link when
offering an applied exegesis of this particular verse.

This transitional stage may very well have enabled the third generation of
amoraim to detach the theme from any connection with pure exegesis. We have seen
above that R. Levi did so, and in the same generation R. Isaac Nappaha, another
rabbi whose midrashim show evidence of interest in Merkabah mysticism, offered
a new interpretation of the verse which was also wholly in the realm of applied
exegesis. His midrash on Zech. 2:9 is reported only in the Babylonian Talmud and
represents the characteristic Babylonian emphasis on halakic thought. Yet it is likely
that R. Isaac, who taught in both Palestine and Babylonia, would have brought a
Palestinian tradition to Babylonia and given it a new development in the light

---

[12] PR 35.2 top and note *ad loc.* in Braude, *Pesikta Rabbati*.

[13] Gen. R 51.2, p. 533, and parallels cited there; PR 42.3 top.

[14] The terms "creative philology" and "creative historiography," in many ways analogous
to Vermes' terms "pure" and "applied" exegesis, are explained by I. Heinemann, *Darkei
Ha'aggadah*, pp. 4—5 and *passim*.

of Babylonian thinking, which, as we shall see, gave the whole tradition a new meaning. The passage in its full context is as follows:

> Rav Ammi and Rav Assi sat before R. Isaac. The former said to him: Let the master teach something of the halaka. The latter said to him: Let the master teach something of the aggada . . . He said to them: I will tell you something which will be equally valuable to both of you. "When fire breaks out and catches in thorns," "breaks out" [implies] by itself, "he that kindled the fire shall make full restitution" (Ex. 22:6). The Holy One, blessed be He, said: I must make restitution for the fire which I kindled. I kindled a fire in Zion, as it is said, "And he kindled a fire in Zion which consumed its foundations" (Lam. 4:11), and I am destined to rebuild her with fire in the future, as it is said, "For I will be to her a wall of fire round about, says the Lord, and I will be the glory within her."[15]

R. Isaac then concludes by giving a purely halakic interpretation of Ex. 22:6 to satisfy Rav Ammi. The emphasis on halakic thinking is evident here not so much in the external linking of aggadic and halakic interpretations as in the nature of the aggadic motif itself.[16] The manifestation of God as a wall of fire is seen here as a legal obligation binding upon God — a repayment of a debt which He has incurred. It is an example of the general aggadic principle of "measure for measure" in the development of history as well,[17] and, as we shall see, this principle plays an important role in the development of our theme. R. Isaac has also added an important new dimension to the idea of God as a wall of fire. He has made explicit what may have previously been implicit — that it is the very same agent which both punishes the sinners and rewards the righteous in the eschatological process. We shall see that this concept is central in a series of later traditions stemming from R. Isaac's tradition; we shall call them collectively the "consolation/recompense"

---

[15] TB Babba Kamma 60b. This may be a midrashic elaboration of a passage inserted into the Amidah prayer on the ninth day of Ab: "For You, O Lord, set her on fire, and with fire You will build her again in the future." (TP Berakot 4,3 8a and Ta'aniot 2,2 65c). However the dating of this passage is very unsure and the prayer of which it is a part underwent many changes in rabbinic times; thus it is possible that the passage was not inserted into the liturgy until after R. Isaac's time. Cf. the discussions of Salo W. Baron, *A Social and Religious History of the Jews*, vol. II, pp. 112, 375 and Joseph Heinemann, *Hat'filah Bit'kufat Hatannaim V'ha'amoraim*, pp. 35–51. In any event, it seems possible that the theme of consolation/recompense introduced by R. Isaac may have influenced later versions of this liturgical passage in which the word "nahem" was inserted; see I. M. Elbogen, *Hat'filah B'yisrael B'hitpathutah Hahistorit*, pp. 42,97 and L. Ginzberg, *Perushim V'hidushim B'yerushalmi*, vol. III, pp. 308–311. Ginzberg cites a manuscript which reads: "For You set her on fire and with fire You will console her in the future."
[16] On halakic influence in Babylonian aggada, see Joseph Heinemann, *Aggadot V'toldotaihen*, ch. 11.
[17] On the concept of "measure for measure" (*middah k'neged middah*) see Heinemann, *Darkei Ha'aggadah*, pp. 64–70; E. E. Urbach, *Hazal*, ch. 15 sec. 2; G. F. Moore, *Judaism*, vol. II, pp. 249–253.

motif. Nowhere in this midrash, however, is there evidence of any interest in esotericism.

We have reviewed four traditions on Zech. 2:9 attributed to four different third century rabbis, and these are in fact the only four traditions attributed to individual rabbis on this passage in all of rabbinic literature. We have seen that Zech. 2:9 entered into rabbinic midrash under the demands of pure exegesis of the Biblical text but passed, in the course of three generations, into the realm of applied eschatological exegesis. In this process, each of the three generations gave a fundamentally new meaning to the text and thus three separate motifs were spawned. We shall now examine the later anonymous traditions on this theme. Ironically, while the "high esteem" motif seems to have been the starting point for midrash on this verse, it was apparently not developed beyond the third century. But the other two motifs each have significant histories in the anonymous texts to which we now turn.

II

R. Isaac's "consolation/recompense" motif was re-worked, sometime during the fourth or fifth centuries, apparently in order to remove the ultimate responsibility for the destructive fire from God. For we find an anonymous tradition cited in both Pesikta d'Rab Kahana and Lamentations Rabbah[18] which says:

> They sinned with fire, as it is written, "The children gather wood and the fathers ignite the fire" (Jer. 7:18). They were stricken with fire, as it is written, "From on high He sent fire" (Lam. 1:13). And they are comforted with fire, as it is written, "For I will be to her a wall of fire round about, says the Lord, and I will be the glory within her."[19]

Here the concept of "measure for measure" has been taken one step further back, and the blame for the punishing fire has been put directly on the sins of Israel. In this way God's manifestation in the form of fire, which R. Isaac had merely stated as a fact, is given an explanation. But the explanation has important theological implications. It builds upon R. Isaac's insight into the unity of the punishing and restoring manifestations of God, explaining this in terms of the classical prophetic view of God's response to Israel's sin: God feels compelled to punish Israel, yet the punishment is always followed by restoration. Israel's deed initiates the act of God, and according to the doctrine of "measure for measure" He punishes with the very same agent with which Israel sinned. Yet Israel's deed also determines the nature of God's restorative redemptive act. Thus the use of fire to denote God's punishing and restoring serves to stress the ambivalence inherent in God's response to Israel's sin.

---

[18] For the dating of these texts, see W. G. Braude and I. J. Kapstein, *Pesikta de-Rab Kahana*, pp. xiv–1; J. Heinemann, *Aggadot*, Appendix; M. D. Herr, "Lamentations Rabbah" *Encyclopedia Judaica*, x, 1378.
[19] PRK 16.11 end; Lam. R chap. 1 end.

Can we fix a more precise date at which this last development took place? Probably not, but there is one conjecture which deserves mention. One of the most significant religious developments in Palestine between the time of R. Isaac and the compilation of the Pesikta d'Rab Kahana was the attempt by the Emperor Julian to have the Temple in Jerusalem rebuilt. This event has left little explicit mark on rabbinic literature, perhaps because of the reticence of the rabbis to endorse the project.[20] But we know from non-Jewish sources that the project was terminated when some kind of accident occurred involving an impressive fire manifestation. Several sources cite "balls of fire" as central in the episode,[21] and Gregory of Nazianzus refers to this as fire from heaven.[22] Is it possible that in some rabbinic circles opposed to the rebuilding of the Temple under human (i. e., non-messianic) auspices, this fire was taken as a sign of God's displeasure? Our midrashic passage would then point to the process of "measure for measure" at work in contemporary fourth-century history; just as God destroyed the illegitimate Temple with fire so He will build the legitimate Temple with fire in the future. This conjecture, however, must remain merely that, for there is no hard evidence to confirm or deny it. But such a context would explain the emphasis on the sin of Israel as the cause of the fire manifestation, an emphasis which is not found in any other version of the tradition.

For R. Isaac's tradition occurs again in Pesikta Rabbati in almost the same form as its original occurrence in the Talmud. Here, however, the context is one of aggadic "creative historiography" alone. The question is which of the patriarchs can comfort Jerusalem, and the answer is that only God Himself can do this, to which He replies:

> It is for me to comfort Jerusalem in keeping with what I have written: "He that kindled the fire shall make full restitution." Since I kindled her, as it is said, "From on high He sent fire," I must comfort her, as it is said, "For I will be to her a wall of fire round about, says the Lord, and I will be the glory within her."[23]

Here there is no mention of Israel's sin or responsibility, only a recompense which she deserves for suffering in the past and which will be granted "measure for measure." A similar idea appears to be the basis for another tradition on Zech. 2:9 which is roughly contemporaneous with the Pesikta d'Rab Kahana tradition:[24]

> The wicked kingdom [i. e., Rome], because it reviles and blasphemes and says, "Who is there in heaven for me?" (Ps. 73:25), is not punished except with fire: "And as I looked,

---

[20] Avi-Yonah, *Jews of Palestine*, p. 197 argues this conclusion persuasively against alternative views.
[21] E.g., Ammianus Marcellinus, *Rerum Gestarum Libri*, XXIII, 1, 2; Rufinus, Historia ecclesiastica, x, 39—40.
[22] Gregory of Nazianzus, Oratio, V. 4 (Migne, *Patrologia Graeca*, vol. 35, col. 669).
[23] PR 30.3.
[24] On the contemporaneous relationship of Lev. R and PRK, see Braude and Kapstein, *Pesikta de-Rab Kahana*, pp. xlix—li.

the beast was slain, and its body destroyed and given over to be burned with fire" (Dan. 7:11).[34] But Israel, because they are despised and lowly in this world, are not consoled except with fire, as it is said, "For I will be to her a wall of fire round about, says the Lord, and I will be the glory within her."[25]

Here we see the other direction in which "creative historiography" could take R. Isaac's tradition. Removing the responsibility for Israel's suffering from God, it does not place that responsibility on sinful Israel but rather on the Romans. Thus the "wicked kingdom" is ultimately responsible for both the negative and positive manifestations of eschatological fire. Yet the theme of consolation and recompense, which is the essence of R. Isaac's tradition, seems to play a secondary role here. The primary motive is to emphasize the single agent by which both punishment of the wicked and reward of the righteous is achieved. There is a clear thematic relationship between this tradition and that of the Pesikta d'Rab Kahana/Lamentations Rabbah. But here the ambivalence does not concern the positive and negative fates of Israel; all is positive as far as Israel is concerned. The central point is rather the ability of God to produce apparently opposite effects by one and the same means. Yet these effects are not, of course, ultimately contradictory; they both serve the single end of Israel's redemption.

This point is stressed explicitly in a later version of the same tradition.[26] The context here is a long piece of aggadic historiography demonstrating that "everyone who raises himself up [i. e., against God] ends up going into fire." The last example is Esau (i. e., the Roman empire), after which the passage concludes:

and Israel, because they made themselves despised and lowly as it is said, "And so I have made you despised and lowly" (Mal. 2:9), are consoled and redeemed with fire, as it is said, "For I will be to her a wall of fire round about, says the Lord, and I will be the glory within her." As soon as Esau vanishes from the world the Holy One, blessed be He, and Israel remain alone, as it is said, "my dove, my perfect one, is unique" (Song 6:9).[27]

While the entire passage is concerned with the many punishing manifestations of fire, it concludes with a statement of the redeeming value of that punishing fire for Israel. This Leviticus Rabbah/Tanhuma tradition as a whole, then, makes two important contributions to our theme. It stresses fire as symbolic of the simultaneous coincidence of contraries in the eschatological process. And it makes the wall of fire a positive reward for Israel; their suffering becomes not merely an unpleasant episode for which they deserve recompense, but rather a positive virtue for which they are rewarded. If we seek the historical context which might have given rise to this tradition, we must obviously look for a time in which Palestinian

---

[25] Lev. R ch. 7 end.
[26] The Tanhuma is especially difficult to date; among recent scholars J. Heinemann (*Aggadot*, Appendix) assigns it to the sixth or seventh century, while M. D. Herr ("Tanhuma," *Encyclopedia Judaica*, 1972, xv, 795) dates it as late as the ninth century.
[27] Tan. Zav 2 end; cf. Tan. B. Zav 4 end, in which the word "and redeemed" is missing.

Jews felt themselves to be suffering at the hands of Rome and had a strong expectation of eschatological reward as a recompense for that suffering. Such an eschatological expectation would serve as a legitimation for suffering, thus giving it a positive value. And in fact, a renewed period of persecution of Palestinian Jewry by Rome did begin, some twenty years after the death of Julian, with the accession of the Emperor Theodosius I in 383; consequent to this there was apparently a new emphasis on eschatological hope within the Jewish community in the late fourth and early fifth centuries. Again, we can only say that such a context seems to be a suitable background for this tradition, but no dating of an anonymous text can be proven conclusively.[28]

If the hypothesized datings for the traditions in the "consolation/recompense" motif offered here are accepted, it appears that this motif went through a clear line of historical development. It began with R. Isaac as a reference to the history of Israel, including both past negative and future positive experiences. It was then developed into a critique of Israel (or at least some segment of the Jewish community) because of her "sin," so that the future reward appears to be unmerited. Finally, it was taken to the other extreme, being a critique of the nations (and especially Rome) and an unqualified positive evaluation of Israel. Thus the theme was returned to its starting point, the totally positive attitude toward Israel shown by R. Joshua b. Levi. If the datings offered here are not accepted, we must still conclude that this motif demonstrates how one midrashic tradition may be developed in opposite directions under different historical conditions (although

---

[28] Avi-Yonah, *Jews of Palestine*, ch. 9 and especially pp. 223–225. Other datings of this tradition are possible, as there were certainly other periods of persecution and eschatological hope as well. In fact, the Tanhuma seems to make a special effort to link the tradition to the Hadrianic persecution and the martyrdom it engendered, for it stresses that they "made themselves" lowly and despised, and in the same pericope it has Israel address Rome: "You decreed that I must worship idols . . . and if I did not worship them you would kill me." However, as the Tanhuma version is quite clearly an expansion of the Leviticus Rabbah version, it can not date from before the late fifth century and thus the reference to martyrdom is probably a retrojection (or a reference to some later historical events). A more serious possibility is a dating to the late third century – the third generation of amoraim – when similar anti-Roman and eschatological feelings ran high. Such a dating is strongly suggested by the attribution of the pericope Lev. R 7.6 to R. Levi; the tradition we have cited appears as the conclusion to this pericope. However it seems probable that this conclusion is a later addition and was not part of R. Levi's original midrash. This is evident from the parallel passage in MT 11.5, where there is no reference to Israel at all; the entire pericope is a listing of those who will be punished by fire, which is precisely the subject of R. Levi's midrash as stated explicitly in Lev. R 7.6. Moreover, we have seen that R. Levi saw Zech. 2:9 as a sign of Israel's "high esteem"; if the conclusion to Lev. R 7.6 were genuinely from R. Levi, we would expect the same term to appear here as well. If, then, the conclusion was added to the pericope after R. Levi's time but before the redaction of Leviticus Rabbah in the mid-fifth century, a dating toward the end of the fourth century seems most likely.

we may be unable to define those conditions). Yet despite these variations, one element remained constant: in every case the wall of fire serves to symbolize the ambiguity in the divine control of history. Whether it be the punishment and subsequent reward of Israel, or the simultaneous punishment of the nations and reward of Israel, the two apparently antithetic processes are carried out by the very same agency.

III

We may now turn to an examination of the other major motif on Zech. 2:9, the "protection" motif initiated by R. Simeon b. Lakish. This motif has no datable occurrence until its appearance in the apocalyptic literature of the early seventh century.[29] Apocalyptic visions are supplied with midrashic proof-texts, as in a passage which describes "the ministering angels guarding the Temple in a wall of fire, as it is said, 'For I will be to her a wall of fire round about.'"[30] This passage is inserted in the text at the crucial turning point between the end of the apocalyptic wars and the beginning of the new, redeemed world which follows the wars. Thus it is hard to say whether the walls of fire serve as protection merely during the wars or rather as an enduring element in the redeemed world. The tradition of R. Simeon b. Lakish, on which this tradition clearly seems to be based, is in reference to the redeemed Jerusalem after the apocalyptic wars. The use of the theme in connection with the Temple seems to imply the postwar situation, since the Temple has already been re-established. Furthermore, a nearly contemporaneous apocalyptic text has the seer claim: "And he showed me the walls of Jerusalem — walls of fire surrounding her"[31] in a context detached from any wars. However a second version of the text presents the unique detail that the wall of fire surrounds "all the small towns of Israel."[32] This innovation in the theme most probably reflects the actual conditions of its author's time, conditions of warfare between Persian and Byzantine forces throughout Palestine. Thus it seems likely that this version is motivated by a concern for protection from apocalyptic war. Yet in this latter version the reference to Zech. 2:9 is placed at the turning point between the war and the institution of the Messianic age. Perhaps in both versions of the text the wall of fire is meant to symbolize divine protection both in wartime and in the redeemed state.[33] In any event, we find that the theme has been revived

---

[29] This literature has been collected and edited by J. Eben-Shmuel in *Midrashei Ge'ulah*.

[30] Perek Eliahu, p. 54, l.103. Eben Shmuel dates the text to 628 A.D. (p. 39), while Avi-Yonah dates it to 607 A.D. (*Jews of Palestine*, p. 261).

[31] Sefer Zerubbabel, p. 85, l.65.

[32] Sefer Eliahu, p. 45, l.56. Two variant readings are cited by Eben-Shmuel (p. 376): "Fire and ministering angels surround them," "Fire and angels of fire surround them."

[33] The passage from the Sibylline Oracles cited above is also placed at the turning point between apocalyptic war and paradisal peace.

in this apocalyptic period with a meaning not given it in any new version since the mid-third century.[34]

However, this revival of the theme makes one crucial change in both textual versions which must be noted. While the original midrash of R. Simeon b. Lakish states that both God and the angels will become a wall of fire (and this is demanded by the "creative philology" underlying the midrash), in the apocalyptic texts it is the angels alone who form the wall (indicating that this tradition, too, has broken free of its roots in "creative philology"). It is highly unlikely (though perhaps possible) that this change was accidental and unconscious. More probably the change was made deliberately to conform to the texts' consistent pattern of having either human beings or angels act as God's agents in the control of human history. Since the angels play a crucial role in the destruction of Israel's enemies, these texts are making the point that God uses the same agency both to punish sinners and protect the righteous. But here the agency of principle interest is the angels, rather than fire. This is underscored by their failure to mention fire in any central way in describing the apocalyptic wars and the sufferings of the wicked.[35]

---

[34] The text in Sefer Eliahu is followed directly by:
> At that time the Holy One, blessed be He, says to Abraham: Just as your descendants descended to the lowest level — "You shall be brought low, you shall speak out of the earth" (Isa. 29:4) — so they will be higher than all the nations — as it is said, "And the Lord your God will place you high above all the nations of the earth." (Dt. 28:1).

The author may have meant this to be related to the immediately preceding midrash on Zech 2:9, but the midrashic contexts are different, and he makes no effort to make the connection apparent. It would seem that he could have drawn directly on the Leviticus Rabbah tradition, in which the two motifs are directly related, if he had meant to emphasize the "consolation/recompense" motif.

[35] The fire image as punishment seems to appear three times in these texts. Both texts cite Ezekiel 39:9 and describe the Israelites fueling their bonfires with the weapons of the defeated Gog and Magog, which is not a direct punishment of the latter. (Sefer Eliahu, p. 46, l.76; Perek Eliahu, p. 54, l.98.) In Sefer Eliahu (p. 47, l.91) punishing fire from heaven is said to descend on the sinners in hell. However, since this text puts the walls of fire image apparently in a pre-judgment, apocalyptic war context, the latter can not be seen as directly related to this post-judgment image of hell-fire. Finally, both texts begin by having the seer carried to "the eastern part of the world" where he sees "a place burning with fire and no creature is able to enter there." (Sefer Eliahu, p. 41, l.5; Perek Eliahu, p. 51, l.7.) Because the Perek Eliahu makes this vision a midrash on Ex. 33:20, "For no man shall see me and live," Eben-Shmuel (note, p. 41) assumes that the place is Jerusalem in which is found "the Temple of fire which has descended from heaven." If Eben-Shmuel is correct we may have here another reference to our theme. But it is not likely that he is correct. Firstly, the author of Perek Eliahu does not use Zech. 2:9 here, while he does use it later on when he wants to relate fire to the Temple in a positive sense. Secondly, nowhere in rabbinic literature do we find the Temple itself burning; rather, it is surrounded by protecting walls of fire. Thirdly, the fire image here has a negative meaning — it keeps Israel out of the Temple (if in fact it refers to the Temple). Fourthly, the passage appears in both

Indirectly, then, these texts emphasize the close connection between punishment and reward in the eschatological process. But the midrash of Zech. 2:9 in itself serves mainly to provide an image of divine protection for Israel in the end of days. It may be under the influence of this version of the theme, with the angels as the wall of fire, that the Yalkut version of R. Simeon b. Lakish's tradition was formed: "And R. Simeon b. Lakish said: That all My family will become a wall for Jerusalem in the future, and I will command the angels to guard her."[36]

There are two other traditions which form part of the "protection" motif, though neither seems to be so directly influenced by R. Simeon b. Lakish's tradition as those we have just considered. Both are found in Exodus Rabbah:

> "And God led the people"[37] (Ex. 13:18). What is the meaning of "led"? That the Holy One, blessed be He, surrounded them, as it says, "For I will be to her a wall of fire round about, says the Lord." It is just as a shepherd who was herding his sheep and saw wolves coming to attack the flock would surround the flock so that they not be injured. So when Israel went out of Egypt, the leaders of Edom and Moab and Canaan and Amalek were conferring on how to attack Israel. When the Holy One, blessed be He, saw this He surrounded them so that they would not be attacked, as it is said, "And God surrounded the people." And not only in this aeon, but in the coming aeon it is so too. How do we know this? Because David says: "As the mountains surround Jerusalem, so the Lord surrounds His people" (Ps. 125:2).[38]

Because this text is anonymous and appears in a late compilation,[39] it is especially difficult to date. It bears some similarity to the apocalyptic texts, because it stresses the wall of fire as protection against military enemies.[40] However it differs significantly from those texts because it is God Himself, not the angels, who surrounds

---

versions at the very beginning of the text as part of a series of visions describing apocalyptic catastrophe, while the Temple descended from heaven is always a paradisal image following the end of the catastrophe (or at least its temporary cessation). Perhaps, then, this passage is a reference to punishment of the wicked by fire (though this is not explicit), but it can not be taken as an eschatological fire image used in a positive sense. If the passage does in fact refer to Jerusalem, it would seem more likely that it describes the Persian firing of Byzantine churches, a sure sign of apocalyptic war to the Jews.

[36] Y. Zech. 2:9.

[37] The word "veyeseb," which in the biblical context means "led," is interpreted in the midrash according to its alternative meaning "surrounded."

[38] Ex. R 20.16.

[39] All of the passages cited here are from the second portion of Ex. R, which has been tentatively dated to the ninth century by J. Heinemann (*Aggadot*, Appendix) and M. D. Herr ("Exodus Rabbah," *Encyclopedia Judaica*, 1972, vi, 1068). However, this dating, like the dating of many rabbinic texts, may have to be altered after further critical study, as pointed out by Saul Lieberman in the introduction to his edition of *Deuteronomy Rabbah*, p. xxiii.

[40] In connection with this parallel between the dangers of the Exodus and those of the apocalyptic era, there is a tradition in PRE, ch. 42, that God sent the angel Michael in the form of a wall of fire to protect Israel against Egypt as they stood before the Sea of Reeds.

and protects Israel; the author of this passage has deleted the mention of the angels from the tradition altogether. All that can be offered is a general observation: since this is the only version of the theme in which the wall of fire explicitly functions solely as protection against the attack of enemies, it might very well come from some time of physical danger to the Jewish community.

The other text from Exodus Rabbah presents a more complex situation:

> "And the Almighty will be your support" (Job 22:25): Make Him your support so that He will be with you in whatever trouble[41] comes upon you, as it is said, "I am with him in trouble" (Ps. 91:15). Another interpretation: "Your support" — That if their enemies attack I will be against them, as it is said, "And the Almighty will be your support." Another interpretation: That He will become your walls, and "your support" means nothing but "walls,"[42] as it is said, "And the high fortress of your walls" (Isa. 25:12). The Holy One, blessed be He, said: I am a wall for them in this aeon, and so will it be in the coming aeon, when Zion is rebuilt I will become a wall for her, as it is said, "for I will be to her a wall of fire round about, says the Lord, and I will be the glory within her."[43]

Here the general context is also one of protection from attacking enemies, but God is explicitly said to make Himself a wall of fire only after Zion is rebuilt; i. e., after the end of the apocalyptic wars. It may be that the last portion of this text (the portion which mentions the wall of fire specifically) was originally a separate interpretation of Job. 22:25, focussing on the theme of divine protection in the world to come. The editor of Exodus Rabbah (or some earlier redactor), who clearly knew the wall of fire motif as a protection against enemies in apocalyptic war, may have joined this originally separate tradition to those now preceding it in order to change the meaning of the tradition. This possibility seems more likely if we survey the development of the "protection" motif as a whole. It was clearly well-known in two different contexts — both during and after the apocalyptic wars. And it could be applied to either of these contexts interchangeably, for its meaning remained rather constant; in either case, it stresses the protection of Israel and the simultaneous destruction of her enemies, and once again we find the central point that both processes occur by means of a single divine agency.

Yet we can not hypothesize an editor of Exodus Rabbah who turned all the traditions on Zech. 2:9 to this single theme of apocalyptic protection. For the text includes another midrash on the verse which is apparently unique and unrelated to any other tradition we have seen:

> What is the meaning of the "Wilderness of Shur" (Ex. 15:20)?[44] Until Israel went out of Egypt the world was a wilderness; as soon as they went out the world became civilized.

---

[41] The term *"baẓar"* ("support") in Job 22:25 is interpreted here as *"b'ẓar"* ("in trouble").

[42] Here the term *baẓar* is interpreted according to its alternative meaning "fortress."

[43] Ex. R 40.4 end.

[44] The name *"Shur"* is interpreted in this text according to various nuances of its basic meaning: a civilized or habitable territory protected by walls and thus set off from surrounding wilderness.

Another interpretation: Until Israel received the Torah the world was a wilderness; as soon as they received the Torah the world became civilized — these are the words of R. Judah b. R. Simon. The Holy One, blessed be He, said: In the future I will also do this for Zion, which is a wilderness, as it is written, "Zion has become a wilderness" (Isa. 64:9), and in the future I will become a wall for her, as it is said, "For I will be to her a wall of fire round about, says the Lord, and I will be the glory within her."[45]

The reference to R. Judah b. R. Simon, a fourth-century amora, indicates that the text can incorporate relatively early material. But the midrash on Zech. 2:9 here seem to have been attached to R. Judah's tradition by a later editor who saw a similarity in themes. This makes it virtually impossible to date the origin of this interpretation. It is rather surprising that this tradition does not appear elsewhere, for it incorporates two complementary themes known in rabbinic literature: redemption as new cosmogony and the cosmogonic symbolism of walls in an eschatological context.[46] However, because it is anonymous and stands alone in rabbinic literature, we can only mention this passage and note that at least one aggadist saw this dimension in the theme of the wall of fire. Finally, the three passages from Exodus Rabbah all share the common trait of exemplifying "creative philology" in the form of exegesis of individual words.[47] However none of these constitutes "creative philology" directly applied to Zech. 2:9. Rather they use an already established theme from the realm of "creative historiography" to elucidate the meaning of a word from another Biblical verse. It seems clear that "creative philology" continued to be an important pursuit even at the time of the compilation of Exodus Rabbah. However these passages do not disprove our observation that an interpretation of Zech. 2:9 motivated by "creative philology" can be dated very early.

IV.

In summary: We have surveyed eleven different traditions occurring in a total of seventeen separate passages in rabbinic literature. The bulk of these can be assigned to one of three general motifs: the wall of fire as a sign of high esteem (two traditions and four total occurrences), as a means of protection (four traditions and six total ocurrences), and as a consolation or recompense (four traditions and six total occurrences). Having studied each motif separately, we may now look at the relationships among them. It would appear that the significant relationships are not to be found in the area of historical causation. In fact, the three motifs seem to have developed quite independently of each other in content (though there may have been an early connection in formal terms, in the influence of pure exegesis

---

[45] Ex. R 24.4 end.

[46] For many examples of these themes in rabbinic eschatology see Ira Chernus, "Redemption and Chaos." Mircea Eliade, in *Cosmos and History* and other works, has developed the phenomenology of these themes at length.

[47] Cf. I. Heinemann, *Darkei Ha'aggadah*, ch. 12.

on applied exegesis). Thus we can not arrange the three motifs in any chronological sequence of cause and effect. Rather we should view them as three independent developments rooted in the third century. The significant relationships appear when we attempt to grasp the entire theme of the divine wall of fire in a pheno-menological survey (which will, of course, be informed by the results of the foregoing historical survey).

Initially, it should be emphasized that the wall of fire consistently represents a visible manifestation of the divine (and in most cases of God Himself) on earth. This indicates one of the primary meanings of the image: the eschatological re-demption carries with it an overcoming of the distance between the divine and the human, between heaven and earth. However this dimension of the theme is always implicit; in each case, the midrash offers an explicit and more precise statement about the meaning of this redemptive manifestation of the divine. In the "high esteem" motif, obviously, the meaning of redemption is that it restores Israel (and Jerusalem as the symbol of the Jewish nation) to the status which is truly hers, but which goes unrecognized in the unredeemed world. It is precisely because of Israel's high esteem that God chooses to descend to earth in the form of a wall of fire, thus bearing witness to the truth of Israel's claim to a superior status. (This claim is re-flected in the widespread belief that Israel would attain political rule of the world in the coming aeon with Jerusalem as world-capital.[48]) In the "protection" motif, God overcomes the distance between Himself and the human world to provide security and thus tranquillity for His people. (Cf. the common rabbinic idea that the coming aeon is "a day which is entirely Sabbath and rest for the life of eternity.")[49] In the "consolation/recompense" motif, it is the actual presence of God which provides consolation for all of the sufferings of Israel in the unredeemed world and which compensates for those sufferings. Perhaps the implication here is that the presence of God in itself is consolation and recompense enough. Or perhaps this motif draws directly on the first two, implying that the vindication of Israel's esteem and the protection of Israel constitute consolation and recompense. But the texts of this motif themselves point to another conclusion: the presence of God provides con-solation and recompense principally because He is manifest as a fire, the very same way in which He manifests Himself to punish sinners, whether they be Israelites of an earlier time or oppressing nations of the present.

All of these motifs also share a common focus on the national corporate aspect of redemption, rather than on individual eschatological reward. But the ambiguity of the third motif is reflected in its variable attitude toward Israel, while the first two motifs maintain a wholly positive attitude. Those traditions which stress Israel's past sin also stress that Israel must experience the divine fire in the future because of the doctrine that God repays "measure for measure." But in those traditions which are wholly positive about Israel, it seems surprising to find any mention of fire, which

---

[48] For examples of this theme, see Chernus, "Redemption and Chaos," ch. 2, sec. 10.
[49] MT 92.2 and parallels cited in Ginzberg, *Legends,* vol. V, p. 128.

was most widely known as a means of eschatological punishment.[50] In this latter case the doctrine of "measure for measure" is not introduced. Rather, the emphasis is on the single means by which God rewards and punishes, and this appears to be the one idea shared by all the traditions concerning the divine wall of fire. All agree that redemption means a direct experience by the Jewish nation of the one God who both punishes and rewards and who assumes the same form for both purposes. (This too reflects a widespread rabbinic concept that God "heals with the very same thing with which He injures.")[51] It is the same God in the same form who is experienced by all mankind in the eschatological events, although with different results. Thus even those who are redeemed must experience the punishing and destroying aspect of God. It would seem that fire has been chosen intentionally for its ability to carry this message of ambivalence in a visible symbol; the ambivalence of fire in terms of its benefit and harm to man is immediately obvious to all.

Yet the forms of divine manifestation are not exactly the same, for God does not appear as a *wall* of fire to punish. The wall in itself seems to be a totally positive symbol of Israel's tranquillity and political superiority in the redeemed world (and, in a single tradition, of new cosmogony too). So we can say more precisely that the experience of redemption is an experience of God as both ambivalent and totally positive. What, then, is the meaning of redemption as expressed in the image of the divine wall of fire? It is a closing of the distance between God and man, providing high esteem, security and tranquillity, consolation and recompense for Israel. All of these results are achieved through Israel's immediate experience of God — a God who is the ambivalent source of life and death, good and evil ("He kills and makes alive at one and the same moment")[52] and yet is at the same time wholly life-giving and good for Israel. But it is only by experiencing God in the potentially destructive form of fire that Israel can receive the ultimate good of redemption.

It may seem that we have strayed far from our initial question — the relationship of esotericism and eschatology in rabbinic midrash. But hopefully this apparent digression has shed some helpful light on the problem. We have found the one consistent idea in all the midrashim on Zech. 2:9 to be the overcoming of distance between God and Israel, and certainly this is in one sense the basic idea in all of Merkabah mysticism as well. But the rabbis were not content with expounding the verse in a general way; rather they gave the basic idea a more specific content which, in each case, seems to have been unrelated to any aspects of Merkabah mysticism. Each of these specific contents, as we have seen, was originated by a third century

---

[50] For a summary of this material, see Paul Volz, *Die Eschatologie der jüdischen Gemeinde im neutestamentlichen Zeitalter,* pp. 318–340; cf. the many references in Louis Ginzberg, *Legends of the Jews,* Index s. v. "Fire of Hell," "Fire, the wicked punished by," "Fire, the names of persons punished by."

[51] Ex. R 23.3; Cf. Ex. R. 26.2; Tan. B'shalah 23–24; Mek. Vayosha 1, p. 156, and parallels cited in note *ad loc.*

[52] Ex. R 28.4; Cf. Tan. Yitro 12 quoting Isa. 45:7.

rabbi who seems to have been interested in esotericism, and so it seems again that there was a conscious decision to develop eschatological midrashim in directions unrelated to esotericism. In reviewing later versions of these motifs, we did not find any evidence that this trend toward separation was reversed.

There is one final point to be made here. In discussing R. Joshua b. Levi's original formulation of this midrashic theme, we pointed out that it bore some similarity to his midrash telling of the Israelites' death at Sinai. In both cases we have an unexpected paradox: a single experience of God, either revelatory or eschatological, which is both destructive and constructive, harmful and helpful, at the same time. We can now define the nature of this paradox more precisely. Throughout both of these midrashic traditions – the death at Sinai and the wall of fire – the consistent theme is that Israel must be willing to accept the experience of God in destructive forms in order to gain the ultimate good of life, be it revelation or redemption. In several cases it seems to have been the same rabbis who advanced this message in both of these traditions, and it seems likely that both were widely known to and accepted by the rabbis in general. Yet, if the interpretations offered here are correct, this message was closely tied to esoteric concerns when revelation was being discussed, but totally divorced from esoteric concerns when redemption was the subject of interest. This indicates the possibility that the idea of God as the coincidence of opposites – the source of both good and evil simultaneously – was an independent theme in rabbinic religious thought and religious experience, one which could be related to various aspects of life, both exoteric and esoteric. Having seen how this theme could be invoked to illuminate the religious experience of the past and future, we would like to know what role it might have played in guiding the rabbinic present. We shall now turn to an examination of the development of a midrashic motif which may offer one answer to that question.

VIII. HISTORY AND PARADOX IN RABBINIC MIDRASH

One of the principles underlying rabbinic thought and the rabbinic world-view is that God guides the events of human history according to certain basic and constant patterns. A corollary to this is that these patterns can be learned by studying God's guidance of history in the past, as recorded in the Bible. One who knows the patterns as manifest in the past can then better understand the historical present and predict the historical future. Thus Johann Maier, in his recent *Geschichte der jüdischen Religion*, begins his discussion of the rabbinic concept of history by saying:

> The frequent recollection of the past *Heilsgeschichte*, as has so often been emphasized, was not based on an emptiness of the historical present; it was not a flight to resigned contemplation of past greatness. The deeds of God in the past were conceived mainly as paradigms of divine activity and as a guarantee and promise of God's intervention in history in the present and in the future.[1]

The searching of the Biblical text for such paradigms of divine activity and promises of divine intervention was a central element in the process of rabbinic midrash. Through what I. Heinemann has termed "creative historiography," many such paradigmatic patterns were discovered,[2] some of which served especially as a guarantee of future redemption for Israel in spite of the disappointments of the present. In fact, one of the most important tasks of the rabbinic *darshanim* was the use of the paradigmatic Biblical past to find connections between the present and the eschatological future. Many Palestinian Jews, especially after the Hadrianic persecutions following the failure of Bar-Kochba's revolt, must have asked how they could realistically expect a fulfillment of the divine promises of redemption when their national fortunes had fallen so low. The rabbis' attempts to prove the reliability of God's promises on the basis of the Biblical past and in light of the present are reflected in various midrashic traditions. We shall examine the history and development of one of these traditions.

Rabbinic literature indicates that the Jews of late antiquity, like their descendants in more recent times, often evaluated contemporary events by the standard of "Is it good or bad for the Jews?". That is, they asked whether a given phenomenon promoted the welfare of the Jewish community in the present and whether it promoted the likelihood of eschatological redemption in the near future. Thus they

---

[1] Johann Maier, *Geschichte der jüdischen Religion*, p. 179.
[2] I. Heinemann, *Darkei Ha'aggadah*, pp. 15—95.

may have tended to impose on the variegated experience of life a fundamentally dualistic value categorization, whereby every phenomenon in their world could be labelled either positive or negative for the Jewish community. (Of course there may have been significant internal disagreement as to precisely which phenomena were good and which were bad for the group as a whole, but the fact of categorization would have been true for all.) It would have been the goal of the community and its leaders to promote the positive, whenever possible, and prevent the negative. This is, of course, the logical response that we would expect any human community to make to its contemporary history.

The tradition we shall examine, however, indicates that at least some of the rabbis did not follow this procedure, for they saw a pattern of divine action in history which was not logical but paradoxical. This pattern was expressed in the proverbial saying: "The Holy One blessed be He, with the very thing with which He injures He heals." In other words, the phenomena of our experience can not neatly be categorized into good and bad "for the Jews," since God uses the very same phenomenon both for positive and for negative purposes. Only the result of an action, not the agency by which the action is carried out, can be judged to be clearly good or bad. This pattern is consistently contrasted with the pattern of human activity, for human beings must use one agency to harm and a different agency to repair harm. Thus we may say that human beings act logically, while God acts paradoxically.

The earliest attributed expression of this tradition in the midrash is that of R. Joshua b. Levi:

> R. Joshua b. Levi said: Come and see that the Holy One blessed be He is not like flesh and blood. A man of flesh and blood injures with a knife and heals with a poultice. But the Holy One blessed be He, with the very thing with which He injures He heals, as it is said, "For I will restore health to you and your wounds I will heal, says the Lord" (Jer. 30:17). Joseph was sold only because of a dream, as it is said, "They said to one another, 'Here comes this dreamer . . . Come let us sell him.'" (Gen. 37:19,27). After he came to reign only because of a dream, as it is said, "after two whole years, Pharaoh dreamed" (Gen. 41:1).[3]

The tradition is often associated with Jer. 30:17 as a proof-text, but nowhere else is it associated with the story of Joseph. Thus it seems unlikely that R. Joshua b. Levi's midrash represents the beginning of the tradition; rather he seems to have been applying a pre-existing tradition (including its proverbial expression and proof-text) to a particular Biblical story which illustrates it.[4]

Perhaps the Mekilta d'Rabbi Ishamel has a *prima facie* claim to embody the oldest version of the tradition, since it is the only tannaitic text in which the tradition appears:

---

[3] Tan. Vayesheb 9 end.

[4] R. Joshua b. Levi may have chosen this particular illustration to stress the importance of dreams, as he did elsewhere; cf. Wilhelm Bacher, PA, III, pp. 181, 188.

"And the Lord looked down upon the host of the Egyptians" (Ex. 14:24): Come and see that the healing of the Holy One blessed be He is not like the healing of flesh and blood. The healing of flesh and blood — he does not heal with that with which he injures. Rather he injures with a knife and heals with a poultice. But the Holy One blessed be He is not like this — that with which He injures is the very thing with which He heals. When He injured Job He only injured him with a whirlwind, as it is said, "For he crushes me with a whirlwind and multiplies my wounds without cause" (Job 9:17). When He healed him He only healed with a whirlwind, as it is said, "And the Lord answered Job from out of the whirlwind" (Job 38:1). When he dispersed Israel He only dispersed them with clouds, as it is said, "How the Lord in his anger has set the daughter of Zion under a cloud" (Lam. 2:1). Yet when He gathers them in He only gathers them in with clouds, as it is said, "Who are these that fly like a cloud and like doves to their windows?" (Isa. 60:8). . . . When He blesses Israel He only blesses them with a look, as it is said, "Look down from your holy habitation, from heaven, and bless your people Israel" (Dt. 26:15). Yet when He punishes Egypt He only punishes them with a look, as it is said, "And the Lord looked down upon the host of the Egyptians."[5]

This pericope is unusual in that it centers on the theme of a single individual or group being both injured and healed by the same agency, which is the central theme of the tradition in all its appearances, but it concludes with an example of the same agency (a divine "look") injuring one group and aiding a different group. This conclusion was necessary to make the tradition applicable to the particular verse (Exod. 14:24) on which it is a comment here. But since the theme had to be altered to make it fit that verse, it seems highly unlikely that the tradition could have originated as a comment on that verse. That is, we do not have the original version of the tradition here either. Again a pre-existing tradition has been applied to a new context, and its point has been changed in the process.[6]

---

[5] Mek. Vay'hi B'shalah 5, pp. 107, 108; cf. Tan. B'shalah 23.

[6] The only other midrash which contrasts Dt. 26:15 and Ex. 14:24 in this way is one attributed to R. Alexandrai:

> R. Alexandrai said: Great is the power of those who tithe, for they turn a curse into a blessing. For wherever the term "look down" is used it is a term denoting suffering, as it is said . . . "And the Lord looked down upon the host of the Egyptians" . . . Except for this one verse: "Look down from Your holy habitation, from heaven, and bless Your people." (Tan. Ki Tissa 14; cf. Ex. R 41.1 and TJ Ma'aser Sheni 56c).

R. Alexandrai seems to have been active in Lydda, where R. Joshua b. Levi taught, and he transmitted many sayings of R. Joshua b. Levi; cf. art. "Alexandrai," *Encyclopedia Judaica*, 1972, I, col. 588 and Bacher, PA, I, p. 194. Thus he must have known the tradition that God injures and heals with the same thing, yet he did not use it here. This may indicate that the combination of that tradition with the Dt. 26:15/Ex. 14:24 tradition occurred after R. Alexandrai's time, perhaps by someone who knew both these traditions circulating in the Lydda school. For post-tannaitic development of the Mekilta, see Ch. Albeck, *Untersuchungen über die halakischen Midraschim*. The inner consistency of the midrashim of both rabbis of Lydda, compared with the inner inconsistency of the Mekilta pericope, makes it unlikely that the latter preceded the former. This would make R. Joshua b. Levi's

It seems, then, that none of our extant texts preserves the original version of the tradition under study. Yet from the early versions which we have just examined we can hypothesize the elements contained in the original version: the proverbial statement contrasting divine and human ways, the mention of the "knife" and "poultice" (which appears in nearly every extant version of the tradition), Biblical illustrations pertaining to the fate of individuals and the Israelite nation going from exile to redemption, and perhaps the reference to Jer. 30:17. Because each version employs different Biblical illustrations, we have no way to determine which Biblical passages were originally associated with the tradition; thus the illustrations are of no help in determining the original context of the tradition. The "knife/poultice" motif indicates that the tradition, as originally conceived, referred to God's actions as analogous to that of a surgeon.[7] God, like the surgeon, is acting for the ultimate benefit of His people, but in the process He must do something that appears to be injurious, although He will then heal the injury. The difference, of course, is God's paradoxical way of using precisely the same agency to injure and heal; there is no difference between that which serves as a knife and that which serves as the poultice. This is really all we can say about the original intent of the tradition.

However its original meaning may be illuminated by another tradition whose origin can be dated more precisely, for we know that its author was R. Simeon b. Gamliel, patriarch of Palestinian Judaism during the second half of the second century. The best preserved version of R. Simeon's tradition appears in the Mekilta d'Rabbi Ishmael as a comment on Exodus 15:23−25: "When they came to Marah [literally "bitterness"] they could not drink the water of Marah because it was bitter . . . and the Lord showed [Moses] a tree and he threw it into the water and the water became sweet." The early rabbinic commentators on this passage were concerned to determine exactly what kind of tree was involved. Before R. Simeon b. Gamliel's time three opinions had been offered that we know of: a willow,[8] an olive,[9] and an *hardapni* (variously identified as ivy, laurel, or oleander).[10] All of these are bitter or

---

midrash the oldest extant version of our tradition, though it is certainly not the original version.

[7] The Hebrew word *'izmal*, translated here as "knife," refers especially to a surgeon's scalpel; cf. Marcus Jastrow, *A Dictionary of the Targumim, the Talmud Babli and Yerushalmi, and the Midrashic Literature*, p. 46.

[8] This was the opinion of R. Joshua, as recorded in Mek. B'shalah Vayosa 1; Mek. RS 103; Ex. R 23.3; Tan. B'shalah 24. Tan. B B'shalah 18 reported R. Joshua's opinion erroneously.

[9] "R. Eliezer of Modi'im says: It was an olive tree, for there is no tree more bitter than the olive tree." This passage appears in all sources cited in the preceding note.

[10] The Targum Pseudo-Jonathan to Exodus 15:25 reads: "And the Lord showed him a bitter tree of *'ardapni*." This tradition was reported in the name of various rabbis in the sources cited in n. 8 above. On the translation of *"hardapni"* (also known as *"'ardapani"* and *"hardopeni"*) see Jastrow, *A Dictionary*, p. 366; S. M. Lehrman, *Midrash Rabbah, Exodus,*

poisonous plants. After recording these and other opinions, the Mekilta pericope
continues:

> R. Simeon b. Gamliel says: Come and see how different are the ways of the Holy One
> blessed be He from the ways of flesh and blood. A man of flesh and blood cures something
> bitter with something sweet, but the Holy One blessed be He cures the bitter with the
> bitter. How can this be? He puts a damaging thing into something damaged in order to
> perform a miracle with it. In the same way you must interpret: "Now Isaiah said, 'Let
> them take a cake of figs and apply it to the boil'" (Isa. 38:21). But isn't it true that if you
> put a cake of figs on living flesh it will immediately decay? What can this mean? He put a
> damaging thing onto something damaged in order to perform a miracle with it. In the same
> way, "Then he went to the spring of water and threw salt in it and said, 'Thus says the
> Lord, "I have made this water wholesome"'" (II Kings 2:21). How is this curing? Isn't it
> true that if you put salt in good water it will immediately be spoiled? What can this mean?
> He put a damaging thing into something damaged in order to perform a miracle with it.[11]

R. Simeon, too, obviously thought that the tree Moses threw in the water was
bitter, but he went on to generalize the principle implicit in this detail and show its
applicability to other Biblical incidents. Here again we have a paradoxical pattern of
divine action in history; did R. Simeon intend it to be a paradigm by which contemporary events could be understood as well? As the highest ranking political
leader of his community he surely must have been deeply concerned with the
political situation of his day, and it seems fair to hypothesize that this concern
would be a major factor in his midrashic activity. Such an hypothesis sheds interesting light on this particular midrash, for it accords well with R. Simeon's political
position and political concerns. Certainly R. Simeon found the rule of Rome a bitter
reality; he is reported to have said of the Jews' sufferings under Rome: "If we had to
write [them] we would never finish."[12] Nevertheless he was against any further
attempts at rebellion and urged his people to acquiesce in Roman rule. His motives
were apparently compounded of political prudence, a concern to maintain his own

---

      p. 558; Louis Ginzberg, *The Legends of the Jews,* vol. III, p. 39. TB Hullin 58b affirms the
      poisonous quality of *hardapni.*

[11] Mek. B'shalah Vayosa 1, p. 156; also with minor variations in Tan. B'shalah 24. The same
      saying appears in the name of R. Ishmael b. R. Johanan b. Brokah, who was an associate of
      R. Simeon b. Gamliel; cf. Herman L. Strack, *Introduction to the Talmud and Midrash,*
      p. 116. R. Ishmael's version as we have it reads: "He puts a thing which is devoured into a
      thing which is devoured in order to perform a miracle with it." The critical apparatus in
      Mek. RS (p. 104) shows many variant readings for this phrase, so it is hard to reconstruct
      the original reading. Perhaps it was "He puts a thing which devours into a devoured thing";
      this would make the most sense. Given the confusion surrounding this passage, it seems
      most likely that the term "devoured" (Hebrew *mitakil*) is an erroneous transmission of
      R. Simeon b. Gamliel's term "damaged" (Hebrew *mithabel*). If so, it would establish that
      R. Simeon b. Gamliel's statement of the tradition was definitely the original version, while
      the version reported in R. Ishmael's name is a confused repetition. An abbreviated version
      of the saying attributed to R. Ishmael appears in Tan. B B'shalah 18.

[12] TB Shabbat 13b.

position of leadership, and a desire to avoid further war.[13] Thus he opposed any attempt to replace the bitter Roman rule with something "sweet" — either a conquering Persian government or a renewed independent Jewish government in Palestine. Rather he hoped to work through the existing government to improve the lot of the Jewish community; he hoped to use something bitter to cure the bitter situation.

It seems plausible that R. Simeon stated the general principle implicit in the Marah episode to prove that he, in pursuing this political course, was acting according to the ways of God rather than man.[14] And in fact the distinction between divine and human modes of activity is central to this midrash. It may reflect the position of the political "moderates" who urged reliance on divine activity to bring redemption and opposed human initiatives to "force the end."[15] But this position did not imply a total cessation of human political activity; certainly R. Simeon was too deeply involved in politics to support such a view. Rather it meant that, since God controls history by working through human political processes, obedience to the divine will should be the first principle of politics. Thus every midrash which claimed to ascertain the pattern of the divine will in history would have politically relevant applications; human beings, having ascertained the divine will, could then act in the political sphere as agents of that will. This seems to be the best context in which to interpret R. Simeon's midrash.

Having made this lengthy excursus, we may now return to our original tradition about God's paradoxical actions in history: "With the very thing with which He injures He heals." This tradition was known in the early third century, when the political "moderate" party was still quite strong and influential,[16] and it must have been understood to carry a meaning very much like that of R. Simeon's midrash.[17]

---

[13] For a discussion of these motives see Michael Avi-Yonah, *The Jews of Palestine,* pp. 67–69. On R. Simeon b. Gamliel's desire for peace, cf. ARN version A, ch. 28, p. 86 and Gen. R 100.8, p. 1293.

[14] Elisha's "curing" of the water, described in II Kings 2 : 21 and referred to by R. Simeon, is understood as *imitatio Dei* in Dt. R 10.3, Gen. R 77.1, p. 910, and Midrash Shmuel Ch. 29.

[15] On the background of this view, see Avi-Yonah, *Jews of Palestine,* pp. 68–71 and Nahum N. Glatzer, "The Attitude Toward Rome in Third Century Judaism," in Alois Dempf *et al.,* eds., *Politische Ordnung und menschliche Existenz.*

[16] Avi-Yonah, *Jews of Palestine,* pp. 70, 71, 128.

[17] While the two midrashic traditions, if taken as abstract theoretical statements, may have different meanings, Palestinian Jews of the late second or early third century would probably have understood their relevance to contemporary history quite similarly. Since they perceived themselves as injured but not yet healed, they would be unaware of the healing properties of that which had injured them, and thus they would perceive it as "bitter." Later tradents apparently understood them as being variants of the same idea, for they were combined rather indiscriminately in the same pericope in several midrash collections: Ex. R 23.3 and 50.3, Tan B'shalah 24, Tan. B B'shalah 18.

Thus we may propose that its original intent should be interpreted in a similar vein. The lesson of the tradition would have been easily understood as politically relevant: since God had used Rome to injure Israel so badly, He could be expected to use Rome to heal Israel as well. To look for another agency (a Persian government or an independent Jewish government) as a remedy for the injury would be a logical but merely human procedure; it would deny the efficacy of paradoxical divine action in history. Thus nations could not simply be categorized as good or bad "for the Jews" — the very nation that had been the depth of evil might yet become the agent of divine redemption.

The later history of this tradition shows that it was not tied to any one political program or viewpoint. If it were seen as merely a theological polemic of the "moderates," we would expect to find it denied or contradicted by more "radical" rabbis and to drop out of currency when the "moderate" group lost influence. Yet nowhere in rabbinic literature is there a denial of its validity, and in fact it was repeated by R. Levi, a leader among the rabbis who shaped their midrash into anti-Roman polemic, at a time when the "moderate" position was in sharp decline:[18]

> R. Joshua of Siknin in the name of R. Levi: . . . A king of flesh and blood punishes a man by means of witnesses[19] but the Holy One blessed be He punishes him by Himself — "I have wounded and I will heal" (Dt. 32:39). R. Berakiah said in the name of R. Levi: A man of flesh and blood wounds with a knife and heals with a poultice, but the Holy One blessed be He, with the very thing with which He injures He heals, as it is said, "For I will restore health to you and your wounds I will heal, says the Lord."[20]

Here again we find the distinction between human and divine activity, and again it seems to be part of an admonition against radical political action. For R. Levi elsewhere interpreted the four "adjurations" of the Song of Songs (2:7, 3:5, 5:8, 8:4) to refer to the four world kingdoms, under each of which God had adjured Israel not to rebel, and to the adjuration "that they should not reveal the end [i.e., calculate the time of the redemption] and that they should not force the end."[21] But R. Levi also indicated that God could act without any assistance from others; this may imply that human beings would have no part in the acts of redemptive history even as agents of God. Such a view accords well with R. Levi's apocalyptic orientation. The apocalyptists did not expect any peaceful or gradual amelioration of Israel's situation produced by human political activity within the existing structure. Rather they expected a sudden and cataclysmic reversal of the existing situation brought about by a breaking-in of the divine which would make human actions irrelevant. However, in accord with the usual apocalyptic view, R. Levi held that these events

---

[18] Avi-Yonah, *Jews of Palestine*, pp. 127–132.

[19] Some of the commentaries suggest amending "witnesses" (Hebrew *'edim*) to "servants" (Hebrew *'abadim*).

[20] Lev. R 18.5.

[21] Tan. B D'barim 3; TB K'tubot 111 a.

would only occur when the situation of the community had become desperate: "R. Levi said: The son of David will only come in a generation which is full of impudence and deserves to be exterminated."[22] Given this view, R. Levi could not have meant that God would use the Roman government, which was injuring Palestinian Jews so badly in his time, as a positive force to bring healing by peaceful political means. But he may very well have meant that the increasing suffering of the people as time went on was a necessary part of the process of redemption; God was using this injury itself as part of the process of healing and thereby using the same historical events to injure (in the short term view) and heal (in the long term view). Any given event could not be classified as good or bad, because its results in the long run might be very different from what they appeared to be in the present. We see, then, that this tradition could be used in different political contexts to make different points. The one constant element was the paradigmatic teaching that God does in fact work in this unique and (by human standards) paradoxical way to control history.

All of the texts we have seen thus far contain an implicit note of theodicy, for they claim that God will eventually compensate Israel for all of the suffering He has imposed upon it, albeit by paradoxical means. However at some indeterminable point[23] the tradition was adapted to make a more specific and elaborate theodicy, centering on the assertion that Israel, not God, was responsible for its own suffering and for the precise mode of suffering:

> "I, I am He who comforts you" (Isa. 51:12). The Holy One blessed be He said: Such is my craft — with the very thing with which I injure I heal . . . How can this be? Come and see: Israel sinned at the brooks, as it is said, "You that burn with lust among the oaks, under every green tree; who slay your children in the brooks, under the clefts of the rocks" (Isa. 57:5), and they were stricken at a brook, as it is said, "And Elijah brought them down to the brook Kishon and killed them there" (I Kings 18:40), yet they will be comforted at brooks, as it is said, "And on the banks on both sides of the river there will grow all kinds of trees for food" (Ezek. 47:12).[24]

The lengthy pericope continues in this vein offering many Biblical illustrations of the pattern of sin-punishment-redemption effected by the same agency.

---

[22] Song R 2.13.4; cf. PR Piska 1 end. In MT 17.10 and Lekah Tob on Numbers 23:17 R. Levi refers to the apocalyptic wars of Gog and Magog.

[23] The attribution at the end of the pericope to R. Tanhuma seems artificial and is most probably pseudepigraphal; Bacher does not include it in his exhaustive list of R. Tanhuma's proems in Pesikta Rabbati (PA, III, pp. 493–499). Thus the attribution is not useful in dating the pericope. Friedmann, in his edition of Pesikta Rabbati (158a n. 160), claims that similar pericopes in Lam. R on 1:22 and PRK 16.11 drew on this pericope; this would give a *terminus ante quem* of the early fifth century. But it seems equally possible that Pesikta Rabbati (compiled in the sixth or seventh century) drew on these fifth-century compilations.

[24] PR 13.13; cf. Aggadat B'reshit 66.

The author's concern for the problem of theodicy apparently caused him to change the focus of the tradition and take a different apparoch to the problem of history. He was not so much concerned with the transition from present suffering to future relief and the divine pattern which guarantees that relief. Rather he looked to the past to discover the cause of present suffering and the dynamic by which past events determine both present and future. The dynamic which he found is actually a compound of two divine patterns — our tradition, which he states explicitly at the outset, and the implicit tradition that God punishes "measures for measure."[25] This latter tradition, which is very common in rabbinic texts, serves to underscore the unity of history by showing that all events are related to each other because all are under the guidance of the one God. It puts "an emphasis on the signs which prove the 'reciprocal interconnection' of matters which appear to be unrelated to each other . . . in order to show the finger of God precisely in events where we would not take it into account."[26] And it seems fair to say that the tradition we have been examining serves the same function of proving the unity in all historical events. It certainly claims that the "finger of God" is at work in situations where we logically would not expect it. By combining these two traditions the author of this pericope has stressed the unity in human history particularly strongly.

In looking to the past and enlarging the scope of relevant historical events, however, the author did not ignore the future redemption. The promise of redemption is central in his theodicy, but he seems to be making the implicit point that future relief from suffering would not have been necessary if Israel had not sinned in the first place. It is sin which has initiated the historical dynamic which makes God's paradoxical work necessary. In a sense, then, the particular form of Israel's sin determined not only the form of punishment — which is logical by human standards — but also the form of redemption and relief from that punishment — which is surely paradoxical by human standards. This pericope, then, uses Biblical paradigms to imply a rather complex theory of history which combines both logical and paradoxical patterns of divine action into a unified conceptual whole. The difficulty in dating the pericope makes it difficult to say anything about what political implications it might have had. The teaching that Israel's political subjugation was due to its own sins had long been known as an idea which would promote political quietism and deter rebellion.[27] We have seen that our tradition, with its distinction between divine and human action, tended to have the same implication. Yet the author of this pericope did nothing to make this point explicit in any way. Moreover, he seems to have chosen Biblical texts to illustrate the redemption pole of his schema with little regard for concrete political-eschatological

---

[25] Cf. Ch. VII, n. 17 above.

[26] Heinemann, *Darkei Ha'aggadah*, p. 69.

[27] For the background of the idea, see Jacob Neusner, *A Life of Rabban Yohanan ben Zakkai*, ch. 7, and S. W. Baron, *A Social and Religious History of the Jews*, vol. II, pp. 113–116, 126–128.

traditions known in rabbinic literature.[28] It would seem that he was more interested in the "philosophical" problems of history and theodicy than the political problems of his day. In pursuing these problems, he discovered that there is both logic and paradox in God's guidance of history; only by using the same thing to both injure and heal (the things by which Israel had sinned) can God be both just and merciful to His people and faithful to the promises by which He guides their destiny.

Thus far we have been concentrating on the relevance of our tradition to the understanding of the history of the Jewish community as a whole. However the tradition may also be applied to the history of individuals' lives; we saw, for example, references to Joseph and Job in texts cited above. Knowing this paradoxical pattern, an individual might evaluate his own experiences quite differently than human logic would suggest. Beyond this, we also find traditions which suggest that individuals who know this pattern would adopt it as a rule for certain actions in their own lives. At least two Biblical figures were found to serve as paradigms for this *imitatio Dei*:

> The Holy One blessed be He cures without a poultice, and Elisha cured Naaman without a poultice. The Holy One blessed be He sweetens the bitter [with the bitter] and Elisha sweetened the bitter [with the bitter].[29]

But the more important paradigmatic figure was Moses, who played a central role in rabbinic life as the paradigm for all proper spiritual conduct:[30]

> You find that a man of flesh and blood injures with a knife and heals with a poultice. But the Holy One blessed be He is not like this; rather with the very thing with which He injures He heals. Thus you find that when they came to Marah . . . the Holy One blessed be He said to Moses: My ways are not like the ways of flesh and blood. Now you have to learn this, as it is said, "And the Lord showed him a tree." It does not say "showed him" [*vayor'ehu*] but "showed him" [*vayorehu*] — He taught him [*horehu*] about His ways . . . And in the same way the righteous, with the very thing with which they provoke they also make amends. You should know that Moses, when he provoked [God] provoked with the word "then," as it is said, "But since then, when I came to Pharaoh to speak in Your name" (Ex. 5:23). Moses said: I provoked with "then" so I will make amends with "then" and sing a song. Therefore it is said, "Then Moses sang" (Ex. 15:1).[31]
> "Then Moses sang." This is what Scripture says: "Your lips distill wild honey, my bride" (Song 4:11). Moses said: Lord of the universe, with the very thing with which I sinned before You I praise You . . . Come and see the way of the righteous: with the very thing

---

[28] In fact the verses were chosen to create an elaborate literary schema unrelated to any political concerns; cf. the notes of Friedmann, PR 157b−158a, and W. G. Braude, *Pesikta Rabbati*, vol. II, p. 658.

[29] Dt. R 10.3. The words in parentheses are supplied on the basis of the parallel in Gen. R 77.1, p. 910. Cf. Midrash Shmuel ch. 29.

[30] See Jacob Neusner, *Talmudic Judaism in Sassanian Babylonia, Essays and Studies*, pp. 53, 62.

[31] Tan. B'shalah 24.

with which they sin they also make amends. Thus: "Your lips distill wild honey, my
bride." From whom do they learn? From the Holy One blessed be He, for with the very
thing with which He injures He heals.[32]

This tradition is particularly enigmatic. It is impossible to date it,[33] and it seems
unrelated to any other rabbinic tradition which might indicate its source or
context.[34] The two pericopes are both composite works incorporating several
traditions which were probably originally separate; the saying "The righteous, with
the very thing with which they sin [provoke] they make amends" was probably one
of these component traditions. This makes it most likely that it circulated as a
proverbial saying for some indefinite time before becoming attached to the other
component traditions found here. Thus even if we could date the pericopes it
would not help us understand the origin of the application of our tradition to "the
righteous." But the problem of dating is not so serious here, because the tradition
has been divorced from any concern with political relevance.

In a sense we might go further and say that it has been divorced from any
concern with history at all. It deals only with the problem of antonement for sin on
the individual level and how the *imitatio Dei* may serve as an effective means of
atonement. It might also be said that the tradition has lost its element of paradox,
since it is quite logical that atonement, like punishment, should be offered "measure
for measure." But there is still some sense of paradox here, for the same phenomenon may become both an agent of sin and an agent of atonement. This version of
the tradition seems to say that if your right hand offends you should not cut it off –
it is not wholly and irredeemably evil – but rather make it a source of atonement –
and thereby experience its positive as well as negative possibilities. Moreover, since
this pattern of behavior is an imitation of God, it is possible to understand God's
actions in history as paradigmatic for this pattern too. An example of this is the
eschatological midrash offered by R. Isaac Nappaha:

> The Holy One blessed be He said: I must make restitution for the fire which I kindled. I
> kindled a fire in Zion, as it is said, "And He kindled a fire in Zion which consumed its
> foundations" (Lam. 4:11), and I am destined to rebuild her with fire in the future, as it is

---

[32] Ex. R. 23.3.

[33] The pericope in Ex. R 23.3 includes a parable attributed to R. Levi b. Hayta; according to
Bacher (PA, III, p. 734) he is the R. Levi b. Hiyya who lived in the late fourth century.
However the point of the parable is not really the same as the point of the pericope as a
whole, so it seems possible that the parable was developed independent of the tradition
about "the way of the righteous," the two having been combined by a later redactor. Thus
we can not use the parable to fix a *terminus ante quem* for the pericope as a whole.

[34] It bears the same resemblance to R. Judah's teaching, cited in TB Yoma 86b, that true
repentance means to refrain from sin in the exact same situation in which one had
previously sinned: "with the same woman, at the same time, in the same place." But the
two are not at all similar enough to suggest any historical filiation.

said, "For I will be to her a wall of fire round about, says the Lord, and I will be the glory within her" (Zech 2:9).[35]

This midrash implies that God's acts of injury against Israel, like the sins of men, demand some kind of atonement, and that the proper atonement is rendered "measure for measure"; the same agency is used both to do injury and to repair the injury. This provides us with another view of the historical process in which logical and paradoxical concepts are harmonized. But the idea that this particular pattern of the divine guidance of history forms the specific paradigm for the atonement of the righteous is never found explicitly in rabbinic literature.

In summary, it seems clear that the conception of God acting paradoxically in history was known and applied throughout the formative period of rabbinic midrash. While it may have originated in one historical situation, it was later employed in a variety of new situations. It is, of course, merely one of many paradigmatic patterns found in rabbinic midrash. While the existence of such paradigms in the Bible was an article of faith common to all the rabbis, the nature of the particular patterns which were true and significant was by no means a matter of common agreement. Any attempt to understand "the rabbinic view of history" must take into account all of the various rabbinic views. The foregoing discussion is an attempt to point up the existence of one such view which has hitherto received little, if any, notice in scholarly discussion on the subject. Many such analyses of different traditions will be necessary before we are in a position to make any comprehensive judgments on the problem of history in rabbinic thought.

---

[35] TB Babba Kamma 60b. The same midrashic motif is incorporated into the ends of PRK 16.11 and Lam. R on 1:22; cf. n. 23 above. It also appears in PR 30.3, and in an ancient version of the Amidah for the ninth of Ab as recorded in TP Berakot 4.3, 8a and TP Taʿaniot 2.2, 65c.

CONCLUSION

The study presented here is a small contribution to a project which is still in its earliest stages: the elucidation of the relationship between Merkabah mysticism and other facets of rabbinic Judaism. Yet I think enough has been said for us at least to frame the questions properly. It seems evident that in the midrash disparate elements of both esoteric and exoteric natures have been fused together. This was not merely an *ad hoc* pastiche of elements which remained incompatible. Rather it was a true synthesis in which the parts were blended to form a new harmonious unity. And this synthesis proceeded as much by the conscious exclusion of esotericism from some midrashim as by the conscious inclusion of it in others. But the literature of midrash is most significant to us as a reflection of the religious experience, value structure, and world view of those who created it. Thus it seems fair to say that in their own lives those who were involved in Merkabah mysticism must have sought and to some extent gained the same kind of harmonious integration.

While the historical questions, particularly of the origins of Merkabah mysticism, will continue to plague us, we can ask some meaningful questions of a relatively non-historical nature. Regardless of when and in what social locus Merkabah mysticism developed, we can ask what the basic experiences, values, and world view inherent in the mystical texts are, and we can ask the same questions about the exoteric rabbinic literature as well. Knowing that at some point these two basic complexes were integrated in individual lives, we can then ask the central question of what a life based upon such an integration would have been like. I have already made a few tentative suggestions along these lines here, but there is much more that needs to be done.

In pursuing this problem, we must remember that Merkabah mysticism, while it was not truly "Jewish Gnosticism," did incorporate a number of elements of Gnosticism, and in some cases this was on a more than superficial level. The values and world view inherent in Gnosticism (and other similar movements of late antiquity) must have exercised a strong attraction upon many Jews. Thus I think the crucial problem is to describe the integration of these attractive features into the enduring structure of exoteric Judaism in both synchronic and diachronic terms. Such a description would show, I think, that some fundamental values of Gnosticism were able to enrich values of rabbinic Judaism, while the opposite process was at work perhaps even more strongly.

In effecting this synthesis of apparent opposites, the Jewish community must have been able to find from the beginning some points of common contact; otherwise it is hard to see how such a synthesis could have ever occurred. Any meaningful description of rabbinic Judaism will have to take into account not only the end product of this process of harmonization, but also its starting point. I have tried to suggest here one potential common basis, and one that is particularly appropriate: the conception of God, and the experience of God, as itself a synthesis of opposites. It has been clear throughout that the divine in the esoteric traditions is markedly "numinous," embracing the opposing elements of *tremendum* and *fascinans*. Yet it also became clear that a similar opposition was posited and reconciled in traditions which seem to show no influence of esotericism. Thus I posit as an hypothesis that this motif existed in rabbinic Judaism independently of the influence of Merkabah mysticism or other esoteric tendencies, though it may well have enabled those tendencies to take root. If we see rabbinic Judaism (or at least one dimension of it) as a complex inter-play of esoteric and exoteric factors, we will want to look closely at the motif of *"coincidentia oppositorum"* in both its esoteric and exoteric manifestations as an important instance of this broader dynamic.

It is difficult to assess just how important this motif was in rabbinic Judaism, though its presence in some degree can not be denied. But I think it is of particular importance that we examine with great care the significance that this paradoxical kind of experience might have had in rabbinic Judaism. Surely one of the greatest values of studying rabbinic literature is the opportunity to understand a wide variety of viewpoints which may differ in important ways from our own. And I think it fair to say that our contemporary culture is based largely on an assumption of the irreconcilability of opposites. We have examined texts which suggest that in understanding the most crucial events of past, present, and future, and in under- standing the relationship of the human community to the divine, the *"coincidentia oppositorum"* points us to a more valid understanding of life. If this message can be found to play a significant role in rabbinic Judaism, it may present us with a new insight into the value of the rabbinic tradition as a challenge to some of our most fundamental assumptions.

In conclusion, I want to suggest one dimension of this challenge which is highlighted by a study of the place of mysticism in rabbinic Judaism. In the modern world (and in the modern study of religion) one often sees life in terms of two assumedly mutually exclusive categories, which may be labelled (though too broadly) as "world-affirming" and "world-denying." The former label is applied to those who, like the rabbis, are committed to playing an active role in the political, economic, and social processes of their community. The latter is given to those who, like the Gnostics, cultivate mystical states as a means of escaping from "this world" and its societal roles. In discussing the midrashim on the "death at Sinai" theme, I suggested that the attraction of the "world-denying" stance may lie largely in its ability to evoke a direct experience of *"coincidentia oppositorum,"* while the attraction of "world-affirmation" may arise from its rejection of *"coin- cidentia oppositorum"* and its consequent ability to provide meaningful structure for the community based on the irreconcilability of opposites. The rabbis found themselves attracted in varying measure to both of these stances, and the history of humanity suggests that both will exercise some attraction in every culture; proponents of both can certainly be found in our own society today.

Yet the rabbis were not bound by the limited choices which the modern person may see: either to reject one alternative altogether, or to alternate between the two by indulging in periodic ecstasies unrelated to one's ongoing societal roles. Rather they sought a true harmonization of these two basic attitudes within their own lives. By integrating the attractive elements of a "world-denying" stance into their basically "world-affirming" tradition, the rabbis were able to effect what I would call the ultimate coincidence of opposites: to affirm and yet simultaneously deny the validity of "*coincidentia oppositorum*" as the basic truth about life. In doing so, they were able to enrich the meaning of mysticism by giving it a grounding in everyday life; their ecstatic states may have been in some sense flights from the world, but more fundamentally they were a means to strengthen the life of the community in the world. Ecstasy and everyday life thus constituted a single continuum, rather than two mutually exclusive states.

If, as some have suggested, the shattering strains and tensions of modern civilization stem from an inability to accept the unification of opposites, the contemporary interest in mysticism and ecstasy may represent a desire to regain this basic insight through direct experience. Yet if ecstatic states remain unconnected to the political, economic, and social life of the community they may prove fruitless and unsatisfying. The well-being of society may not be advanced by those who choose a "world-denying" path any more than by those are only "world-affirming." But neither can it be advanced by those who alternate between these two as mutually exclusive states. The challenge posed to us by the rabbinic tradition may be to discover some way in our own day to affirm both ecstasy and the ordinary life of society in an integrated way – to affirm and yet simultaneously deny the coincidence of opposites as the foundational truth for human society and human life.

In the final analysis, the value of my studies will be judged by their ability to provoke further investigation of these kinds of problems, as well as by their ability to point in some small way toward satisfactory solutions.

BIBLIOGRAPHY

Primary Sources Cited

Abot D'Rabbi Nathan, Ed. S. Schechter. 1887; 3rd Rev. Ed., New York, 1967.

Aggadat B'reshit, Ed. S. Buber. Cracow, 1902.

Aggadat Shir Hashirim, Ed. S. Schechter. Cambridge, 1896.

Beit Hamidrash, Ed. Adolph Jellinek. 1853–1877; 3rd Ed., 6 vols., Jerusalem: Wahrmann Books, 1967.

Deuteronomy Rabbah, Wilna (Romm), 1887.

Deuteronomy Rabbah, Ed. Saul Lieberman. 1940; 3rd Ed., Jerusalem: Wahrmann Books, 1974.

Ecclesiastes Rabbah, Wilna (Romm), 1887.

3 Enoch or the Hebrew Book of Enoch, Ed. H. Odeberg. 1928; Reprint, New York: Ktav Publishing Co., 1973.

Esther Rabbah, Wilna (Romm), 1887.

Exodus Rabbah, Wilna (Romm), 1887.

Genesis Rabbah, Ed. J. Theodor and Ch. Albeck. 1903–1936; 2nd Ed., 3 vols., Jerusalem: Wahrmann Books, 1965.

Heikalot Rabbati, Ed. A. Jellinek. *Beit Hamidrash*, vol. III, pp. 83–120.

Heikalot Rabbati, Ed. S. A. Wertheimer. *Battei Midrashot*, vol. I, pp. 67–137.

Lamentations Rabbah, Wilna (Romm), 1887.

Leviticus Rabbah, Ed. M. Margulies. Jerusalem, 1953.

Ma'aseh Merkabah, Ed. G. Scholem. *Jewish Gnosticism, Merkabah Mysticism, and Talmudic Tradition*, pp. 103–117.

Maseket Heikalot, Ed. A. Jellinek. *Beit Hamidrash*, vol. II, pp. 40–47.

Mekilta D'Rabbi Ishmael, Ed. H. S. Horowitz and I. A. Rabin. 1930; 2nd Ed., Jerusalem: Wahrmann Books, 1970.

Mekilta D'Rabbi Simeon Bar Yohai, Ed. J. N. Epstein and E. Z. Melamed. Jerusalem, 1955.

Midrash Hagadol on Exodus, Ed. M. Margulies. Jerusalem, 1967.

Midrash Lekah Tob, Ed. S. Buber. Wilna, 1879.

Midrash Tanhuma. 1833; Reprint, Jerusalem: Lewin Epstein, 1974.

Midrash Tanhuma Haqadom, Ed. S. Buber. Wilna, 1885.

Midrash T'hillim, Ed. S. Buber. Wilna, 1891.

Midrashei Ge'ulah, Ed. J. Eben-Shmuel. 2nd Ed.; Jerusalem: Hozeit Mosad Bialik, 1954.

Midrash Shmuel, Ed. S. Buber. Lemberg, 1893.

Mishnah, New York, 1965.

Numbers Rabbah, Wilna (Romm), 1887.

Perek Eliahu, Ed. J. Eben-Shmuel. *Midrashei Ge'ulah*, pp. 49–54.

Pesikta D'Rab Kahana, Ed. B. Mandelbaum. 2 vols., New York: Jewish Theological Seminary of America, 1962.

Pesikta D'Rab Kahana, Ed. S. Buber. Lyck, 1868.

Pesikta Rabbati, Ed. M. Friedmann. 1880; Reprint Tel-Aviv, 1963.

Pirkei D'Rabbi Eliezer, Ed. D. Luria. Warsaw, 1852.

Re'uyot Yehezkiel, Ed. I. Gruenwald. *Temirin* 1 (1972), pp. 101–139.

Ruth Rabbah, Wilna (Romm), 1887.

Seder Eliahu Rabbah, Ed. M. Friedmann. Vienna, 1902.

Sefer Eliahu, Ed. J. Eben-Shmuel. *Midrashei Ge'ulah*, pp. 29–48.

Sefer Merkabah Shelemah, Ed. S. Mussaioff. Jerusalem, 1921.

Sefer Zerubbabel, Ed. J. Eben-Shmuel. *Midrashei Ge'ulah*, pp. 55–88.

Sifre on Deuteronomy, Ed. L. Finkelstein. Berlin, 1939.

Sifre on Numbers, Ed. H. S. Horowitz. 1917; Reprint, Jerusalem: Wahrmann Books, 1966.

Song of Songs Rabbah, Wilna (Romm), 1887.

Babylonian Talmud, New York, 1923.

Palestinian Talmud, Krotoshin, 1866.

Tosefta, Ed. M. S. Zuckermandel. 1881; New Ed., Jerusalem: Wahrmann Books, 1970.

Yalkut Shimeoni, 2 vols., Jerusalem, 1970.

Ammianus Marcellinus, *Rerum Gestarum Libra*, Ed. Eyssenhardt. Berlin, 1871.

Gregory of Nazianzus *Oratio* (Migne, *Patrologia Graeca,* vol. 35).

Philo *De Posteritii Cainii.*

Philo *De Somniis.*

Philo *Quaestiones et Solutiones in Exodam.*

Rufinus *Historia Ecclesiastica.*

Secondary Sources Cited

Albeck, Chanoch. *Untersuchungen über die halakischen Midrashim.* Berlin: Akademieverlag, 1927.

Alexander, P. S. "The Historical Setting of the Hebrew Book of Enoch." *Journal of Jewish Studies.* 28 (1977).

"Alexandrai." *Encyclopaedia Judaica.* 1972. Vol. 2.

Aptowitzer, A. "Beit Miqdash Shel Ma'aleh Al Pi Ha'aggadah." *Tarbiz.* 2 (1930).

Avi-Yonah, Michael. *The Jews of Palestine.* New York: Schocken Books, 1976.

Bacher, Wilhelm. *Die Agada der Palästinensischen Amoräer.* 1892; reprint ed., 3 vols. Hildesheim: Georg Olms Verlagsbuchhandlung, 1965.

Baron, Salo W. *A Social and Religious History of the Jews.* 2nd ed., rev. and enl. 16 vols. New York: Columbia University Press, 1952ff.

Braude, W. G., Trans. *Pesikta Rabbati.* Yale Judaica Series, Vol. XVIII. New Haven: Yale University Press, 1968.

Braude, W. G., Trans. *The Midrash on Psalms.* Yale Judaica Series, Vol. XIII. 2 vols. New Haven: Yale University Press, 1959.

Braude, W. G. and I. J. Kapstein, Trans. *Pesikta de-Rab Kahana.* Philadelphia: Jewish Publication Society of America, 1975.

Bultmann, Rudolph. "Zur Geschichte der Lichtsymbolik im Altertum." *Philologus* 97 (1948).

Chernus, I. "Redemption and Chaos: A Study in the Symbolism of the Rabbinic Aggada." Ph. D. Dissertation, Temple University, 1975.

Cohen, A. Trans. *Midrash Rabbah, Lamentations.* London: Soncino Press, 1939.

Eben-Shoshan, Abraham, *Hamilon Hehadash.* 7 vols. Jerusalem: Kiryath Sepher, 1967.

Elbogen, I. M. *Hat'filah B'yisrael B'hitpathutah Hahistorit*. Translated by Yehoshuah Amir. Tel Aviv: Hozeit D'vir, 1972.

Eliade, Mircea. *Rites and Symbols of Initiation: The Mysteries of Birth and Rebirth*. Translated by Willard R. Trask. Harper Torchbooks. New York: Harper and Row, 1965.

Eliade, Mircea. *Myths, Dreams and Mysteries*. Translated by Phillip Mairet. Harper Torchbooks. New York: Harper and Row, 1967.

Eliade, Mircea. *The Sacred and the Profane*. Translated by Willard R. Trask. Harper Torchbooks. New York: Harper and Row, 1961.

Eliade, Mircea. *Cosmos and History*. Translated by Willard R. Trask. Harper Torchbooks. New York: Harper and Row, 1959.

Friedlander, Gerald, Trans. *Pirke de Rabbi Eliezer*. 1916; reprint ed., New York: Hermon Press, 1965.

Ginzberg, Louis. *The Legends of the Jews*. 7 vols. Philadelphia: The Jewish Publication Society of America, 1909–1938.

Ginzberg, Louis. *On Jewish Law and Lore*. Meridian Books. Cleveland and New York: The World Publishing Co., 1962.

Ginzberg, Louis. *Perushim V'hidushim B'yerushalmi*. 4 vols. New York: Jewish Theological Seminary of America, 1941.

Glatzer, Nahum N. "The Attitude Toward Rome in Third Century Judaism." *Politische Ordnung und menschliche Existenz*. Edited by Alois Dempf *et al*. Munich: Beck, 1962.

Goldberg, A. M. *Untersuchungen über die Vorstellung von der Schekhina in der frühen rabbinischen Literatur*. Studia Judaica, vol. 5. Berlin: Walter de Gruyter & Co., 1969.

Goldin, Judah, Trans. *The Fathers According to Rabbi Nathan*. New York: Schocken Books, 1955.

Gruenwald, Ithamar. "Knowledge and Vision." *Israel Oriental Studies* 3 (1973).

Gruenwald, Ithamar. Review of *Rivalität zwischen Engeln und Menschen*, by P. Schäfer. *Kiryat Sefer* 51 (1976).

Gruenwald, Ithamar. Review of *Rivalität zwischen Engeln und Menschen*, by P. Schäfer. *Études Juives* 132 (1973).

Gruenwald, Ithamar. "Yannai and Hekhaloth Literature." *Tarbiz* 36 (1967).

Halperin, David. "Merkabah and Ma'aseh Merkabah, According to Rabbinic Sources." Ph. D. Dissertation, University of California, Berkeley, 1977.

Heinemann, I. *Darkei Ha'aggadah*. 2nd ed. Jerusalem: Hozeit Magnes, 1954.

Heinemann, Joseph. *Aggadot V'toldotaihen*. Jerusalem: Keter Publishing House Ltd. 1974.

Heinemann, Joseph. *Hat'filah Bit'kufat Hatannaim V'ha'amoraim*. 2nd ed. Jerusalem: Magnes Press, 1967.

Herr, M. D. "Exodus Rabbah." *Encyclopaedia Judaica*. Vol. 6.

Herr, M. D. "Lamentations Rabbah." *Encyclopaedia Judaica*. Vol. 10.

Herr, M. D. "Tanhuma Yelammdenu." *Encyclopaedia Judaica*. Vol. 15.

Heschel, Abraham Joshua. *Torah Min Hashamayim B'aspeklaryah shel Hadorot (Theology of Ancient Judaism)*. 2 vols. London and New York: Soncino Press, 1962.

Jastrow, Marcus. *A Dictionary of the Targumim, the Talmud Babli and Yerushalmi, and the Midrashic Literature*. 1903; reprint ed., New York: The Judaica Press, 1971.

Jonas, Hans. "Delimination of the Gnostic Phenomenon – Typological and Historical." *Le Origini dello Gnosticismo*. Edited by Ugo Bianchi. Leiden: E. J. Brill, 1967.

Jonas, Hans. *The Gnostic Religion*. Third printing. Boston: Beacon Press, 1970.

Kadushin, Max. *The Rabbinic Mind*. New York: The Jewish Theological Seminary of America, 1952.

Klausner, Joseph. *The Messianic Idea in Israel.* Translated by W. F. Stinespring. New York: Macmillan Co., 1955.

Lehrman, S. M., Trans. *Midrash Rabbah, Exodus.* Soncino Press, 1939.

Lieberman, Saul. "Mishnat Shir Hashirim." In *Jewish Gnosticism, Merkabah Mysticism, and Talmudic Tradition* by Gershom Scholem.

Maier, Johann. *Geschichte der jüdischen Religion.* Berlin: Walter de Gruyter, 1972.

Maier, Johann. *Vom Kultus zur Gnosis.* Salzburg: Otto Müller Verlag, 1964.

Marcus, Ralph, Trans. Philo, *Questions and Answers on Exodus.* Cambridge: Harvard University Press, 1953.

Moore, G. F. *Judaism in the First Centuries of the Christian Era.* 3 vols. Cambridge: Harvard University Press, 1927.

McNamara, M. "Targums." *Interpreter's Dictionary of the Bible, Supplementary Volume.* Nashville: Abingdon Press, 1976.

Neher, Andre. "Le Voyage Mystique de Quatres." *Revue de l'Histoire des Religions* 140 (1951).

Neusner, Jacob. *A History of the Jews in Babylonia.* 5 vols. Studia Post-Biblica, vols. 9, 11, 12, 14, 15. Leiden: E. J. Brill, 1965–1970.

Neusner, Jacob. *A Life of Rabban Yohanan ben Zakkai.* 2 ed. compl. rev. Leiden: E. J. Brill, 1970.

Neusner, Jacob. *Talmudic Judaism in Sassanian Babylonia, Essays and Studies.* Leiden: E. J. Brill, 1976.

Puech, H. C. "Gnosis and Time." *Man and Time, Papers from the Eranos Yearbooks.* Bollingen Series xxx, edited by Henry Corbin, vol. 3. Princeton: Princeton University Press, 1957.

Saldarini, Anthony J., Trans. *The Fathers According to Rabbi Nathan. Version B.* E. J. Brill, 1975.

Sanders, E. P. *Paul and Palestinian Judaism: A Comparison of Patterns of Religion.* Philadelphia: Fortress Press, 1977.

Schäfer, Peter. *Rivalität zwischen Engeln und Menschen.* Studia Judaica, vol. 8. Berlin and New York: Walter de Gruyter, 1975.

Scholem, Gershom. *Jewish Gnosticism, Merkabah Mysticism, and Talmudic Tradition.* 2nd ed. New York: The Jewish Theological Summary of America, 1965.

Scholem, Gershom. "Jewish Theology Today." *The Jewish Tradition and its Relevance to Contemporary Life.* Santa Barbara, CA: The Center for the Study of Democratic Institutions/The Fund for the Republic, Inc., n. d.

Scholem, Gershom. *Kabbalah.* New York: Quadrangle/The New York Times Book Co., 1974.

Scholem, Gershom. *Major Trends in Jewish Mysticism.* 3rd ed. rev. New York: Schocken Books, 1961.

Scholem, Gershom. *The Messianic Idea in Judaism and Other Essays on Jewish Spirituality.* New York: Schocken Books, 1971.

Scholem, Gershom. *Von der Mystischen Gestalt der Gottheit.* Zürich: Rheinverlag, 1962.

Schubert, Kurt. "Jüdischer Hellenismus und jüdische Gnosis." *Wort und Wahreit* 6/7 (1963).

Schultz, Joseph P. "Angelic Opposition to the Ascension of Moses and the Revelation of the Law." *Jewish Quarterly Review* LXI (1971).

Silver, Daniel Jeremy and Martin, Bernard. *A History of Judaism.* 2 vols. New York: Basic Books, 1974.

Simon, Maurice, Trans. *Berakoth.* London: Soncino Press, 1940.

Simon, Maurice, Trans. *Midrash Rabbah, Song of Songs*. London: Soncino Press, 1939.

Spiegel, Shalom. *The Last Trial*. Translated by Judah Goldin. New York: Schocken Books, 1967.

Strack, Herman L. *Introduction to the Talmud and Midrash*. 1931; reprint ed., Harper Torchbooks, New York: Harper and Row, 1965.

Urbach, E. E. *Hazal, Pirke 'Emunot V'de'ot*. Jerusalem: Magnes Press, 1969.

Urbach, E. E. "Hamasoret al Torat Hasod Bit'kufat Hatannaim." *Studies in Mysticism and Religion presented to Gershom Scholem*. Edited by E. E. Urbach. Jerusalem: Magnes Press, 1967.

Van Baaren, Th. P. "Toward a Definition of Gnosticism." *Le Origini dello Gnosticismo*. Edited by Ugo Bianchi. Leiden: E. J. Brill, 1967.

Vermes, G. "Bible and Midrash: Early Old Testament Exegesis." *The Cambridge History of the Bible*. Vol. 1, Edited by P. R. Ackryod and C. F. Evans. London: Cambridge University Press, 1970.

Vermes, G. *Scripture and Tradition in Judaism*. Studia Post-Biblica, Vol. 4. Leiden: E. J. Brill, 1961.

Volz, Paul. *Die Eschatologie der Jüdischen Gemeinde im neutestamentlichen Zeitalter*. Tübingen: J. C. B. Mohr, 1934.

Wewers, G. A. *Geheimnis und Geheimhaltung im rabbinischen Judentum*. Berlin and New York: Walter de Gruyter, 1975.

Zunz, L. *Had'rashot B'yisrael*. Translated by Chanoch Albeck. Jerusalem: Mosad Bialik, 1947.

INDEX

MODERN SCHOLARS

RABBIS

SUBJECTS

teaching of, in heavenly academy 93–94, 94n
transcendence of 3, 31, 51
word of, as source of resurrection 41–43
Golden calf 4

Hadrianic persecution 36, 117n, 126
Heikalot, thresholds of 5, 7
Heimarmene 14
Heresy, danger of 13, 39, 47

Immortality
given to Israelites at Sinai 6n, 24–25, 52, 59, 82n
and Merkabah mysticism 24, 52, 59, 91
Isaac, binding of 35–36, 40
Isaiah 13, 14, 21

Jerusalem, in world to come 95–96, 109n, 110, 118, 119n, 123
Jewish Gnosticism 13, 15n, 16, 32, 74–75, 138
Job 128
Joseph 127
Julian, Emperor 115

Kabbalah 54

Levi, tribe of 28–29
Light, symbolism of 78, 83–84, 91–93; *see also* Shekinah, splendor of
Lightning 6, 7, 8, 42

Ma'aseh Merkabah 1, 21, 22, 27, 28, 30, 31, 40n, 82
Measure for measure, principle in aggada of 113, 123, 134, 137
Merkabah
ascent (descent) to 5–7, 10–13, 15, 24, 30, 39, 76, 81, 89–93
chambers (sections) of 20, 49
descent of, on Sinai 11, 19, 27–29
ox in 4
Metatron 9, 99
Moral interpretations of esoteric traditions 23, 43

Moses 3, 4, 11, 58, 68, 129–130, 135
as mediator of revelation 33, 34, 54, 55, 71; *see also* Revelation
"feeding" on Shekinah 83–86; *see also* Shekinah, splendor of

Naaman 135
Nadab 83–84
Nations (gentile) 43–44, 63, 65–66, 71–72, 117
Ninth day of Ab 113n
Numinous quality 3, 11, 79, 90, 106, 139

Paradigms, Biblical 126, 134–137
Isaac as 36, 40
Moses as 54, 130
Sinai revelation as 13–16, 36, 40, 51, 56, 86
Passover 36
Persians 118, 120n, 131–132
Philo 42, 82
Pure exegesis 35, 103, 110–113

Rabbi, role of 53–56
Redemption 15–16, 74–77, 79n, 86–87, 107, 123, 125, 126, 132–134
Reed Sea
God revealed at 21–22, 27, 100
wall of fire at 120n
Revelation
according to power of recipient 42, 67–70
limited 41–43, 53–56
unlimited 42–43, 46, 53–56, 68; *see also* Moses as mediator of revelation
Rome 36, 99, 111, 115–117, 130–133

Salvation, Soteriology; *see* Redemption
Seals, theurgic use of 5, 40
Seven
Heavens (firmaments) 19–20, 58, 95–96
partitions of fire 26
Shabbat 77, 90, 123
Shekinah
equivalent to God 109, 109n
"feasting upon," 83–85
seen by angels 78
seen by Merkabah mystics 75
splendor of, nourishment by ("feeding upon") 75–78, 79n, 82–85

BIBLICAL REFERENCES

RABBINIC LITERATURE REFERENCES

Philon
Philonis Alexandrini

Opera quae supersunt. Editio maior
Edid. Leopoldus Cohn et Paulus Wendland

7 volumes. Octavo. 1896–1930. Reprint 1962.
Cloth DM 380,– ISBN 3 11 005105 2

Vol. I: De opificio mundi. Legum allegoriarum lib. I–III. De cherubim. De sacrificiis Abelis et Caini. Quod Deterius potiori insidiari soleat. Edid. Leopoldus Cohn. – CXIII, 298 pages, 1 chart. 1896

Vol. II: De posteritate Caini. De gigantibus. Quod deus sit immutabilis. De agricultura. De plantatione. De ebritate. De sobrietate. De confusione linguarum. De migratione Abrahami. Edid. Paulus Wendland. – XXXIV, 314 pages. 1897

Vol. III: Quis rerum divinarum heres sit. De congressu eruditionis gratia. De fuga et inventione. De mutatione nominum. De somniis liber I. De somniis liber II. Edid. Paulus Wendland. – XXII, 306 pages. 1898

Vol. IV: De Abrahamo. De Josepho. De vita Mosis lib. I. De vita Mosis lib. II. De decalogo. Edid. Leopoldus Cohn. – XXXII, 307 pages. 1902

Vol. V: De specialibus legibus lib. I–IV. De virtutibus. De fortitudine. De humanitate. De poenitentia. De nobilitate. De praemiis et poenis. De exsectationibus. Edid. Leopoldus Cohn. – XXXI, 376 pages, 2 charts. 1906

Vol. VI: Quod omnis probus liber sit. De vita contemplativa. De aeternitate mundi. In Flaccum. Legatio ad Gaium. Edid. Leopoldus Cohn et Sigofredus Reiter. – LXXVII, 223 pages. 1915

Vol. VII: Indices ad Philonis Alexandrini opera. Compos. Ioannes Leisegang. – Pars I: VIII, 338 pages. 1926. – Pars II: 539 pages. 1930

Philon
Index Philoneus

By Günter Mayer

Octavo. X, 312 pages. 1974.
Cloth DM 165,– ISBN 3 11 004536 2

Preisänderungen vorbehalten

Walter de Gruyter   Berlin · New York

Beihefte zur Zeitschrift für die alttestamentliche Wissenschaft

Tomoo Ishida

The Royal Dynasties in Ancient Israel

A Study on the Formation and Development of Royal-Dynastic Ideology

Large-octavo. XII, 211 pages. 1977. Cloth DM 82,– ISBN 3 11 006519 3 (Volume 142)

Charles Francis Whitley

Koheleth

His Language and Thought

Large-octavo. VIII, 199 pages. 1979. Cloth DM 86,– ISBN 3 11 007602 0 (Volume 148)

Prophecy

Essays presented to Georg Fohrer on
his sixty-fifth birthday September 6, 1980
Edited by J. A. Emerton

Large-octavo. VIII, 202 pages, frontispiece. 1980. Cloth DM 92,–
ISBN 3 11 007761 2 (Volume 150)

Gerald T. Sheppard

Wisdom as a Hermeneutical Construct

A Study in the Sapientializing of the Old Testament

Large-octavo. XII, 178 pages. 1980. Cloth DM 78,– ISBN 3 11 007504 0 (Volume 151)

J. A. Loader

Polar Structures in the Book of Qohelet

Large-octavo. XII, 138 pages. 1979. Cloth DM 62,– ISBN 3 11 007636 5 (Volume 152)

Philip J. Nel

The Structure and Ethos of the Wisdom Admonitions in Proverbs

Large-octavo. XII, 142 pages. 1982. Cloth DM 74,–
ISBN 3 11 008750 2 (Volume 158)

Preisänderungen vorbehalten

Walter de Gruyter Berlin · New York